ASIANT A

I fy holl gefndryd a chyfnitherod bach
sydd wastad yn ysbrydoliaeth

1
FEDRI DI GADW CYFRINACH?

Helô! Pwy wyt ti? Na, paid â dweud wrtha i. Beth am gadw hynny'n gyfrinach? Ac am rŵan, gei di fy ngalw i'n… ymmm… Alys. Ia, dyna ni, Alys Phillips.

Dwi'n dda iawn am gadw cyfrinachau. Dyna ydi fy swydd i. Oes, mae gen i swydd bwysig, er nad ydw i'n ddim ond 14 mlwydd oed. Er bod fy swydd i'n dibynnu ar gadw cyfrinachau, dwi'n torri 'mol isio dweud wrth rywun. Mae Mam yn gwybod pob dim, wrth gwrs. Roedd hi'n gwybod cyn fi hyd yn oed. A rŵan dwi am rannu'r gyfrinach. Ond, er lles pawb, gan gynnwys chdi, dydw i ddim wedi defnyddio enwau go iawn yn y stori yma, iawn?

Ti'n gweld, mi fedra i ddringo'n gynt na wiwer, cuddio yn y llefydd lleia posib, neidio fel mwnci a dwi'n ddigon slic i fedru baglu oedolyn chwe throedfedd a'i ddal ar y llawr. Mi fedra i agor drysau sydd wedi'u cloi a dwi'n dweud celwydd fel taswn i'n dweud y gwir. Dwi'n andros o glyfar ond fues i erioed mewn ysgol cyn i mi fod yn 11 mlwydd oed. Mam ddysgodd bob dim i mi adra. Ond ro'n i'n dysgu mor sydyn fel y dechreuodd hi roi gwersi ychydig yn wahanol i mi.

Dechreuodd yr holl beth pan o'n i tua 6 oed. Roedd yn rhaid i mi godi am 6.30 y bore a mynd i redeg, yna gwneud pob math o waith ffitrwydd a chryfder... bob diwrnod! Roedd o fel artaith am yr wythnos neu ddwy gynta – roedd fy nghoesau i'n llosgi ac yna fel jeli. Ro'n i'n chwysu chwartiau, a'r unig beth ro'n i isio'i wneud oedd aros yn fy ngwely. Wnes i hyd yn oed ystyried cario ymlaen i redeg rhyw fore a pheidio byth â dod adra. Ond, gydag amser, mi ddes i arfer â'r boreau cynnar ac, yn wir, wnes i hyd yn oed ddechrau mwynhau.

Yna, fe ddatblygodd y gwersi. Cefais wersi ymladd a sut i amddiffyn fy hun. Ro'n i'n cael gwersi dringo rhydd ac yn dysgu sut i fynd o un pen i ystafell i'r pen arall heb gyffwrdd y llawr. Ro'n i'n gorffen pob diwrnod gyda gêm o guddio ond roedd Mam yn gwybod am bob twll a chornel yn ein tŷ ni. Mae o'n dŷ anferth ac er bod digonedd o lefydd i guddio, roedd Mam wastad yn dod o hyd i mi. Ond, un tro, llwyddais i wasgu fy hun o dan y bwrdd pŵl, codi fy hun i fyny oddi ar y llawr a bachu fy melt ar damaid o'r bwrdd er mwyn i hwnnw gymryd y rhan fwya o'r pwysau. Ro'n i yno am bron i awr yn cuddio. Yn y diwedd, safodd Mam yn y cyntedd a gweiddi dros y tŷ:

"Iawn! Dwi'n *give up!*"

Diolch i'r drefn, meddyliais innau wrth ollwng fy hun i lawr a llusgo fy nghorff allan. Ro'n i'n ofnadwy o falch nad o'n i wedi cael fy nal y tro hwnnw, felly cerddais i'r cyntedd yn dalsyth a chyhoeddi ble bues i'n cuddio. Ond beth oedd ymateb Mam?

"Dim ond un waith roedd yn rhaid i mi weiddi i dy gael di allan! Be fasat ti wedi'i neud os faswn i'n rhywun drwg oedd isio dy ddal di a dy werthu di i ffatri gwneud tedis?!"

"Y?!" gofynnais innau'n syn.

"... a ddylat ti byth gyfadda lle fuest ti'n cuddio. Ti 'di colli'r guddfan yna am byth rŵan. Mi fydda i'n edrych yn fan'na bob tro o hyn 'mlaen!"

Dwi'n gwybod erbyn heddiw fod y gwersi ro'n i'n eu cael gan Mam yn anarferol ond, ar y pryd, doedd gen i ddim syniad. Ro'n i'n meddwl bod pawb yn dysgu'r pethau hyn ar ryw adeg yn eu bywyd.

Unwaith, dwi'n cofio mynd i'r archfarchnad efo Mam ar brynhawn dydd Sadwrn, ac fe ges i fynd i'r gornel chwarae tra oedd hi'n siopa. Roedd yna dwneli, ffrâm ddringo, rhaffau, peli lliwgar a phob math o bethau, ac ro'n i'n neidio a hongian o un peth i'r llall. Ro'n i'n medru llamu a throelli yn yr awyr cyn glanio ar blatfform a rholio i lawr y twnnel, yna gwibio i fyny rhaff. Ro'n i'n hedfan rownd a rownd heb sylweddoli'r hyn oedd yn digwydd o 'nghwmpas. Roedd y plant eraill i gyd wedi stopio chwarae. Roedd 'na rieni wedi dod draw i edrych. Roedd rhai wedi codi eu ffonau symudol i ffilmio hyd yn oed. Ond do'n i ddim wedi sylwi ac ro'n i'n dal i neidio o gwmpas y lle. Ar ôl ychydig o funudau, a finnau'n malio dim, clywais lais Mam yn gweiddi:

"Alys!"

Stopiais yn stond a throi i weld Mam yn sefyll yng nghanol y gynulleidfa. Roedd y lle mor ddistaw â phwll nofio heb blant, a phawb yn edrych arna i.

Cochais at fy nghlustiau, ac ro'n i isio cuddio. Rhedais at Mam, yn methu deall beth oedd yn digwydd. Gafaelodd Mam yn fy llaw a'm harwain o'r archfarchnad. Ddywedodd hi ddim gair nes iddi gau drws y car.

"Alys, be ddaeth dros dy ben di'n tynnu'r fath sylw atat ti dy hun? Gwneud sioe wirion fel'na o flaen pawb!"

"Ond Mam…"

Ceisiais egluro nad o'n i'n gwybod beth ddigwyddodd. Ond roedd Mam yn flin.

"Paid ti byth â gwneud rhywbeth fel'na eto, ti'n dallt?"

"Yndw. Sori," atebais yn bwdlyd. Ond do'n i ddim yn deall. Roedd Mam yn gwylltio fel hyn weithiau, yn gwylltio am bethau bach oedd yn ymddangos yn ddigon diniwed i mi.

Mam yw un o'r merched delia i mi eu gweld erioed. Mae ganddi wallt tywyll, syth fel papur a llygaid glas tywyll fel inc. Mae hi'n dal ac yn hynod o heini. Ond pa bynnag reswm oedd gan Mam i fod yn flin y diwrnod hwnnw, o leia roedd hi'n gwybod bod y gwersi symud a dringo wedi gweithio.

Bob dydd Mercher ro'n i'n cael gwersi sut i ddarllen pobol. Roedd yn rhaid dysgu beth oedd yr arwyddion pan fyddai pobol yn dweud celwydd a dysgu sut i guddio'r arwyddion hynny pan fyddwn i'n dweud celwydd. Os oedd rhywun yn edrych ar ei draed neu'n cyffwrdd ei wyneb pan fyddai'n dweud rhywbeth, roedd hi'n debygol iawn ei fod yn dweud celwydd. Dysgu sut i wrando ar rhythm anadlu. Pe bai anadlu rhywun yn cyflymu neu'n trymhau, roedd o'n arwydd ei fod yn nerfus, o bosib oherwydd ei fod yn dweud celwydd.

Bywyd felly oedd gen i. Ro'n i'n gorfod bod yn barod am unrhyw beth. Doedd gen i ddim ffrindiau. Roedd plant yr ysgol gynradd leol yn chwarae yn y parc dafliad carreg o'n tŷ ni weithiau ac er nad oedden nhw'n siarad llawer efo fi, ro'n i'n cael ymuno mewn ambell gêm bêl-droed. Ond roedd hynny'n reit ddiflas a dweud y gwir. Doedd neb yn pasio'r bêl i mi, a phan fyddwn i'n cael fy nhroed arni doedd neb yn medru fy nal.

Ond doedd dim ots gen i. Fy hoff beth i yn y byd oedd darllen a gwylio rhaglenni ditectifs neu raglenni oedd yn gwneud i mi chwerthin nes 'mod i'n sâl. Ond roedd 'na rai rhaglenni yn fy ngwylltio. Roedd un comedïwr ar y teledu rownd y rîl ac yn andros o boblogaidd. Roedd o'n mynd dan fy nghroen i. Roedd ambell jôc neu stori yn ddoniol ond doedd o ddim yn eu dweud nhw'n iawn – roedd o'n meddwl gormod ohono fo'i hun i werthfawrogi pam roedd y jôcs yn ddoniol. Yr unig beth doniol amdano oedd ei enw – Rhodricês Llywethin. Ha!

Ta waeth, un diwrnod tua tair blynedd yn ôl a hithau'n ddiwedd haf, galwodd Mam arna i i ddod i'r gegin. Wrth y bwrdd roedd dynes mewn siwt ddu yn eistedd, a phaned yn ei llaw. Roedd y ddynes ddiarth wedi tynnu ei gwallt yn ôl yn gwlwm tyn ar gefn ei phen. Roedd ganddi drwyn main, hir a gwefusau coch, tenau, fel petai rhywun wedi tanlinellu ei thrwyn efo beiro goch.

"Alys," meddai Mam wrtha i gan nodio tuag at gadair wag oedd wrth y bwrdd. "Eistedda am funud bach, dwi isio i ti gwrdd â rhywun."

Eisteddais, gan sylwi bod y ddynes ddiarth yn syllu arna i heb flincio.

"Dyma Mrs Pi."

Am enw hurt, meddyliais.

"Mae hi'n ffrind da i mi ac mae ganddon ni rywfaint o newyddion i ti."

Edrychais ar y ddynes ddiarth. Roedd hi'n eistedd mor syth, a'i gwefusau hi mor fain, fel y dechreuais amau fod Mrs Pi isio pi-pi... neu o leia angen taro rhech. Cefais ysfa i chwerthin wrth edrych ar y ddynes od â'i henw odiach.

"Mrs Pi?" holais.

"Ie, Mrs Pi," meddai'r ddynes ddiarth, "yn briod efo Mr Pi ac yn fam i ddau Pi bach."

Bu bron i mi dagu, ond roedd Mrs Pi a Mam yn dal i edrych yr un mor ddifrifol.

"Rwyt ti'n mynd i'r ysgol fory," meddai Mam, heb ddangos unrhyw emosiwn o gwbwl. Dim hapusrwydd, dim sioc, dim cynnwrf, felly atebais gydag...

"O."

Edrychodd Mrs Pi arna i.

"Dwyt ti ddim wedi bod mewn ysgol erioed, naddo, Lleucu."

"Naddo. Ond dwi wedi dysgu mwy adra efo Mam na 'run o'r plant sy'n y cae chwarae ar bnawn dydd Sul."

"Alys," meddai Mam gyda'i hwyneb paid-â-bod-yn-bowld.

"Wel, mae hi'n amser i ti fynd i'r ysgol... ond nid i gael addysg," cyhoeddodd Mrs Pi yn gadarn.

Pwy oedd y ddynes yma? Roedd hi a Mam i fod yn ffrindiau da, ond doedd yr awyrgylch rhyngddyn nhw ddim yn un cyfeillgar iawn. Gafaelodd Mam yn fy nwy law cyn dweud,

"Alys, rwyt ti wedi dysgu llawer efo fi, ti'n iawn. Ond nid y pethau arferol. Rwyt ti wedi cael dy ddysgu i fod yn ysbïwr."

"Y?" Ro'n i'n siŵr ei bod hi'n dechrau colli arni. "Be? Fel sbei?"

"Ia," crawciodd Mrs Pi.

"Peidiwch â bod yn hurt!" meddwn i wrth y ddwy, yn methu credu'r hyn ro'n i'n ei glywed.

"Paid ti â meiddio siarad mor bowld o flaen Mrs Pi..." dechreuodd Mam, cyn i Mrs Pi dorri ar ei thraws.

"Na, mae hi'n iawn, Lynwen."

Synnais wrth glywed Mrs Pi yn galw Mam yn Lynwen. Lyn fyddai pawb arall yn ei galw. Wel, a bod yn onest, enw cwbl wahanol sydd ganddi go iawn, ond er mwyn diogelwch, Lynwen ydi hi yn y stori yma! Ta waeth, do'n i ddim hyd yn oed yn siŵr a oedd unrhyw un arall yn gwybod mai Lynwen oedd ei henw llawn.

Ro'n i isio chwerthin eto, gan fod yr holl sefyllfa'n

wallgo. Roedd 'na ddynes o'r enw Mrs Pi, oedd yn edrych fel ei bod hi isio pi-pi, yn eistedd yn ein cegin ac roedd hi a Mam dan yr argraff 'mod i'n mynd i fod yn ysbïwr?!

"Dwi wedi gwybod erioed dy fod ti am fod yn ysbïwr, Alys," meddai Mam o nunlla.

"Am be ti'n fwydro, Mam?" gofynnais o ddifri.

"Wel..." a dechreuodd adrodd ei stori.

Pan oedd Mam yn yr ysgol, roedd hi wedi mynd i drwbwl am ddwyn ac wedi cael ei gyrru i garchar i droseddwyr ifanc. Un diwrnod, daeth Mrs Pi i mewn i'r carchar a dewis tair o ferched i fynd i fyw gyda hi mewn plasty anferth wedi ei guddio gan goed yng nghanol nunlla. Roedd Mam yn un o'r tair. Yn y plasty anferth, roedd Mrs Pi wedi rhoi addysg dda iddyn nhw a dysgu'r merched sut i edrych ar ôl eu hunain, sut i beidio mynd i drwbwl a sut i ymladd. Ymhen ychydig flynyddoedd, datgelodd Mrs Pi wrthyn nhw eu bod wedi cael eu hyfforddi i fod yn ysbïwyr, a dyna fu.

"Fedra i ddim dweud mwy wrthat ti am y gwaith wnaethon ni, ond wedi deng mlynedd o weithio fel ysbïwr dyma fi'n cyfarfod dy dad, a dyma ti. Felly, mi ddysgais i bopeth ro'n i'n ei wybod i ti."

"A be? Dach chi'n disgwyl i mi fod yn ysbïwr? Un ar ddeg ydw i, os na dach chi 'di sylwi!" meddwn i'n reit bigog.

13

"Yn union," meddai Mrs Pi, oedd heb grawcian gair ers meitin. "Ti'r union beth 'dan ni angen ar gyfer y dasg gudd nesa. Ti'n gweld, Alys, mae 'na bethau rhyfedd iawn yn digwydd yn Ysgol Breifat Pen y Rhych sydd y tu allan i'r dref."

"Wel, mae pawb yn gwybod hynny. Maen nhw'n cael llwyth o bres o rwla ac mae'r plant yn anarferol o glyfar. Mae hi fel ysgol i robotiaid, yn ôl pob sôn!" oedd fy ymateb wrth glywed am Ben y Rhych.

"Yn union, Alys," meddai Mrs Pi. "Ers tua pum mlynedd mae 'na brifathrawes newydd, a phan ddaeth hi fe ddaeth set gyfan o staff newydd hefyd, i gyd yn ddiarth i'r ardal. Mae'r arian sy'n cael ei bwmpio i mewn i'r ysgol wedi cynyddu'n aruthrol – gymaint felly nes ei fod wedi codi clustiau'r llywodraeth – heb sôn am gyflog y brifathrawes a rhai o'r staff..."

"Sut dach chi'n gwybod hyn i gyd?" gofynnais, cyn i Mam arthio,

"Tydi hynny'n ddim o dy fusnes di, Alys. Gwranda."

"Diolch, Lynwen. Rhywbeth arall anarferol iawn am yr ysgol hon – fel rwyt ti wedi sôn – ydi bod perfformiadau addysgol y plant yn anhygoel. Ond, hefyd, eu bod nhw fel robotiaid. Dydyn nhw ddim yn chwerthin, nac yn gwenu hyd yn oed."

"Be?" Ro'n i mewn tipyn o sioc erbyn hyn ac, yn eironig iawn, ro'n i isio chwerthin.

"Rydyn ni wedi llwyddo i osod meicroffonau bychan yn y neuaddau, mewn ambell stafell ddosbarth ac yn y coridorau i wrando am bethau anarferol. Roedden ni wedi gobeithio gosod rhai drwy'r ysgol gyfan, ond mae ein hysbïwr ni wedi diflannu... heb gysylltu na dim."

Aeth Mrs Pi'n ddistaw am ychydig cyn tynnu anadl ddofn a chario ymlaen.

"Ta waeth, doedd dim yn anarferol yn y recordiadau sain gawson ni, oni bai nad oedd 'na ddim chwerthin, dim chwarae, dim tynnu coes... dim sŵn arferol plant."

Felly'n union yr oedd hi yn ein cegin ni yr eiliad honno. Dim chwerthin na chwarae. Yna, gofynnais,

"Ond be dach chi'n disgwyl i mi neud?"

Do'n i ddim yn deall ac, am y tro cynta, do'n i ddim yn siŵr o'n i isio deall chwaith. Pam oedden nhw f'angen i? Pam na chawn i aros adra efo Mam?

"Am mai chdi ydi'r ysbïwr 11 oed gora yn y wlad... yn y byd, efallai. Dyma'r dasg gudd berffaith i ti," meddai Mrs Pi.

"Chdi *ydi'r* gora, Alys, a 'dan ni'n dibynnu arna chdi. Mae'r plant mewn peryg, ac ella mai chdi ydi'r unig un fedrith eu hachub nhw," meddai Mam gan edrych arna i efo'i hwyneb ti-werth-y-byd, sy'n codi cywilydd o'r mwya arna i.

"Ond be os dwi ddim isio bod yn sbei?"

Edrychodd y ddwy arna i a dweud efo'i gilydd:

"Tyff!"

Y noson honno, es i fy ngwely am y tro ola yn ferch arferol 11 mlwydd oed, achos y bore wedyn ro'n i'n codi o fy ngwely fel ysbïwr... neu, i roi fy enw swyddogol i mi, Asiant A.

2
MAE YSBÏWR DA YN ANWELEDIG

Deffrais i sgrech fy nghloc larwm. Roedd '6:00' yn fflachio'n goch dros fy ystafell, yn union fel petai'r lle ar dân. Roedd y bore wedi dod yn gynt na'r gwynt y diwrnod hwnnw. Yn sydyn, cofiais ei bod hi'n ddiwrnod arbennig, a chyn i mi gael cyfle i ddiffodd y cloc larwm dyma floedd o'r gegin.

"Alys, cwyd. Brysia!"

Mam, unwaith eto, yn meddwl nad ydi cloc bach sy'n cael sterics wrth fy nghlust i yn mynd i 'neffro i! Codais a newid i ddillad rhedeg er mwyn mynd allan am hanner awr fach cyn cael brecwast.

"I be ti'n gwisgo'r rheina?" gofynnodd Mam, fel tasa hi erioed wedi 'ngweld i'n gwisgo fy nillad rhedeg. "Tydan ni ddim yn mynd i redag, siŵr. Rhaid i ti gadw dy egni ar gyfer dy ddiwrnod cynta. Beth bynnag, ma 'na wisg briodol i chdi… hwda."

Rhoddodd Mam dwmpath bach o wisg Ysgol Breifat Pen y Rhych i mi, oedd yn ddu fel ei selsig barbeciw hi.

"Rŵan, cer i newid yn reit handi neu mi fydd Mrs Pi 'di cyrraedd."

Lluchiais y dillad amdana i. Bois bach, roedden

nhw'n cosi, fel tasa rhywun wedi rhoi plu bach, bach y tu mewn iddyn nhw i gyd. Pan edrychais arnaf fy hun yn y drych, ro'n i'n teimlo fel pawb arall am y tro cynta. Do'n i ddim yn adnabod fy hun.

Es i lawr y grisiau ac ar fwrdd y gegin roedd 'na fag ysgol mawr newydd. Mi afaelais yn y bag, ac roedd o'n drymach nag ro'n i wedi'i ddisgwyl.

"Be ar wynab y ddaear sy'n y bag 'ma?"

Wrth i mi drio'i roi ar fy nghefn, clywais grawc o ddrws yr ardd.

"Dy offer di, Alys. Eistedda, mae ganddon ni dipyn o betha i fynd trwyddyn nhw."

Roedd Mrs Pi'n swnio'n gadarn, felly eisteddais heb ddweud gair. Daeth hi i mewn a thynnu'r bag yn ddarnau. Roedd 'na becyn casglu data oedd yn cynnwys camera bach oedd yn tynnu lluniau ac yn ffilmio drwy'r adeg. Ond roedd ganddo hefyd feicroffon hynod o bwerus oedd yn medru recordio deg trac sain ar yr un pryd gan gyrraedd pellter o gan metr pe bai raid. Roedd popeth oedd yn cael ei recordio yn cael ei anfon yn ôl at Mrs Pi.

"Anfon yn ôl i lle?" gofynnais, heb feddwl dim.

"Tydi hynny'n ddim o dy fusnes di," atebodd Mrs Pi heb edrych arna i.

Roedd Mam yn ddistaw, yn cadw ei hun yn brysur o gwmpas y gegin – yn rhoi brecwast ar y bwrdd, yna golchi llestri, glanhau, yna rhoi mwy o fwyd ar y bwrdd. Ro'n i a Mrs Pi yn bwyta fesul tamaid wrth i Mrs Pi bentyrru'r holl wybodaeth arna i. Ond ro'n i'n gwybod bod Mam yn gwrando'n astud ar bob gair hefyd.

Roedd y pecyn casglu data ar fy mag ysgol yn medru dod yn rhydd.

"Felly, mi fedri di ei adael o yn y llefydd mwya defnyddiol heb i neb sylwi dy fod ti wedi colli dy fag," eglurodd Mrs Pi.

Roedd 'na declynnau anhygoel yn rhan o'r bag. Roedd 'na ddyfais i agor clo unrhyw ddrws heb wneud difrod. Roedd 'na botyn bach oedd yn medru rhyddhau drewdod aruthrol er mwyn gwagio ystafell. Roedd 'na saeth â gwifren yn sownd iddi. Roedd modd ei chysylltu ag adran arall o'r bag a'i saethu dros bellter o ugain metr er mwyn creu ffordd i ddianc ar ei hyd pe bai angen. Roedd yr holl declynnau wedi eu cuddio'n llwyr yn y bag fel na fyddai neb cyffredin yn medru eu gweld, dim ond y rheini oedd yn gwybod y gyfrinach.

"Gwranda, Alys, y gwahaniaeth mwya rhwng ysbïwr a, ddeudwn ni, plisman neu dditectif, ydi ein bod ni'n cael ein hyfforddi i fod yn anweledig, ac yn cael ein hyfforddi i beidio bod mewn sefyllfa lle mae rhywun yn ein hamau, yn ein bygwth, ac yn bendant yn ein dal. Ond, wrth gwrs, mae bod yn ysbïwr yn waith peryglus. A dwi'n gwybod o dy wersi ymladd a hunanamddiffyn dy fod ti'n ddigon tebol i edrych ar ôl dy hun."

Edrychais ar y ddwy ohonyn nhw. Roedd wyneb Mam yn edrych mor esmwyth i gymharu â wyneb Mrs Pi.

Ro'n i isio gweiddi arnyn nhw, "DIM OND 11 OED YDW I!", ond roedd y ddwy'n edrych mor obeithiol rywsut.

"Iawn," atebais yn dawel, gan droi at fy Nghoco Pops a throi'r teledu ymlaen i geisio gwylio rhywbeth fyddai'n rhoi gwên ar fy wyneb. Ond yr unig beth oedd ar y sgrin oedd wyneb annioddefol Rhodricês Llywethin. Diolch byth bod Mam wedi diffodd y teledu cyn iddo agor ei geg.

Eisteddais yn bwyta tra oedd Mrs Pi yn mynd trwy bopeth. Dangosodd lun o'r brifathrawes, Miss Glein, i mi. Llun i hyrwyddo'r ysgol oedd o ac arno roedd y geiriau 'Miss Glein, yn rhoi sglein ar fywydau ein plant'.

Ych, meddyliais, chwydfa. Roedd hi'n ddynes dal, siapus gyda gwallt coch tywyll a sbectol ar flaen ei thrwyn. 'Miss', meddyliais – dim gŵr felly.

"Dim teulu o gwbwl, 'dan ni wedi cael cryn drafferth dod o hyd i unrhyw gefndir iddi a dweud y gwir. Ar hyn o bryd, hi yw'r prif berson sydd dan amheuaeth…"

Aeth Mrs Pi ymlaen ac ymlaen efo mwy a mwy o wybodaeth am Miss Glein, y staff eraill, yr ysgol a'r disgyblion. Roedd y disgyblion i gyd yn dod o deuluoedd cyfoethog ac roedd rhieni'r rhan fwya ohonyn nhw yn tu hwnt o brysur (yn rhy brysur i edrych ar ôl eu plant). Roedd eraill yn dod o deuluoedd clyfar a llwyddiannus ac am i'w plant gael yr addysg orau bosib.

"Rwyt ti'n ffitio'n berffaith. Rwyt ti'n glyfar ac rwyt ti a dy fam yn byw bywyd cyfforddus iawn yn y tŷ yma," crawciodd Mrs Pi gan edrych tuag at Mam.

Dechreuais feddwl o ddifri am y tro cynta sut yn union roedd Mam yn medru fforddio cymaint o bethau, a hithau byth yn gweithio. Ro'n i'n amau bod gan hynny rywbeth i'w wneud â Mrs Pi.

"Dyma dy gefndir di," meddai Mam, gan roi ffolder i mi. "Mae o'n weddol syml a ddim yn rhy bell o'r gwir felly does gen ti ddim lot i'w ddysgu, heblaw mai dyn ym myd busnes gwerthu olew yw dy dad a'i fod yn gweithio oddi cartra yn aml. Does gen ti ddim llawer o berthynas ag o ond mi ydach chi mewn cysylltiad."

Roedd Mam mor ddideimlad wrth ddweud hyn. Doedd hi byth yn siarad am Dad – pwy bynnag ydi hwnnw – a dyma hi rŵan yn siarad mor sych am fy nhad dychmygol. Ond nid dyma'r amser i ddechrau holi am hynny. Roedd gen i fy ngwaith fy hun i feddwl amdano.

Do'n i ddim wedi ystyried y byddwn i'n aros yn yr ysgol am y tymor cyfan. Dim ond ychydig filltiroedd i ffwrdd oedd hi, wedi'r cyfan. Ond roedd Mam wedi pacio cês mawr i fynd efo fi ac wedi rhoi popeth allweddol yn y bag ysgol mawr. Roedd popeth yn digwydd mor gyflym a finnau heb gael eiliad i feddwl bron iawn. Roedd Mam a Mrs Pi wedi trefnu popeth.

Cododd Mrs Pi ar ei thraed pan oedd Mam a fi'n barod i fynd, gan ddweud wrtha i,

"Cofia gadw dy ben i lawr ond dy glustiau a'th lygaid ar agor. A chofia fod ysbïwr da yn anweledig."

Rhoddodd ei llaw ar fy ysgwydd a rhoi nòd pendant i mi. Rhoddais innau nòd yn ôl. Cerddodd Mrs Pi allan drwy'r drws a dyna ni, do'n i ddim yn mynd i'w gweld hi eto hyd nes y byddwn i wedi gorffen y dasg gudd. Ond roedd hi a Mam wastad yn mynd i fod ar ben arall y gwifrau, yn derbyn yr holl wybodaeth ro'n i'n ei chasglu yn Ysgol Breifat Pen y Rhych.

3
YSGOL BREIFAT 'HYNOD LEWYRCHUS' PEN Y RHYCH

Wnaeth Mam ddim dod i mewn hefo fi. Wnaeth hi ddim hyd yn oed gyrru i fyny'r lôn fach tuag at yr ysgol, na 'ngollwng i wrth y gatiau. Stopiodd hi'r car rownd y gornel, wrth ymyl y brwgaij a dyfai'n wyllt.

"Iawn. Cofia di bob dim rŵan. A ti'n gwybod sut i gael gafael arnan ni, yn dwyt? A chofia yrru adroddiad am un ar ddeg o'r gloch bob nos. Ma hynny'n bwysig – dwyt ti ddim isio i Mrs Pi ddangos ei hochr annifyr…"

"Mam. Dwi'n iawn. Paid â phoeni."

Tynnodd Mam anadl ddofn cyn gwyro tuag ata i a rhoi clamp o sws a charu mawr i mi a dweud:

"Edrych ar ôl dy hun, achos neith neb arall, iawn?"

"Iawn," meddwn i, cyn neidio o'r car gyda'r bag pwysig ar fy nghefn a rholio'r cês ar f'ôl.

Ro'n i'n methu dallt pam roedd Mam mor emosiynol tan i mi gerdded o'r car tuag at y gatiau mawr crand. Dyna pryd wnaeth o 'nharo i. Do'n i erioed wedi bod i ffwrdd o'r blaen. Erioed wedi bod yn aros yn nhŷ ffrind, yn nhŷ unrhyw nain na dim.

Doedd o ddim yn fy mhoeni i rhyw lawer, ond roedd o'n amlwg yn poeni Mam. Felly, cyn i mi fynd o'r golwg rownd y gornel, dyma fi'n troi'n ôl unwaith eto i godi llaw ar Mam a gwenu'n ddel arni. Ro'n i isio iddi weld 'mod i'n hapus fy myd. A dyna ni, roedd y gwaith yn dechrau.

Cefais gryn drafferth i agor y gatiau. Edrychais i wneud yn siŵr nad oedd neb o gwmpas cyn taflu fy nghês dros y giât, ei wylio'n glanio ar y glaswellt yna bagio'n ôl ychydig gamau. Wedi i mi dynhau'r bag pwysig ar fy nghefn, dechreuais redeg at y giât a chyda thri cham i fyny ro'n i wedi cyrraedd y top ac wedi rhoi fy nwylo rhwng y pigau er mwyn taflu fy nghoesau i'r ochr arall. Yna naid, glanio a rholio unwaith cyn codi yn ôl ar fy nhraed heb lol. Llusgais fy nghês i fyny'r lôn fach tuag at yr adeilad mawr, dychrynllyd.

Roedd Pen y Rhych fel rhyw fath o blasty ac eglwys mewn un. Ac roedd o'n dywyll, fel craig fawr bigog yn erbyn yr awyr las. Roedd yr ysgol yn ddistaw hefyd, a dim enaid byw i'w weld o gwmpas y lle.

Ar ôl tua pum munud o gerdded, ro'n i'n sefyll o flaen y drws, yn syllu arno. Doedd 'na ddim dwrn drws i mi afael ynddo, felly ceisiais ei wthio, ond doedd dim yn tycio. Gyda lwc, dyma fi'n sylwi ar raff oedd yn hongian ger y drws. Y gloch, wrth gwrs.

Rhoddais blwc iddi a chlywed sŵn rhywbeth yn canu ym mherfeddion y graig.

Arhosais cyn clywed tip-tapian yn y pellter. Roedd y sŵn yn cryfhau, a rhywun ar ei ffordd i agor y drws. Sefais yn syth gan ddisgwyl i'r drws agor ac imi gael fy nghroesawu â gwên. Ond pan gyrhaeddodd y tip-tapian y drws, peidiodd y sŵn. Distawrwydd.

"Helô!" meddwn i'n ddiniwed.

"Tro 'nôl..." sibrydodd y llais yr ochr arall i'r drws.

"Dwi'n dechra ym Mlwyddyn 7. Dwi'n gwybod 'mod i fymryn yn hwyr ond..."

"Tro 'nôl..." Roedd y llais bron yn erfyn.

"Pwy sy 'na?" gofynnais.

"Tro 'nôl... Ma gen ti amser..." Roedd y llais yn gryfach erbyn hyn.

Ond cyn i mi gael amser i holi mwy, clywais ochenaid, yna'r tip-tapian yn distewi a diflannu. O'r pellter, daeth sŵn traed trymach yn agosáu — bwmp-di-bwmp yn dod yn nes at y drws ac, yn sydyn, y drws yn agor yn ddidrafferth.

"Croeso i Ysgol Breifat Hynod Lewyrchus Pen y Rhych."

O fy mlaen roedd 'na lwmp o ddyn mawr tew a'i wallt yn gylchoedd melyn fel creision Hula Hoops ar ei ben. Roedd ei lygaid yn disgleirio wrth i'r haul beintio gwên wan ar ei wyneb. Edrychodd arna i ac yna edrych o'i gwmpas. Roedd o i'w weld yn nerfus. Roedd ei lais wedi distewi ac roedd o'n siarad yn gyflym.

"Wel, wel, un arall... Ti damed bach yn hwyr. Ma'r gwasanaeth wedi dechre. Oes rhywun 'da ti?"

Edrychodd dros fy ysgwydd i chwilio am riant neu gar neu unrhyw beth heblaw cês newydd sbon.

"Ym, nag oes. 'Mond fi. Mi o'dd Mam... Mae Mam... wedi gorfod mynd... cyfarfod... ymmm..."

Am ryw reswm, dechreuais faglu dros fy ngeiriau. Roedd y dasg gudd wedi dechrau go iawn. Roedd yn rhaid i mi gallio a meddwl fel ysbïwr, nid merch 11 oed yn dweud celwydd.

"Paid â phoeni, nid dim ond dy rieni di sy'n dewis gadael eu plant mewn lle fel hyn heb fawr o ddiddordeb," atebodd y dyn gan afael yn fy nghês ag un llaw a'm harwain i mewn i Ysgol Breifat Pen y Rhych heb edrych arna i. Roedd o'n dal i barablu'n nerfus. Roedd o'n siarad mor dawel, do'n i ddim yn siŵr ai siarad efo fi neu efo fo'i hun yr oedd o.

"Mr Bylbs ydw i, a na, sai'n arbenigwr ar fylbie – ond *roedd* fy hen, hen, hen dad-cu i, ac am ryw reswm, rywle ar hyd fy llinach, daeth y ffugenw Mr Bylbs yn gyfenw. Be amdanot ti?"

"O, Alys Phillips, a dwi ddim yn meddwl bod

gen i stori cystal â honna am fy enw. Ond dwi'n licio bylbs… a gola yn gyffredinol… a…"

O, mam bach, ro'n i'n mwydro eto. Bob tro ro'n i'n agor fy ngheg ro'n i'n panicio.

"Ym, Mr Bylbs, ddaeth 'na rywun arall at y drws cyn chi?" gofynnais.

"Beth? Na, sai'n credu. Mae pawb yn y neuadd. Dere, well i ni hastu."

Aeth Mr Bylbs â mi i ystafell fach wag yn gynta, er mwyn i mi adael fy magiau. Do'n i ddim isio gadael fy mag ysgol yno ond roedd Mr Bylbs yn mynnu.

"Na, na, so ti angen bag yn y gwasanaeth. Galli di ddod i'w hôl nhw'n nes 'mlân."

Roedd Mr Bylbs ar frys, felly roedd yn rhaid i mi adael popeth yno a mynd heb yr offer ysbïo. Cerddais ar ei ôl ar hyd y coridor hir. Roedd hi'n dawel a dim ond sŵn ein traed yn clecian mynd.

"Dyma ni," meddai Mr Bylbs a'i law ar ddwrn drws derw mawr, trwm. Rhoddodd ei fys ar ei geg gan ddweud, "Ssshh!"

Agorodd y drws ac ymddangosodd rhesi ar resi o ysgwyddau a chefn pennau cannoedd o blant. Ro'n i yng nghefn y neuadd. Pwyntiodd Mr Bylbs at sedd wag a'i chefn ar y wal. Sleifiais gyda'r wal ac eistedd. O'm sedd ro'n i'n medru gweld pawb yn eu dillad du fel haid o frain ar wifrau trydan, yn eistedd yn llonydd a'u dwylo ar eu gliniau. Roedden nhw i gyd yn edrych i lawr i ben pella'r neuadd tuag at un person oedd yn sefyll wrth bulpud bach.

Wrth y pulpud roedd 'na ddynes ifanc dal a siapus. Roedd ganddi wallt coch tywyll fel gorchudd dros ei hysgwyddau. Hon oedd y brifathrawes – y prif berson dan amheuaeth, Miss Glein.

"… a thra bod ein disgyblion newydd yn ymgartrefu mae'n hanfodol bod y gweddill ohonon ni'n gwneud popeth o fewn ein gallu i sicrhau eu bod nhw'n teimlo eu bod nhw'n perthyn yma."

Roedd ei llais hi'n hufennog, a dim ond weithiau y byddai hi'n trafferthu anadlu. Roedd ganddi sbectol ar flaen ei thrwyn er mwyn darllen oddi ar y pulpud, ond pan fyddai hi'n edrych ar ei chynulleidfa roedd hi'n edrych dros ei sbectol. Roedd ei hewinedd hi'n ffug ond yn rhai drud, wedi eu peintio'n union 'run lliw â'i gwallt. Doedd ganddi ddim gemwaith, heblaw am gadwyn fach aur. Roedd ei dillad wedi cael eu smwddio'n fanwl, heb grychau, ac roedd ei hesgidiau'n rhai newydd sbon ac yn pinsio ei thraed hi rhyw fymryn. Ro'n i'n nodi pob manylyn amdani yn y cyfrifiadur yn fy mhen.

"Rydyn ni eto'r tymor yma yn croesawu dau athro Gwyddoniaeth newydd. Mae Mr Pritch a Miss Wil yn ymuno â ni o'r coleg."

Y tu ôl iddi roedd Mr Pritch a Miss Wil yn eistedd ar gadair yr un. Roedd Mr Pritch mor fyr fel nad oedd ei draed yn cyffwrdd y llawr ac roedd Miss Wil mor nerfus roedd hi'n edrych fel petai hi bron â chrio. Wel, ro'n i'n gwybod yn syth y byddai Mr Pritch yn cael ei alw'n Pritch Titch, a Miss Wil? Roedd ei henw hi'n dweud y cyfan – Miss Swil!

Doedd neb yn ymateb i ddim roedd Miss Glein yn ei ddweud, heblaw am gnewyllyn bach o blant Blwyddyn 7 oedd yn eistedd reit o flaen ei phulpud. Roedd y rheini'n gwingo i gyd, ond roedd pawb arall yn hollol dawel a llonydd.

"Dydd da i chi i gyd."

Camodd Miss Glein oddi wrth y pulpud bach a cherddded yn syth, heb edrych ar neb, drwy ddrws yng nghefn y neuadd. Cododd Mr Pritch a Miss Wil yn ara deg a phetrus ac edrych o'u cwmpas, gan ddisgwyl i rywun ddweud wrthyn nhw beth i'w wneud.

Ro'n i'n disgwyl i'r lle lenwi efo sgwrsio a chwerthin a sŵn disgyblion ysgol. Ond doedd 'na ddim sŵn, dim smic. Dim ond sŵn y cadeiriau'n crafu'r llawr a phlant yn codi a gadael fesul rhes ar ôl eu hathro. Pawb heblaw disgyblion Blwyddyn 7, oedd yn dal i eistedd yn eu seddi.

Wrth i bawb adael y neuadd ro'n i'n medru gweld

cyrls Mr Bylbs yn bownsio i lawr y neuadd. Yna cymerodd ei le wrth y pulpud.

"Blwyddyn 7! Arhoswch lle y'ch chi am nawr. Wedi i bawb arall fynd i'w gwersi fe gewch chi awr i fynd yn ôl i'ch stafelloedd i orffen dadbaco ac yn y blân. Ow... Mr Pritch a Miss Wil..."

Cerddodd o'r pulpud tuag at y ddau athro newydd a rhoi ei freichiau am eu hysgwyddau a'u harwain o'r neuadd.

Ro'n i'n dal i eistedd yng nghefn y neuadd, a phawb arall o Flwyddyn 7 yn y pen arall. Ond, yn hytrach na mynd draw atyn nhw, penderfynais fod yn rhaid i mi gael fy mag ysgol. Felly, dyma fi'n sleifio trwy'r drws cefn ac ar hyd y coridor hir i chwilio am yr ystafell lle roedd fy mag a 'nghês. Cyrhaeddais yno'n sydyn, heb weld neb ar y ffordd. Llithrais i mewn yn ara deg a gweld fy mag a 'nghês yn yr union fan y gadewais i nhw. Ond, wrth i mi fynd yn nes, sylwais nad oedd sip fy mag ysgol wedi ei gau'n iawn. Roedd rhywun wedi agor y bag. Gafaelais ynddo a'i astudio'n fanwl. Oedd unrhyw beth wedi mynd? Oedd unrhyw un o'r darnau cudd wedi cael eu darganfod?

Yn sydyn, agorodd rhywun y drws y tu ôl i mi a dweud:

"Wel, wel, wel! Un bach newydd arall ar goll. Sobor o beth ydi bod ar goll!"

A chyn i mi fedru yngan gair, cerddodd tri bachgen mawr, hyll ata i. Roedd un mor llydan â bwrdd a'r ddau arall fel dwy stôl bob ochr iddo. Gafaelodd dau ohonyn nhw – y stolion – yn fy mag a 'nghês tra safodd yr un hylla a'r mwya swnllyd reit o fy mlaen i. Roedd o'n sefyll mor agos ata i nes fy mod i'n gallu arogli nionod ar ei anadl.

"Be fedra i neud i chi?" gofynnais yn garedig.

"O ho ho ho!"

"Pwy ti'n feddwl wyt ti? Siôn Corn?!" atebais.

"Ma hon yn meddwl ei bod hi'n glyfar. Ych-a-fi, dach chi'n medru arogli hynna, bois? Ma hon yn drewi 'fyd. Hyll ac yn drewi… graduras," meddai'r hyllaf eto.

"Ti'n siŵr nad dy ddrewdod dy hun ti'n arogli?" holais innau heb symud, tra oedd y ddau arall yn taflu fy mag ysgol yn ôl ac ymlaen dros fy mhen.

"Yli di'r gnawas fach wirion, tydi atab yn ôl ddim yn beth call iawn, nac 'di? Dwyt ti ddim isio bod yn bowld hefo fi, sdi, neu 'nei di ddim para'n hir iawn yn yr hen le 'ma…"

Wrth iddo fo siarad roedd o'n pwnio'i fys ar fy ysgwydd, yn fwy hegar â phob gair. Felly, dyma fi'n gafael yn ei fys a'i droi, yn union fel roedd Mam wedi dangos i mi. Yna, camais ymlaen a rhoi fy nhroed y tu ôl i'w droed nes iddo ddisgyn fel sach o datws ar ei gefn ar lawr. Ro'n i'n dal i afael yn ei fys – oedd fel selsigen heb ei choginio – a rhois fy nhroed ar ei wddw.

"Be oeddat ti'n ddeud, sori?"

Roedd y ddau arall wedi gollwng y bag a rhedeg oddi yno.

"Clyw!" meddwn i wrth y bwli oedd ar lawr o dan fy nhroed a'i fys yn fy llaw. "Ti'n clywed y ddau linyn trôns 'na'n deud bo chdi 'di cael cweir gan hogan fach Blwyddyn 7? Os gwnawn ni wrando'n astud, ella glywn ni pawb yn chwerthin ar dy ben di!"

"Hy… go brin y clywi di'r ffasiwn beth yn fama. A beth bynnag, mae 'na betha tipyn gwaeth…"

Cyn iddo orffen, a chyn i mi gael cyfle i'w arteithio ychydig bach yn fwy, daeth y ddau linyn trôns yn ôl i mewn gyda Mr Bylbs.

Rhythodd y tri arna i ac yna ar y bwli dan fy nhroed. Camais oddi arno a gollwng ei fys. Gwenais, ond dim ond syllu'n gegrwth arna i wnaeth y tri. Roedd pethau'n mynd i fod yn ddiflas iawn yn yr ysgol hon, meddyliais.

4
CHWERTHIN PERYGLUS

Wedi i Mr Bylbs anfon yr hogiau oddi yno, gafaelodd yn fy magiau. Roedd o wedi cynhyrfu'n waeth na fi.

"Beth ddigwyddodd?! Pe byddai Miss Glein wedi'ch gweld chi... O, bois bach, dyw'r Twm Ffrancs 'na'n ddim ond trwbwl!"

Twm Ffrancs? Roedd o'n debycach i Twm Ffat!

"Dim ond chydig o ddadla," meddwn i.

"Wel, os oes 'da ti rywfaint o synnwyr, cadwa mas o drwbwl."

Agorodd y drws a chario ymlaen i barablu wrtho'i hun. Roedd nerfau Mr Bylbs yn rhacs.

"Dere nawr, i dy stafell," arthiodd arna i.

Ddywedodd o ddim un gair wrtha i wedyn, yr holl ffordd ar hyd coridor hir yr ystafelloedd gwely, dim ond mwmian ambell air wrtho'i hun. Doedd dim sŵn arall. Dim smic. Neb yn chwarae, neb yn sgwrsio, neb yn rhedeg.

"Lle mae pawb?" gofynnais.

"Blwyddyn 7 yn dadbaco a phawb arall yn eu gwersi... 'Co ti. Stafell 25."

Gollyngodd fy magiau a throi oddi wrtha i heb ddweud gair yn rhagor, gan drotian yn ei ôl ar hyd y coridor hir. Syllais ar y rhif 25 ar y drws cadarn. O wel, meddyliais, o leia ga i lonydd i feddwl am ychydig.

Gwthiais y drws gyda fy ysgwydd i'w agor a llusgo fy nghês ar f'ôl. Bu bron i mi neidio o 'nghroen wrth glywed llais bach yn dweud:

"Helô!"

Do'n i ddim yn disgwyl y byddai neb yn fy ystafell, ond wrth i mi godi 'mhen i edrych yn iawn gwelais ddau wely. Roedd un fel amlen o daclus ac yn gwgu fel athrawes ysgol Sul arna i. Ond ar y llall eisteddai merch denau, lwydaidd a chanddi wallt lliw dŵr budur. Roedd pob dim amdani'n llwyd: ei chroen, ei dillad, ei hesgidiau.

"Sori... do'n i ddim yn trio dy ddychryn di!"

Roedd hyd yn oed ei llais yn llwyd.

"Lleucu dwi."

Bu bron i mi dagu. Lleucu Llwyd go iawn!

"Haia, Alys dwi," atebais heb symud o'r drws na gollwng fy mag.

"'Dan ni'n rhannu," meddai Lleucu Llwyd wedyn.

"O, ydan?" meddwn i am ryw reswm gwirion, achos roedd hi'n eithaf amlwg ein bod ni'n rhannu ystafell.

Llusgais fy nghês i mewn a phloncio fy hun a'm

34

bag ar y gwely. Roedd yr ystafell yn binc. Pinc diflas. Efallai ei fod yn arfer bod yn binc cyffrous ond bod presenoldeb llwydaidd y llipryn Lleucu wedi llwydo'r lle. Doedd yna ddim ffenest ac roedd hi'n llethol o dawel a llonydd. Doedd dim byd yno heblaw am ddau wely, cist wrth droed y ddau a chwpwrdd uchel yr un i hongian dillad â droriau ar y gwaelod ar gyfer dillad wedi'u plygu. Ac yn swatio fel rhyw greadur ofnus yn y gornel roedd sinc bach, seimllyd, fel tasa 'na blymar wedi tisian ar yr ystafell.

"Ma'r lliw pinc 'ma'n od, dydi?" Ro'n i'n chwilio am unrhyw beth i gynnal sgwrs.

"Dwi'n licio fo. Ma stafelloedd y merched i gyd yn binc."

Ydyn mae'n siŵr, meddyliais – dim dychymyg o gwbwl!

"Ac mae'n siŵr bod stafelloedd y bechgyn yn las!" wfftiais.

Gan fod y sgwrs rhyngdda i a Lleucu mor fywiog â phêl droed heb wynt ynddi dechreuais ddadbacio, gan gadw fy mag ysgol yn saff ar y gwely.

"Ma hwnna'n fag ysgol mawr," meddai Lleucu ymhen hir a hwyr.

Chymerais i fawr o sylw ohoni. Ro'n i wedi sylwi ei bod hi wedi dadbacio ei phethau hi i gyd ac wedi eu cadw nhw'n daclus o'r golwg – naill ai hynny neu doedd ganddi ddim byd efo hi.

Lluchiais fy nghês ar fy ngwely. Y cês newydd sbon oedd wedi ei bacio gan Mam. Doedd gen i ddim syniad beth oedd y tu mewn iddo ac, yn anffodus, doedd gen i ddim syniad sut i'w agor o chwaith. Roedd 'na sip ond welwn i ddim lle roedd y sip yn dechrau nac yn gorffen. Roedd 'na focs bach dros ran o'r sip. Edrychais dros fy ysgwydd ar Lleucu. Roedd hi'n dal i eistedd yno ar ei gwely heb symud modfedd. Do'n i ddim isio iddi feddwl 'mod i mor ddi-glem fel 'mod i'n methu agor fy nghês fy hun. Ceisiais agor y bocs bach, yn araf a gofalus i ddechrau. Wedyn, ar ôl i mi fethu, a methu eto, a methu am y tro ola, ro'n i'n dechrau berwi. Rhoddais un droed ar y cês, gwthio fy ewinedd o dan y bocs bach a thynnu nes i mi stopio anadlu. Doedd dim yn tycio, felly rhoddais un plwc sydyn arall. Daeth y bocs yn rhydd! Ond ar yr un pryd daeth fy nwylo a 'nhroed oddi ar y cês a chyn pen dim ro'n i'n gadach ar lawr yr ystafell.

Yn sydyn, clywais sŵn y sip yn agor. Roedd rhyddhau'r bocs yn gwneud i'r sip agor ar ei ben ei hun bach, ac o fewn saith eiliad agorodd y cês yn llydan agored fel ceg crocodeil. Syllais i a Lleucu ar y cês am ryw eiliad neu ddwy, cyn i mi ddechrau chwerthin.

Roedd o mor ddoniol, ro'n i bron â phi-pi yn fy nhrowsus! Do'n i erioed wedi gweld y ffasiwn beth. Edrychais ar Lleucu a disgwyl ei gweld hithau'n chwerthin hefyd, ond doedd hi ddim. Roedd hi'n edrych fel petai hi wedi gweld ysbryd.

"Be sy?" gofynnais drwy fy chwerthin.

"Dim byd, jyst tria beidio chwerthin gymaint. Ti'n gneud sŵn," atebodd.

Wrth gwrs, ro'n i'n gwybod nad oedd neb i fod i chwerthin, ond doedd Lleucu ddim yn gwybod fy mod i'n gwybod hynny, nag oedd? Felly roedd yn rhaid i mi ymateb drwy ofyn:

"Pam?"

"Jyst stopia chwerthin," meddai hi'n bigog gydag ychydig o banig yn ei llais.

Penderfynais ufuddhau ac eisteddon ni'n dwy'n ddistaw. Doedd gen i ddim clem beth oedd i fod i ddigwydd nesa.

Ar ôl i ni gario ymlaen â'n gêm bêl droed ddiwynt o sgwrs am rhyw ddeg munud (oedd yn teimlo fel deg awr), daeth cnoc ar y drws. Neidiodd y ddwy ohonon ni fymryn.

Pan agorais ddrws ein hystafell roedd Mr Bylbs yn sefyll yno'n gwenu'n ansicr, yn union fel y tro cynta i mi ei weld pan agorodd y drws mawr i mi. Roedd o'n edrych fel clown: ei wallt yr un mor gyrliog ag erioed a'i fochau'n goch a chwyslyd. Roedd hwn yn greadur od ar y naw!

"Nawr 'te, Alys a Lleucu, mae pawb yn aros amdanoch chi. Dewch nawr."

Edrychodd Lleucu arna i fel petai hi'n disgwyl i mi benderfynu oedden ni am adael yr ystafell neu beidio. Codais fy ysgwyddau arni a dilyn Mr Bylbs. A chyn i mi hyd yn oed edrych yn ôl, ro'n i'n gallu teimlo Lleucu yn anadlu wrth fy ysgwydd. Roedd hi fel cysgod llwyd.

Wrth i ni gerdded i lawr y coridorau, ceisiais roi popeth ro'n i wedi ei weld a'i glywed mewn stordy trefnus yn fy meddwl.

Y peth rhyfedd cynta yr oedd yn rhaid ei nodi oedd y llais ddaeth at y drws. Llais merch yn fy rhybuddio i beidio mynd i mewn i'r ysgol. Roedd hynny'n cadarnhau bod 'na rywbeth od yn digwydd yn yr ysgol. Ond wedi dweud hynny, dim ond cymeriadau od ar y naw ro'n i wedi eu cyfarfod hyd yn hyn, felly gallai'r llais fod wedi bod yn unrhyw un o'r disgyblion diflas. Eto i gyd, roedd o'n swnio'n debyg iawn i lais Lleucu...

Yr ail beth od oedd yr hyn ddywedodd Twm Ffrancs wrth i mi sôn am chwerthin: "Go brin y clywi di'r ffasiwn beth yn fama. A beth bynnag, ma 'na betha tipyn gwaeth..." Roedd o'n gwybod fod 'na bethau od yn digwydd yma felly.

Wedi i ni gyrraedd y neuadd, lle roedd pawb o

Flwyddyn 7 yn eistedd, gadawodd Mr Bylbs. Doedd dim un athro nac oedolyn yn agos at y lle. Roedd pawb yn dawel i ddechrau, yna dechreuodd y disgyblion sibrwd sgwrsio ymysg ei gilydd. Gydag amser fe gynyddodd y sŵn nes bod y neuadd yn swnio fel cwt ieir. Roedd Lleucu a finnau'n dal i eistedd yn dawel.

Fe ges i'r teimlad ymhen tipyn fod rhywun yn ein gwylio. Doedd 'na ddim ffenestri heblaw am y rhai uchel uwch ein pennau ni, yn cyffwrdd â'r nenfwd. Roedd y drysau i gyd wedi'u cau'n sownd ac roedd y rhai oedd â phaneli gwydr ynddyn nhw wedi cael eu gorchuddio gan bosteri. Yna, o gornel fy llygad, sylwais ar rywbeth bach du yn symud, yn uchel yng nghornel y neuadd. Roedd un ym mhob cornel. Camerâu. Roedd rhywun yn ein gwylio ni.

Edrychais o 'nghwmpas. Roedd pawb yn sgwrsio a chwerthin a thynnu coes. Roedd pawb yn gyffrous, wedi cyrraedd ysgol newydd a chwrdd â ffrindiau newydd. Drws nesa i mi roedd 'na ddwy ferch siaradus tu hwnt ac roedden nhw'n edrych yn union 'run fath.

"Haia, Celi dwi…"

"… a Ceri dwi…"

"… ond pan o'n i'n fach doeddwn i methu deud 'r'…"

"… felly roedd Celi yn galw fi'n Celi hefyd…"

"... er na Ceri o'dd hi..."

"... ond o'n i'n atab i Ceri a Celi am fod Celi'n galw fi'n Celi yn lle Ceri..."

"... o'dd Mam yn drysu ei phen yn lân efo ni..."

"... o, sori, nathon ni anghofio deud – 'dan ni'n efeilliaid."

Wel, meddyliais, doedd dim rhaid i mi fod yn ysbïwr gorau'r wlad i sylweddoli hynny! Roedd y ddwy ohonyn nhw'n siarad ar draws ei gilydd ac yn giglo'r un pryd. Roedden nhw wedi cyffroi'n lân a fedrwn i ddim peidio â chwerthin hefo nhw a dweud y gwir. Roedden nhw fel un person ond yn ddwy.

Dyma fi'n troi i wynebu Lleucu er mwyn ei chyflwyno hi i Celi a Celi... sori, Celi a Ceri. Ond roedd golwg swp sâl arni, ac roedd hi'n edrych o'i chwmpas fel peth gwyllt. Penderfynais drio siarad efo hi i'w thawelu, gan adael Celi a Ceri i fwydro.

"Ti'n licio'r ysgol?" Dyna'r cwestiwn cynta ddaeth i 'mhen i, er nad oedden ni ddim ond wedi bod yno ers ychydig oriau.

Ddywedodd Lleucu ddim gair. Edrychodd o'i chwmpas yna codi ei hysgwyddau, fel petai hi'n trio hel y llwch oddi arnyn nhw.

"Ti 'di bod yma o'r blaen?" gofynnais wedyn.

"Do," atebodd yn swta.

Ro'n i ar fin colli amynedd yn llwyr efo sgwrsio

rhechlyd Lleucu pan ddywedodd hi, "Mae 'mrawd i yma."

Haleliwia, meddyliais, ateb call o'r diwedd – ac ateb defnyddiol iawn hefyd. Ond cyn i mi gael cyfle i holi mwy, agorodd prif ddrws y neuadd a daeth Miss Glein i mewn, a Mr Bylbs wrth ei chynffon.

Caeodd pawb eu cegau'n syth bìn, fel tasa rhywun wedi pwyso *pause*. Cerddodd Miss Glein ar hyd y neuadd gan edrych ar bawb. Doedd ganddi ddim emosiwn ar ei hwyneb. Dim byd. Ro'n i'n ei chael hi'n anodd penderfynu oedd hi'n hapus, yn falch o'n gweld ni, neu'n flin. Roedd Mr Bylbs yn trotian ar ei hôl a'i ben i lawr. Roedd ei gyrls yn cael disgo bach ar ei ben. Cyrhaeddodd Miss Glein y pulpud a safodd Mr Bylbs wrth ei hymyl fel plentyn wedi cael cam.

"Croeso."

Tywalltodd y gair fel hufen o'i cheg. Roedd hi'n amhosib peidio gwrando arni.

"Croeso i Ysgol Breifat Hynod Lewyrchus Pen y Rhych. Fi ydi Miss Glein a fi sy'n rhoi'r sglein ar y lle 'ma, ac arnoch chi. Gobeithio eich bod wedi cadw eich pethau yn y mannau priodol ac wedi cyfarfod â'r cyfaill sy'n rhannu ystafell gyda chi. Cyn i chi gael eich amserlen mae'n rhaid i chi ddeall un peth am ysgol Pen y Rhych. Rydyn ni'n ysgol arbennig, yn ysgol ysgubol o lwyddiannus, ac mae disgyblaeth a gallu academaidd yn allweddol. Does dim lle i unrhyw ddisgybl nad yw'n cydymffurfio â rheolau'r ysgol mewn unrhyw ffordd, a does dim lle i unrhyw ddisgybl nad ydi o neu hi'n cymryd pob agwedd o fywyd yr ysgol o ddifri."

Ro'n i'n teimlo fel gweiddi "Diiiiiflas!" dros bob man ond cofiais am eiriau olaf Mrs Pi – "cofia fod ysbïwr da yn anweledig…"

Wrth i Miss Glein ddod i ddiwedd ei haraith ddiflas daeth gwich dros y lle, yna sŵn chwerthin yn atseinio. Edrychodd pawb i fyny mewn sioc ar yr uchelseinydd. Roedd rhywun yn chwerthin lond ei fol, a chyn pen dim roedd 'na biffian chwerthin o gwmpas y neuadd. Os glywi di rywun yn chwerthin, mae hi'n dipyn o gamp i beidio chwerthin dy hun. Roedd pawb yn rhyw hanner chwerthin, heblaw am Miss Glein, oedd yn edrych fel petai ei hwyneb a'i gwallt coch am droi'n un belen fawr o fflamau. Gafaelodd Mr Bylbs yn ei braich a'i harwain hi o'r neuadd ar frys. Dyna pryd y dechreuon ni i gyd chwerthin nerth ein pennau. Peidiodd y sŵn o'r uchelseinydd, ond roedd y chwerthin yn dal i glochdar yn ein clustiau ni yn y neuadd.

Doedd gen i ddim syniad pam ro'n i'n chwerthin, ond roedd clywed chwerthiniad ambell ddisgybl yn gwneud i mi chwerthin mwy a mwy. Roedd rhai'n rhochian trwy eu trwynau. Roedd ambell un ar nodyn uchel, gwichlyd ac yn swnio fel anifail gwyllt, tra bod ambell un arall yn swnio fel tractor. Ond fy hoff chwerthiniad i oedd un hogyn boliog oedd yn chwerthin yn fwy na neb a'i geg ar agor led y pen a'i goesau i fyny wrth iddo siglo 'nôl a 'mlaen. Ond – a hyn oedd yn rhyfedd – doedd dim sŵn o gwbwl! Ond doedd Lleucu ddim yn chwerthin. Roedd hi'n gwenu ychydig ond edrychai'n debycach i wên nerfus na gwên hapus.

Daeth Mr Bylbs yn ei ôl i'n tawelu, a'i wyneb yn welw fel dŵr golchi llestri. Rhannodd bawb i grwpiau a rhoi amserlen yr un i ni. Yna, cyn gadael, dywedodd ei bod hi'n amser rhydd a'i fod yn awgrymu y dylen ni fynd i'r llyfrgell i gael y llyfrau yr oedd eu hangen arnon ni ar gyfer gwersi'r prynhawn.

"Dyna i gyd am y tro. Bydd cinio ymhen hanner awr yn y ffreutur, trwy'r drysau dwbwl 'na," meddai'n siort, cyn brysio o'r neuadd.

"Ti'n gwybod ble ma'r llyfrgell, Lleucu?" gofynnais.

"Mae ganddon ni fap ar gefn ein hamserlen. Ond ydw, dwi'n gwybod lle mae o."

Roedd rhywbeth annwyl am Lleucu, ond roedd hi mor sych a diflas roedd hi'n gwneud i mi fod isio mynd i 'ngwely ac aros yno trwy'r dydd. Beth oedd yn ei phoeni hi tybed? Gan ei bod hi mor dawel, cefais y cyfle i hel meddyliau wrth grwydro hefo hi am y llyfrgell.

Roedd Lleucu'n cerdded a'i phen i lawr, yn edrych ar ei thraed, ac ro'n i'n hollol groes i hynny – yn syllu ar bob cornel, yn edrych a chofnodi yn fy mhen lle roedd y camerâu. Yn sydyn, daeth y ddwy ohonon ni wyneb yn wyneb â Twm Ffrancs, y twmffat. Roedd fel petai wedi bod yn rhedeg ac roedd 'na ddeigryn bach o chwys ar ei dalcen a'i wyneb fel balŵn goch bron â byrstio, ond roedd ei anadlu'n bwyllog.

Ro'n i'n barod amdano yn syth bìn, ond do'n i ddim am i'r twmffat ddechrau cega ar rywun mor ddiniwed â Lleucu.

"A lle dach chi'n mynd?" gofynnodd Twmffat.

Ond cyn i mi fedru dweud wrtho am sticio'i drwyn i le nad ydi'r haul yn sgleinio, atebodd Lleucu,

"Y llyfrgell. Pam? Lle ti 'di bod?"

Edrychais ar Lleucu gan feddwl nad oedd hi'n gall ond, er mawr syndod i mi, atebodd Twmffat,

"Paid â holi! Be ti'n neud efo hon? Dydi hi ddim yn gall, sdi."

Roedd o'n siarad amdana i.

"Oi! Cau hi!"

"Dach chi wedi cwrdd?" gofynnodd Lleucu.

"Ydach *chi*?!" meddwn i a Twmffat efo'n gilydd.

"Alys… dyma Twm, fy mrawd. Twm… dyma Alys, sy'n rhannu stafell efo fi."

"O," meddai'r ddau ohonon ni gan edrych ar ein gilydd.

"Twm, lle ti 'di bod?" gofynnodd Lleucu eto yn fwy pendant.

Edrychodd Twm arna i ac yna ar Lleucu eto.

"Ma hi'n iawn," meddai Lleucu, er nad o'n i'n siŵr iawn beth oedd hynny i fod i'w feddwl. "Oeddach chdi rwbath i neud efo'r chwerthin 'na?" gofynnodd iddo wedyn.

Tynnodd Twm anadl ddofn a dweud "Dowch i'r ffreutur."

5
AMSER CINIO, AMSER YSBÏO

Roedd y ffreutur yn weddol wag pan gerddais i, Lleucu a Twm y twmffat i mewn. Doedd amser cinio heb ddechrau eto ac felly dim ond ambell un oedd yn eistedd yma ac acw'n darllen neu'n siarad, ac un neu'n ddau'n eistedd yn gwbwl lonydd, yn edrych ar ddim byd. Roedd rhywbeth arswydus, anghyfforddus am y lle.

Arweiniodd Twm ni i eistedd yng nghanol yr ystafell, ddim yn rhy agos at neb a ddim yn rhy agos at yr ochr — er mwyn osgoi edrych yn amheus, meddai.

Cefais y teimlad nad oedd Twm isio i neb ein clywed ni'n siarad. Yna, cofiais am Mrs Pi yn sôn bod meicroffonau wedi eu gosod ynghudd mewn gwahanol lefydd yn yr ysgol. Oedd un yn agos aton ni rŵan, tybed? Cofiais hefyd am yr asiant cudd oedd wedi gosod y meicroffonau a'r ffaith ei fod wedi diflannu'n ddirybudd.

Roedd Twm yn edrych o'i gwmpas, yn syllu ar bawb arall yn ofalus. Ro'n i'n edrych i fyny. Roedd 'na gamera ym mhob cornel yn cadw llygad arnon ni. Roedd Lleucu'n eistedd yn agos iawn ata i ac yn edrych ar Twm.

"Twm, be nest ti?"

"Ches i ddim fy nal... mae'n iawn," atebodd ei brawd.

Do'n i ddim yn siŵr iawn am beth oedden nhw'n siarad, ond roedd o rywbeth i'w wneud â'r chwerthin ar yr uchelseinydd.

"Neith rhywun ddeud wrtha i be sy'n mynd 'mlaen, plis?"

"Wel, Twm wnaeth dorri mewn i swyddfa Miss Glein a chwerthin dros yr uchelseinydd."

Er 'mod i'n gwybod nad oedd chwerthin yn rhywbeth oedd yn digwydd yn yr ysgol yma, do'n i ddim isio i Lleucu na Twm wybod 'mod i'n amau unrhyw beth.

"Pam nest ti hynna?! A be 'di'r ots? Roedd o'n eitha doniol, o feddwl mai chdi oedd y tu ôl i'r peth," meddwn i'n goeglyd.

Gwenodd Twm yn hyll arna i, cyn sobri.

"Alys, dwyt ti ddim wedi sylwi bod petha'n od yma? Ei bod hi'n ysgol sy'n rhyfedd o dawel?" gofynnodd, a'i fol tew yn bownsio wrth iddo siarad.

Ceisiais gogio 'mod i'n hollol ddiddeall, ac aeth Twm yn ei flaen i egluro.

"Dyma fy mhedwaredd flwyddyn i yma rŵan ac oni bai am yn yr wythnos gynta un ym Mlwyddyn 7, does neb o fy mlwyddyn i wedi chwerthin. Ti ddim yn meddwl bod hynny'n od? Dydw i ddim yn deud bod pawb yn drist, ond does neb yn chwerthin... byth! Mae'r athrawon yn rhyfedd hefyd. Does yna'r un athro Gwyddoniaeth wedi para blwyddyn. Ac mae Miss Glein yn ddrwg, dwi'n siŵr o hynny. Mae hi'n *casáu* sŵn chwerthin. A rywsut, dwi ddim yn gwybod sut, ond mae hi'n llwyddo i wneud i bawb anghofio sut i chwerthin."

"Wel, nid pawb..." meddai Lleucu.

"Na. Ti'n iawn. Nid pawb. Beth bynnag mae Miss Glein yn ei wneud, tydi o ddim yn effeithio ar bawb. Tydi o ddim wedi effeithio arna i a dwi'n eitha siŵr fod 'na rai eraill nad ydyn nhw wedi cael eu heffeithio chwaith," meddai Twm.

Roedd gen i gymaint o gwestiynau i'w gofyn ac roedd cymaint o bethau'n mynd rownd a rownd yn fy mhen. Ro'n i'n torri 'mol isio gyrru adroddiad at Mrs Pi y funud honno. Ro'n i hefyd yn flin nad oedd fy mag ysgol gen i i recordio popeth roedd Twm yn ei ddweud. Dim ond gobeithio bod y meicroffonau cudd yn gwrando.

"Iawn," meddwn i. "Ydach chi wedi deud wrth rywun? Eich rhieni?"

Edrychodd y ddau arna i fel taswn i newydd ddweud bod gen i gynffon.

"Does gan Mam na Dad ddim math o ddiddordeb

be 'dan ni'n feddwl o'r ysgol. Hon ydi'r ysgol sy'n cael y canlyniadau gora yn y wlad a tydyn nhw ddim yn gorfod ein dioddef ni drwy'r tymor, dim ond ein gadael ni yma," meddai Lleucu, hyd yn oed yn fwy llwyd nag arfer.

"A be bynnag, wyt ti erioed wedi trio dweud wrth dy fam bod dy brifathrawes di'n hypnoteiddio pawb i beidio â chwerthin?" Torrodd Twm ar draws llith lwyd Lleucu.

"Ti'n meddwl mai dyna sy'n digwydd go iawn?" gofynnais.

"Dwi ddim yn gwybod, ond be bynnag ma hi'n neud, tydi hi ddim wedi fy nghael i, a dwi'n benderfynol o'i gwylltio hi a gwneud i bawb yn y lle 'ma chwerthin ar ei phen hi."

Roedd Twm yn swnio'n benderfynol. Roedd o'n edrych yn filain — yr un olwg ag oedd ar ei wyneb pan ddaeth o o hyd i mi efo fy magiau yn gynharach yn y dydd.

"Pam na 'nei di jyst cadw dy ben i lawr a chadw'n dawel? Nest ti roi pawb ym Mlwyddyn 7 mewn trwbwl efo busnes yr uchelseinydd." Roedd Lleucu yn amlwg yn golygu pob gair roedd hi'n ei ddweud ond ddaru hi ddim codi ei llais o gwbwl.

"Be? Yn union fel ti 'di bod yn neud? 'Nes i weld chdi'n trio rhybuddio pwy bynnag oedd wedi cyrraedd yn hwyr bora 'ma," meddai Twm, ac yn sydyn sylweddolais fod fy amheuon i'n gywir – Lleucu oedd y llais wrth y drws yn gynharach!

"Chdi oedd honna?! Pam nest ti hynny? A sut nest ti Twm lwyddo i dorri mewn i swyddfa Miss Glein heb i un o'r cannoedd o gamerâu sydd yma dy ddal di?" gofynnais. Mae'n rhaid ei fod wedi bod yn andros o slei i fedru osgoi pob un ohonyn nhw.

Eglurodd Twm bod y camerâu wedi cael eu haddasu'n arbennig i sylwi ar unrhyw beth anarferol – popeth heblaw am blant diflas yn cerdded ar hyd y coridorau. Roedd gan Twm bêl ac, o'r tu ôl i ddrws, fe daflodd y bêl i lawr y coridor o flaen swyddfa Miss Glein. Dilynodd pob camera'r bêl a cherddodd Twm yn hamddenol at y drws. Ystafell a desg Mr Bylbs oedd trwy'r drws ac yna roedd drws arall yn arwain i swyddfa Miss Glein. Ond roedd hwnnw wedi ei gloi ac roedd angen cod arbennig i fynd i mewn. Torri i mewn i swyddfa Miss Glein oedd bwriad Twm yn wreiddiol ond roedd hi'n amhosib agor y drws felly penderfynodd ddefnyddio meicroffon yr uchelseinydd oedd ar ddesg Mr Bylbs. Doedd o ddim yn gallu meddwl am ddim i'w ddweud felly dechreuodd chwerthin.

"Oooo, roedd o'n deimlad braf, sdi. Chwerthin dros bob man. 'Nes i ddim chwerthin am yn hir gan 'mod i'n gwybod y byddai rhywun ar ei ffordd i 'nal i," dywedodd wrth ddod at ddiwedd ei antur, a Lleucu a finnau'n gwrando'n astud.

"Ond sut fedri di fod yn siŵr nad oedd yna'r un camera wedi dy weld di? Ma raid bod o leia un yn swyddfa Mr Bylbs?"

"Wel, fedra i ddim bod yn siŵr. Ond dwi'n eistedd fan hyn, yn siarad efo chi, a does neb wedi dod i chwilio amdana i, er eu bod nhw'n gwybod yn iawn lle ydw i." Edrychodd dros fy ysgwydd ar gamera oedd yn syllu'n syth arnon ni'n tri.

Yn sydyn, agorodd y drysau dwbwl efo'i gilydd a daeth dwy ddynes foliog allan, yn wên o glust i glust. Roedden nhw'n edrych yn union 'run fath â'i gilydd.

"Dewch nawr, 'te... Ni 'di bod yn slafo trw'r bore i chi gael llond eich bolie. Rhes daclus, os gwelwch yn dda. Y rhai bach newydd i'r blân. Blwyddyn 7 yn gynta!"

"Wel, mae'r ddwy yma'n hapus," meddwn i wrth Lleucu, yn methu credu eu bod nhw mor fywiog o'u cymharu â phawb arall.

"Blod Sglods a Meri Grefi ydi'r unig bethau da am yr ysgol 'ma... ac am ryw reswm, maen nhw'n cael llonydd gan Miss Glein," meddai Twm, cyn neidio ar ei draed a mynd i gefn y rhes o ddisgyblion eiddgar oedd yn disgwyl i gael eu bwyd.

"Chi'ch dwy..." gwaeddodd Blod Sglods (neu Meri Grefi, do'n i ddim yn siŵr pa un), "i'r blân. Chi'n Blwyddyn 7, nag y'ch chi?"

Aeth Lleucu a finnau'n ufudd tuag at y ddynes fawr, annwyl.

"Nawr, peidwch becso, fe edrychwn ni'n dwy ar eich hole chi," meddai un ohonyn nhw.

"Rhaid i bawb gael digon o fwyd, i gadw nerth, on'd yfe?" meddai'r llall.

Rhoddwyd hambwrdd yr un i ni ac aeth Blod a Meri i sefyll y tu ôl i'r bwyd a chodi llond llwyaid fawr o gaserol cig oen i ni.

"Nawr 'te, sglods?" gofynnodd Blod, dwi'n cymryd.

"Ia, plis," meddwn i cyn symud ymlaen i gael llwyaid o foron.

"A digon o bwdin i ti... cwstard ychwanegol!" meddai'r llall.

"O na, dim diolch. Dwi ddim yn licio cwstard," atebais cyn i'r hylif trwchus melyn gyrraedd fy hambwrdd.

"Iyffach, ddim yn lico cwstard? Beth yw d'enw di nawr 'te, bach?" gofynnodd Meri Grefi mewn anghrediniaeth.

"Pam?" gofynnais.

"Wel, i mi gael cofio peidio rhoi peth i ti yn y dyfodol, on'd yfe?"

"O. Alys Phillips. Diolch yn fawr!" meddwn i.

Rhoddodd Meri Grefi bowlennaid fawr o sbwng melyn wedi'i foddi mewn cwstard trwchus, melys i Lleucu a hyd yn oed mwy o gwstard i Celi a Ceri ar ei hôl hi.

Roedd yn rhaid cyfaddef bod y bwyd yn edrych yn fendigedig. Ac er nad o'n i wedi meddwl unwaith am fy mol drwy'r bore, ro'n i'n llwglyd iawn mwya sydyn. Wrth i mi godi fy hambwrdd i adael y gegin sylwais ar fachgen ifanc swil yr olwg a chanddo wallt fel bwgan brain yn golchi llestri y tu ôl i Meri a Blod. O'i gymharu â'r ddwy gogyddes hwyliog, roedd o'n edrych yn ddigalon iawn. Ond dyna ni, meddyliais, mi faswn *i'n* ddigalon iawn hefyd petawn i'n gorfod golchi llestri drwy'r dydd.

Aeth Lleucu a finnau i eistedd bron i'r union fan lle roedden ni wedi bod yn siarad efo Twm. Roedd fy mhen i'n troi ar ôl sgwrsio â'r ddau a do'n i ddim yn awyddus i siarad mwy. Roedd yn rhaid i mi gael trefn ar fy meddyliau cyn y medrwn i lyncu unrhyw beth heblaw am fy nghinio. Mae'n rhaid bod Lleucu'n teimlo yr un fath achos ddywedodd hi ddim gair trwy'r holl amser roedden ni'n bwyta.

Wrth i Lleucu orffen ei môr o gwstard daeth Twm i eistedd aton ni, a'r ddau dwmffat arall oedd efo fo'n gynharach yn sefyll y tu ôl iddo. Roedd yntau wrthi'n bwyta ei bwdin.

"Ges i ddau bwdin gan Meri heddiw!" meddai cyn dweud y byddai'n ein gweld ni'n nes ymlaen. Diflannodd gyda'r ddau arall, oedd yn edrych fel petai rhywun wedi eu taro â sosban.

Er ei fod o'n frawd i Lleucu, ac er ei fod o wedi dweud popeth wrtha i, ro'n i'n dal i feddwl mai twmffat oedd Twm. Ond ta waeth, roedd yn rhaid i mi gael munud o lonydd cyn gwersi'r prynhawn.

"Dwi am fynd i'n stafell am chydig. Dwi angen nôl ambell beth," dywedais wrth Lleucu gan ollwng fy hambwrdd yn y man priodol.

"Ocê. Ddo i efo chdi," meddai honno'n ddidaro.

"Na!" meddwn i braidd yn fyrbwyll. "Na, na, mae'n iawn. Dos di i'r llyfrgell. Ti angen llyfra ar gyfer gwersi'r pnawn. Ac… os nad ti'n meindio… alli di gael fy rhai i hefyd?"

"Iawn," meddai Lleucu gan roi gwên wan i mi.

Ro'n i'n cofio fy ffordd o amgylch yr ysgol yn iawn, er ei bod yn hynod o gymhleth gyda'i holl goridorau. Ro'n i wedi creu mapiau yn fy mhen. Felly, cyrhaeddais ystafell rhif 25 yn sydyn. Welais i neb ar y daith ond roedd rhywun yn fy ngwylio i. Ro'n i'n gallu teimlo'r camerâu bach yn fy nilyn, bron fel petai ganddyn nhw fywyd eu hunain.

Unwaith i mi gau'r drws y tu ôl i mi ro'n i'n gallu ymlacio mymryn. Roedd heddiw wedi bod yn rhyfeddol, a dim ond amser cinio oedd hi! Gafaelais yn fy mag ysgol a thynnu'r pecyn casglu data ohono. Ar yr olwg gynta, roedd o'n edrych fel cas pensiliau go fawr. Doedd dim byd ond tywyllwch ar y camera ond roedd y recordydd llais yn fflachio. Gwasgais y botwm bach triongl a gwrando. Sŵn sip yn agor. Rhywun yn anadlu. Sŵn papurau a phethau'n symud. Mae'n rhaid bod rhywun wedi bod yn fy mag. Yna, cofiais fod sip fy mag fymryn yn agored pan es i i'w nôl ar ôl y gwasanaeth. Doedd dim posib dweud pwy oedd wedi bod yno, ond roedd gen i deimlad mai anadl merch oedd y sŵn. Ond pam? Do'n i heb roi rheswm i unrhyw un fy amau. Oedd bagiau pawb arall yn cael eu harchwilio fel hyn?

Roedd yn rhaid i mi gael trefn ar bopeth ro'n i wedi ei glywed er mwyn gyrru adroddiad manwl i Mrs Pi am un ar ddeg o'r gloch. Roedd hynny'n mynd i fod yn sialens gyda Lleucu o gwmpas, a byddai angen imi baratoi. Felly, ysgrifennais restr:

1. Merch yn fy rhybuddio wrth y drws.

2. Rhywun yn ymyrryd â fy mag ysgol

3. Athrawon Gwyddoniaeth newydd – Mr Pritch a Miss Wil Athrawon Gwyddoniaeth yn newid bob blwyddyn, yn ôl ymchwil

4. Disgyblion yn rhyfedd o dawel yn y gwasanaeth. Neb yn gwenu na chwerthin.

5. Mr Bylbs yn gwenu (weithiau), felly hefyd Meri Grefi a Blod Sglods (merched cinio).

6. Twm Ffrancs a Lleucu Ffrancs (Blwyddyn 10 a Blwyddyn 7) yn ymwybodol fod rhywbeth od yn digwydd ac yn credu bod Miss Glein o bosib yn hypnoteiddio plant i beidio â chwerthin. Ond nid yw'r hyn mae Miss Glein yn ei wneud yn amharu ar bawb. Nid yw wedi amharu ar Twm Ffrancs.

7. Twm Ffrancs wedi chwerthin drwy'r uchelseinydd gan achosi i bawb ym Mlwyddyn 7 chwerthin.

Ar ôl creu'r rhestr a'i chadw'n daclus o dan fatras fy ngwely, tynnais y pecyn casglu data o 'mag a rhoi ambell feiro, pensil, rhwbiwr a phren mesur ynddo fel ei fod yn edrych fel cas pensiliau go iawn. Roedd gen i dipyn o waith o fy mlaen, ond dim ond hanner diwrnod oedd wedi mynd heibio. Roedd dau beth yn bendant – do'n i ddim am aros yn yr ysgol fymryn yn hirach nag oedd raid, ac o hyn ymlaen byddwn yn mynd â'r cas pensiliau i bob man.

6
DYSGU GWERS

Ro'n i a Lleucu yn dod ymlaen yn dda efo'n gilydd, ac ro'n i'n dechrau dod i ddeall sut deimlad oedd cael ffrind. Ond wrth gwrs, do'n i ddim yn medru datgelu fy nghyfrinach wrthi hi na neb arall a bob nos roedd yn rhaid imi fynd i'r ystafell ymolchi i anfon adroddiad at Mrs Pi, ymhell o olwg Lleucu a'r camerâu. Llusgai'r dyddiau'n ara deg, fel malwen yn ceisio dianc o bwll o fêl. Roedd y prynhawn penodol yma yn waeth na'r un. Tair gwers mor ddiflas â'i gilydd – Mathemateg, Llenyddiaeth Saesneg a Daearyddiaeth. Roedd yr athrawon wedi diflasu hefyd, fel petaen nhw wedi laru ar ddysgu. Sut yn y byd oedd canlyniadau'r ysgol mor dda a phawb mor glyfar?

Roedd egwyl cyn y wers ola, ond awgrymodd Mr Bylbs yn gryf ein bod ni i gyd yn mynd i'r llyfrgell i ddarllen.

"... a chofiwch mai rheol aur y llyfrgell yw tawelwch."

Wrth eistedd yn y llyfrgell, roedd Lleucu ar bigau'r drain am ryw reswm, yn syllu i gyfeiriad y drws bob dwy funud. Fel arfer byddai hi'n syllu i'r un lle am hydoedd.

"Be sy'n bod arnach chdi?" gofynnais. Roedd hi'n dechrau mynd ar fy nerfau i wir.

"Meddwl lle mae Twm ydw i. Mae gen i deimlad drwg. Dwi heb ei weld o drwy'r dydd."

"Mae'n siŵr ei fod o wedi mynd i bigo ar ryw blant bach diniwad yn rhywle," meddwn i dan fy ngwynt.

"Dwi'n poeni bod rhywbeth yn bod."

"Lleucu, paid â bod yn wirion. Ty'd, rhaid i ni fynd i'r wers ola."

Heddiw oedd diwrnod cynta'r clybiau ar ôl gwersi. Ar ôl y wers ola, byddai pawb yn rhydd i fynd i nôl rhywbeth i'w fwyta o'r ffreutur cyn mynd i ba bynnag glwb roedden nhw wedi ei ddewis. Cyn dechrau'r flwyddyn ysgol roedd yn rhaid i bob disgybl gofrestru ar gyfer clwb i ddysgu sgìl newydd. Roedd yna Glwb Karate, Clwb Gitâr, Clwb Gwnïo, Clwb Adeiladu… pob math o glybiau gwahanol. Doedd gen i ddim syniad ym mha glwb ro'n i – Mam a Mrs Pi oedd wedi penderfynu hynny. Felly, roedd yn rhaid i mi fynd i edrych ar y rhestrau oedd wedi eu gosod ar y wal y tu allan i swyddfa Mr Bylbs a Miss Glein.

Ro'n i'n gobeithio y byddai fy enw ar restr y Clwb Rhedeg neu'r Clwb Karate, neu o leia yn y Clwb Gitâr, i mi gael dysgu rhywbeth newydd. Ond o na, roedd gan Mam a Mrs Pi syniadau eraill ar fy nghyfer...

"Clwb Coginio?!"

Roedd yn gas gen i goginio. Beth ydi'r pwynt dysgu sut i goginio? 'Nes i erioed weld James Bond yn coginio. Mam sy'n trio bod yn ddoniol, meddyliais. Sgwn i oes 'na Glwb Comedi?! Go brin, yn yr ysgol hon, meddyliais wedyn gan edrych o ddifri ar y rhestr. Yr unig enwau oedd yn gyfarwydd i mi ar restr y Clwb Coginio oedd rhai Celi a Ceri, yr efeilliaid siaradus. Ceisiais edrych am enw Lleucu. Byddai hi'n siŵr o fod yn aelod o'r Clwb Gwnïo neu'r Clwb Celf neu efallai'r Clwb Darllen. Ond doedd hi ddim. Cyn i mi droi oddi wrth y rhestrau, fflachiodd enw Lleucu Ffrancs ata i o waelod rhestr enwau'r...

"Clwb Bocsio?!"

Lleucu Llwyd, a edrychai cyn gryfed â gwymon, yn bocsio?! Rhyfeddol, meddyliais, gan gofio eto mai Clwb Coginio oedd o fy mlaen i. Ych! Ond o leia mai Meri Grefi a Blod Sglods oedd yn cynnal y clwb, felly byddwn i'n siŵr o glywed chwerthin. Gwenais wrth feddwl am y ddwy'n siarad ar draws ei gilydd wrth ein dysgu ni sut i wneud sglodion a grefi.

Wrth i mi sefyll yno a gwên fach yn sbecian rhwng fy mochau, camodd rhywun allan o swyddfa Mr Bylbs – rhywun main, tal, yn arogli fel cnau a llefrith wedi suro. Edrychais i fyny a gweld Miss Glein yn syllu arna i. Dyma'r tro cynta i mi fod mor agos â hyn ati. Roedd hi'n rhyfeddol o ddrewllyd ac ystyried ei bod hi'n rhoi argraff mor grand ohoni hi ei hun pan oedd hi'n sefyll wrth y pulpud. Wrth edrych arni'n agos, gwelais fod ei chroen hi'n smotiau coch, yn grachod ac yn sych i gyd. Ond roedd hi'n edrych dipyn gwaeth oherwydd yr holl golur ar ei hwyneb. Roedd hi'n edrych fel bara brith oren.

Peidiais â gwenu ar unwaith a dal ei llygaid. Ro'n i'n gafael yn dynn yn fy nghas pensiliau gan wybod bod hwnnw'n cofnodi popeth.

"Helô," meddai Miss Glein yn ddiemosiwn, gan edrych arna i fel taswn i ddim yno bron iawn.

"Helô," atebais yn yr un modd.

"Alys Phillips, ie?"

"Ia, Miss Glein."

"Dere gyda fi."

Trodd ar ei sawdl a cherdded drwy swyddfa wag Mr Bylbs a thrwy ddrws mawr trwm ei swyddfa. Dilynais hi fel cynffon. Arweiniodd fi i sefyll o flaen ei desg a chau'r drws y tu ôl i mi. Roedd ei hystafell yn weddol wag a thywyll, er bod un ffenest uchel uwchben. Dim ond desg, cadair iddi hi ac un gadair arall yng nghanol yr ystafell oedd yno. Ond roedd lluniau mawr, trawiadol yn hongian ar bob wal –

heblaw am y wal y tu ôl iddi. Roedd y wal honno'n hollol foel, heb unrhyw farc nac addurn arni.

"Sut mae pethau'n mynd, Alys?" gofynnodd Miss Glein yn ei llais hufennog.

Pam ar wyneb y ddaear oedd hi wedi fy ngalw i'w swyddfa i holi hynny? Yn ôl yr hyn ro'n i wedi ei glywed, roedd swyddfa Miss Glein yn lle diarth iawn i ddisgyblion. Dechreuodd fy meddwl rasio fel gafr ar daranau. Oedd hi'n gwybod? Oedd hi'n gwybod mai ysbïwr oeddwn i a 'mod i, Mam a Mrs Pi'n ceisio ei dal hi? Yna, cofiais yn sydyn. Mae'n rhaid mai hi oedd wedi agor fy mag ysgol ar y diwrnod cynta. Ceisiais gofio rhythm yr anadlu oedd wedi ei recordio ar y pecyn casglu data a gwrando arni hithau'n anadlu.

"Oes rhywbeth yn bod, Alys Phillips?" gofynnodd Miss Glein wrth fy ngweld i'n syllu arni, wedi dal fy anadl fy hun er mwyn gwrando ar ei hanadlu hi.

Dychrynais fymryn pan sylweddolais nad o'n i wedi ei hateb.

"Na, sdim yn bod. Dwi'n iawn. Petha'n mynd yn iawn, diolch."

Ro'n i isio gwenu er mwyn ei pherswadio 'mod i'n hapus fy myd yn Ysgol Breifat Pen y Rhych. Ond roedd gen i'r teimlad mai gwenu fyddai'r peth gwaetha posib i'w wneud (oni bai am chwerthin). Roedd y cas pensiliau'n dal yn fy llaw.

"Wyt ti'n cael digon o ginio?" gofynnodd wedyn.

Am gwestiwn gwirion, meddyliais.

"Ydw, diolch," atebais yn gwrtais gan geisio meddwl ble fyddai'n lle da i guddio fy nghas pensiliau.

Ond yna, gofynnodd Miss Glein gwestiwn nad o'n i'n ei ddisgwyl o gwbwl.

"A sut mae dy fam?" Rhythodd arna i.

"Mam? Ydach chi'n adnabod Mam?" O na, o na, roedd hi'n gwybod popeth, mae'n rhaid! Ro'n i'n dechrau chwysu. Roedd rhywbeth od iawn yn digwydd yn fan hyn.

"Ro'n i'n ei hadnabod hi erstalwm," meddai Miss Glein. "Ydi dy fam yn siarad am erstalwm weithiau?" gofynnodd wrth gulhau ei llygaid a dod yn agos ata i.

Roedd drewdod cnau a llefrith wedi suro yn dawnsio rhwng blew bach fy ffroenau. Roedd yn rhaid i mi gallio a dechrau meddwl fel ysbïwr go iawn.

"Dim llawer," meddwn i er mwyn gweld ei hymateb.

Ro'n i'n siŵr i mi weld cysgod o ryddhad ar ei hwyneb, felly gofynnais yn ddiflewyn-ar-dafod: "Oeddach chi yn y carchar i droseddwyr ifanc hefyd?"

Sythodd Miss Glein yn sydyn ac aeth ei gwefusau'n fain. Trodd ei hwyneb bara brith oren i ryw fath o biws. Yna, dywedodd yn araf a miniog:

"Paid ti â meiddio gofyn cwestiynau mor haerllug, y gnawes fach."

Am ddynes ddychrynllyd! Trodd ei chefn a cherdded i ochr arall y ddesg. Gwelais fy nghyfle. Gollyngais y pecyn casglu data ar y llawr wrth fy nhroed dde a phesychu i guddio'r sŵn.

"Mae'n ddrwg iawn gen i, ond... ymmm... newydd gyfaddef ei bod hi wedi bod yn y carchar mae hi, ac rydw i'n dal ychydig bach yn flin am y peth. Tydi hi'n dweud dim wrtha i – does ganddon ni ddim perthynas dda iawn, dach chi'n gweld."

Wrth i mi raffu celwyddau, gwthiais y pecyn casglu data gyda fy nhroed nes ei fod o dan ei desg.

"Alys, tydw i ddim yn dwp. Ond tydw i ddim chwaith yn siŵr pam dy fod ti yma. Mae gan yr ysgol fas-data eang iawn ar bob disgybl ac mae dy ganlyniadau academaidd di yn rhy dda o lawer i Flwyddyn 7 – hyd yn oed Blwyddyn 7 Ysgol Breifat Hynod Lewyrchus Pen y Rhych. Ond fedra i yn fy myw â darganfod pa ysgol fynychaist ti cyn dod yma."

Sut yn y byd oedd hi wedi darganfod unrhyw beth o gwbwl? Ro'n i fymryn yn flin nad oedd Mrs Pi wedi medru dileu unrhyw wybodaeth am fy nghefndir i oddi ar y we.

"Fel y dywedais i, tydw i a Mam ddim yn dod ymlaen efo'n gilydd yn dda iawn a dwi'n meddwl ei bod hi jyst isio cael gwared arna i. Unwaith o'n i'n ddigon hen i ddod i'r ysgol yma, wel... i ffwrdd â fi. Mae Ysgol Pen y Rhych yn enwog am ei safonau uchel − ac fe fydd y safonau'n uwch nag erioed efo rhywun o fy ngallu i yma." Ro'n i'n fodlon dweud unrhyw beth er mwyn ei pherswadio hi nad oedd unrhyw beth amheus amdana i, ac i geisio tynnu ei sylw oddi wrth fy nghefndir addysgol. Ro'n i'n gweld olwynion ei meddwl hi'n troi ac yn ystyried yr hyn ro'n i newydd ei ddweud. Cymerais gipolwg ar leoliad y pecyn casglu data. Roedd yn saff ac o'r golwg o dan y ddesg.

"Ella wir. Basa'n well i ti fynd i dy Glwb... Coginio?" Edrychodd arna i fel tasa hi angen eglurhad pam 'mod i wedi dewis y Clwb Coginio.

"O ia... Dwi wrth fy modd yn coginio. Tydi Mam ddim yn licio gwastraffu egni yn gwneud bwyd."

Ro'n i'n cael modd i fyw yn palu celwyddau wrthi, rŵan bod fy hyder i'n dod yn ei ôl.

"Wel, dos 'ta. Ond cofia, os wyt ti'n ceisio fy nhwyllo i mewn unrhyw ffordd, fe ddysga i wers go iawn i ti."

Cerddais oddi yno, heb wenu na dim, a mynd yn syth am y gegin yn y ffreutur, yn barod ar gyfer y

Clwb Coginio. Eisteddais wrth ymyl Celi a Ceri gan ddisgwyl i'r ddwy ddechrau parablu a chwerthin a giglo. Ond roedd yr efeilliaid yn dawel a digyffro.

"Haia!" meddwn i gan geisio codi sgwrs.

"Haia," atebodd Ceri neu Celi.

"Dach chi'n iawn?" holais.

"Iawn, diolch," atebodd y llall yn swta.

Doedd 'na ddim chwarter cymaint o hwyliau arnyn nhw o'i gymharu â'r bore cynta. Roedd golwg bell yn eu llygaid ac roedd y lliw wedi mynd o'u bochau. Oedden nhw'n iawn, neu oedd Miss Glein wedi tywallt ei hud dychrynllyd drostyn nhw? Edrychais o 'nghwmpas – roedd pawb yn edrych yr un mor ddiflas â'i gilydd. Beth bynnag roedd Miss Glein yn ei wneud, roedd o wedi dechrau gweithio ar Flwyddyn 7. Ond roedd Meri a Blod yn bownsio o gwmpas, gan chwerthin a gwenu wrth fynd ymlaen â'r wers.

Penderfynais wneud y gorau o'r clwb a cheisio mwynhau fy hun. Ond bob tro ro'n i'n hanner gwenu neu'n mwynhau rhyw jôc, ro'n i'n cael y teimlad nad o'n i i fod i fwynhau. Roedd Meri a Blod yn fy anwybyddu i. Roedd pawb arall yn cael cymorth, er nad oedd yr un o'r disgyblion eraill yn chwerthin ar eu jôcs nhw. Ro'n i, ar y llaw arall, yn gwneud ymdrech i ymuno yn yr hwyl ond roedd y ddwy'n edrych arna i fel tasa gen i ddim hawl chwerthin.

Wrth i'r awr ddod i ben, a finnau heb ddysgu sut i gracio wy heb sôn am wneud cinio dydd Sul, gwichiodd yr uchelseinydd dros yr ysgol. Llais Mr Bylbs oedd yno, yn gofyn i ddisgybl ddod i'w swyddfa cyn gynted â phosib. Pwy oedd y disgybl? Ia, fi!

Ro'n i'n gwybod beth oedd yn bod. Roedden nhw wedi dod o hyd i fy nghas pensiliau. Ond y cwestiwn mawr oedd: oedden nhw wedi darganfod be'n union *oedd* fy nghas pensiliau?

Wrth i mi gerdded tuag at swyddfa Mr Bylbs, roedd fy nghalon yn curo fel petai eliffant yn rhedeg ras y tu mewn i mi. Cyrhaeddais y drws a rhoi cnoc cyn camu i mewn.

"A… Alys… Shwd wyt ti, bach? Ymm… Dere 'ma."

Roedd Mr Bylbs yn goch at ei glustiau ac yn chwys diferol. Roedd o wedi bod yn rhedeg ac roedd 'na ddrewdod ar ei ddillad. Nid drewdod chwys ond rhyw arogl melys fel pwdin. Roedd o'n sibrwd hefyd, ac yn gwneud i mi deimlo braidd yn anghysurus.

"Ai ti sydd berchen hwn?" gofynnodd yn frysiog. Roedd o'n gafael yn fy nghas pensiliau.

"W, ia! Diolch, syr. Lle gawsoch chi o?" Ceisiais swnio'n ddidaro.

"Yn swyddfa Miss Glein. Pam oeddet ti yno... yn ei swyddfa hi?"

"Miss Glein nath fy ngwahodd i. Roedd hi isio holi sut roedd petha'n mynd," atebais yn ddiniwed.

"O. Reit. Wel, gwna'n siŵr na fyddi di'n gadael unrhyw beth ar ôl yno 'to. *Os* byddi di byth yn ei swyddfa hi 'to, hynny yw. Cer!"

Diolch byth, wnaeth o amau dim am y cas pensiliau, ac ar ôl i mi edrych yn fanwl roedd popeth yn edrych yn iawn, heb ei gyffwrdd. Ffiw! Ro'n i wedi chwysu heb i mi sylwi ond, creda fi, ro'n i bron iawn yn sgipio 'nôl i fy ystafell. Ro'n i'n teimlo cymaint o ryddhad fy mod wedi llwyddo i adael y pecyn casglu data yn swyddfa Miss Glein ac wedi ei gael o'n ôl heb i neb amau dim. Dim ond gobeithio bod rhywbeth o werth wedi'i gofnodi arno. Y cyfan oedd angen ei wneud rŵan oedd gwrando ar y tâp a gyrru adroddiad llawn i Mrs Pi a Mam am un ar ddeg o'r gloch.

Ychydig a wyddwn i ar y pryd ei bod hi'n mynd i fod yn noson brysur iawn!

7
NOS DA, NOS DRWG

Roedd hi'n tynnu at hanner awr wedi chwech erbyn hyn, a do'n i ddim wedi gweld Lleucu ers amser. Dychmygais ei bod hi gyda'r nyrs ar ôl iddi gael llygad ddu yn y Clwb Bocsio. Ond ro'n i'n ddiolchgar nad oedd hi yno, a dweud y gwir, er mwyn i mi gael llonydd i wrando ar yr hyn roedd y pecyn casglu data wedi ei gasglu.

Yn lwcus i mi, roedd y camera a'r meicroffon yn medru dangos pryd yn ystod y recordiad roedd 'na symudiad neu sŵn mawr. Felly ro'n i'n medru chwarae'r recordiad yn syth o'r pwynt hwnnw, yn hytrach na gorfod gwrando ar ddistawrwydd am hydoedd. Doedd dim llawer wedi ei gofnodi gan y camera, dim ond traed Miss Glein, ond ro'n i'n gallu clywed popeth yn glir:

Drrrrring drrrrring. Ffôn yn canu.

"W!" Llais Miss Glein. "Heliiiw! Rhods, shwd wyt ti, cariad?!"

Roedd yn rhaid i mi wasgu *pause* am eiliad i ysgrifennu nodyn:

Miss Glein yn swnio'n hapus, efallai'n gwenu! Ac mae ganddi acen ddeheuol gref. Pwy yw Rhods?

Gwasgais y triongl bach unwaith eto.

"Ie, ie, Rhods bach, wrth gwrs. Bydd y ffeiliau sain yn dy gyrraedd di ddiwedd yr wthnos… Wel, beth am i fi ddod draw atat ti?… Falle ddim felly, ife?… Ow, owcei 'te… Wel, ffona fi nes 'mlân… Helô?"

Clywais y ffôn yn cael ei osod ar y ddesg. Ysgrifennais yn fawr ar fy nodiadau:

Ffeiliau sain?

Yna, gwaeddodd Miss Glein:

"Barri!"

Daeth rhywun i mewn i'r ystafell.

"Ie, Carys? Be sy nawr?"

Mr Bylbs, dwi'n siŵr! Yn crynu yn ei sgidiau. Ysgrifennais nodyn:

Mr Bylbs = Barri Bylbs.

Miss Glein = Carys Glein.

"Ble ti 'di bod?"

Roedd hi'n swnio'n flin eto.

"Ma'n ddrwg 'da fi, Carys, ond dwi wedi bod yn gwneud yn siŵr fod popeth yn ei le ar gyfer heno. Mae pob stafell yn barod nawr."

"Wel, mae angen i ti fynd i sorto'r bachgen Ffrancs 'na mas. Nawr."

Ac wrth iddi ddweud 'nawr' daeth ei llaw o dan y ddesg a phwyso botwm coch. Yna, y tu ôl i'w choesau,

gwelais y wal foel yn llithro yn agored. Doedd y
camera ddim yn medru gweld be'n union oedd y tu
ôl i'r wal, ond ro'n i'n medru gweld gwaelod drws
arall. Agorodd Miss Glein y drws a cherddodd Mr
Bylbs trwyddo. Roedd sŵn gweiddi yn y pellter. Ai
Twm oedd yno? Oedd Miss Glein a Mr Bylbs wedi
dal Twm?

Caeodd Mr Bylbs y drws y tu ôl iddo, a chaeodd
Miss Glein y wal. Yna gadawodd y swyddfa. Roedd
yr ystafell yn wag. Neidiodd y tâp ymlaen hanner awr,
yna dechreuodd redeg eto. Agorodd y wal a daeth Mr
Bylbs yn ôl i mewn i'r ystafell gan anadlu'n drwm,
fel petai newydd redeg i fyny grisiau. Daeth ei law i'r
golwg o dan y ddesg, â hances ynddi. Gollyngodd yr
hances wrth chwilio am y botwm coch i gau'r wal.

"O, damo! Be sy'n bod arna i?" dywedodd cyn
dod ar ei bengliniau o dan y ddesg. Pwysodd y
botwm coch ac ymbalfalu am ei hances, yna'n sydyn
cafodd y camera ei daro. Edrychodd Mr Bylbs i fyw
fy llygaid. Roedd wedi darganfod y pecyn casglu data.
Dychrynais. Yna clywais ei lais yn dweud:

"Pwy sydd wedi gadael hwn fan 'yn?" Gafaelodd
ynddo a'i droelli'n ofalus. "Fi 'di gweld hwn o'r blân.
Alys Phillips, greda i. O, na...! Beth ma'r ferch 'na
wedi wneud nawr?!" Gadawodd yr ystafell gyda fy
nghas pensiliau yn ei feddiant.

Wel wir, meddyliais, roedd tipyn o wybodaeth wedi ei chasglu, ac fe fyddai gen i adroddiad llawn iawn i'w roi i Mrs Pi a Mam heno am y tro cynta ers dyddiau. Ond roedd gen i gymaint o gwestiynau. Beth oedd Mr Bylbs wedi bod yn ei wneud yn yr ystafelloedd? Pa ystafelloedd? Ein hystafelloedd gwely ni? Beth am Twm? Roedd yn rhaid i mi chwilio am Lleucu. Ble bynnag roedd hi wedi bod, ro'n i'n siŵr o'i gweld hi yn y ffreutur amser swper. Cadwais y pecyn casglu data yn ofalus.

Roedd y ffreutur yn llawn, ond roedd hi'n rhyfeddol o dawel yno. Roedd hyd yn oed criw Blwyddyn 7 wedi colli pob sbarc erbyn hyn. Beth ar wyneb y ddaear oedd wedi digwydd iddyn nhw i gyd? O'n i wedi methu rhywbeth? Gwelais Celi a Ceri a gofyn oedden nhw wedi gweld Lleucu. Roedd y ddwy'n llowcio cwstard.

"Pwy?" meddai un.

"Na," meddai'r llall gan gario ymlaen i fwyta'r cwstard.

Roedd gen i deimlad drwg iawn erbyn hyn. Wrth i mi adael y ffreutur, gwelais Lleucu.

"Lleucu! Lle wyt ti wedi bod?!"

Edrychodd Lleucu arna i'n ddiflas, yn ôl ei harfer, gan ddweud:

"Gwena."

"Sori?" gofynnais.

"Dwi angen i chdi wenu cyn y medra i dy drystio di."

Gwenais arni, a diolch byth, gwenodd hithau'n ôl a diflannodd y llwydni. Beth bynnag oedd wedi digwydd i bawb arall, doedd o ddim wedi effeithio arnon ni.

"Wyt ti wedi gweld Twm?" gofynnodd Lleucu.

"Naddo, ond dwi'n meddwl 'mod i'n gwybod lle mae o."

"Beth?"

"Alla i ddim egluro popeth rŵan ond dwi'n meddwl bod Miss Glein a Mr Bylbs wedi dal Twm."

"O na! Be 'dan ni am neud?"

"Wel, ei achub o. Ty'd!"

Do'n i heb feddwl am gynllun iawn ond ro'n i'n gwybod lle i ddechrau.

Aeth Lleucu a finnau tuag at swyddfa Mr Bylbs a Miss Glein. Doedd neb o gwmpas ac roedd ias yn rhedeg i lawr fy nghefn, fel petai 'na bluen yn disgyn rhwng fy nghrys a 'nghroen. Cnociais ar ddrws mawr swyddfa Mr Bylbs. Daeth neb i'w ateb a phan geisiais ei agor sylweddolais ei fod dan glo ond, diolch byth, rydw i'n giamstar am agor cloeon ac roedd y drws yn agored mewn chwinciad.

"Sut nest ti hynna?!" gofynnodd Lleucu.

Anwybyddais hi a mynd yn syth i geisio agor drws swyddfa Miss Glein. Ond roedd hynny'n amhosib heb y cod.

"Dwi ddim yn meddwl bod hyn yn syniad da iawn, Alys."

"Sh, Lleucu. Edrycha am unrhyw beth fasa'n profi bod Twm wedi bod yma."

Dechreuodd y ddwy ohonon ni chwilio o amgylch swyddfa Mr Bylbs: yn y cypyrddau, o dan y ddesg, y tu ôl i'r planhigion, rhwng yr argraffydd a'r copïwr. Do'n i ddim yn siŵr am be'n union roedden ni'n chwilio nes i Lleucu ddweud fy enw:

"Alys!"

Roedd ei llais hi'n gryndod. Edrychais arni ac roedd hi'n sefyll yno gyda bag ysgol Twm yn ei llaw. Roedd hi wedi dod o hyd iddo yn nrôr isa'r cwpwrdd ffeilio.

"O na," meddwn i dan fy ngwynt. "Oes rhywbeth o'r bag ar goll?"

"Dwn i'm... Fel be?"

Roedden ni'n dwy ar ein gliniau ar lawr yn chwilota drwy fag Twm, yn chwilio am unrhyw fath o gliw, pan deimlais law ar fy ysgwydd. Dwylo meddal, chwyslyd Mr Bylbs.

"A beth y'ch chi'n meddwl y'ch chi'n neud fan 'yn?" Roedd ei lygaid yn fawr a phanig yn cripian yn ara deg dros ei wyneb.

"O, Mr Bylbs…"

Ceisiais feddwl am esgus ond cyn i mi gael cyfle cododd Lleucu ar ei thraed.

"Lle mae Twm? Be dach chi 'di neud iddo fo?"

"Nawr, nawr, Lleucu Ffrancs…"

Cymerodd Mr Bylbs gam tuag ati i geisio'i thawelu, am wn i, ond cododd Lleucu ei dyrnau fel petai hi mewn sgwâr bocsio. Rhoddodd Mr Bylbs sgrech!

"Lle mae Twm?" gofynnodd Lleucu, a'i dyrnau i fyny wrth ei hwyneb.

"Lleucu… Paid â bod yn wirion…" meddwn i, wedi dychryn braidd o'i gweld hi'n codi ei dyrnau.

"Na, Alys. Maen nhw wedi gneud rhywbeth i Twm."

Roedd Mr Bylbs yn fflapian ei freichiau fel adenydd aderyn gwyllt. Ceisiodd afael ym mreichiau Lleucu, ond cyn iddo fedru gwneud dim roedd Lleucu wedi gosod ei dwrn yn slic ac yn gadarn ar ochr ei drwyn.

"Aaaaa!" sgrechiodd Mr Bylbs a rhoi ei wyneb yn ei ddwylo, ac yn ara deg dechreuodd cochni lifo rhwng ei fysedd.

"Lleucu! Ma'i drwyn o'n gwaedu! Ti ddim yn gall!" meddwn i gan afael yn Mr Bylbs a'i roi i eistedd wrth ei ddesg. Dwi'n siŵr ei fod o wedi dechrau crio! Wrth i mi wneud hynny, agorodd drws swyddfa Miss

Glein a daeth sgrech hyll fel cloch rydlyd o geg y brifathrawes.

"BETH SY'N MYND 'MLAEN?! Lleucu Ffrancs ac Alys Phillips!"

"Fi 'nath," meddai Lleucu, "ond dwi'n gwybod 'ych bod chi wedi neud rwbath i Twm. Lle mae o?"

Ro'n i'n meddwl bod Lleucu wedi colli ei phwyll yn lân a bod pethau'n siŵr o fynd o ddrwg i waeth. Ond yna, fel angel yn canu, daeth llais Twm o'r tu ôl i Miss Glein.

"Lleucu, dwi fan hyn."

Edrychais i a Lleucu â'n cegau'n agored ar Twm yn camu tuag aton ni o'r tu ôl i Miss Glein.

"Mae Twm wedi bod yn ein helpu ni gydag arbrawf bach, er nad ydi hynny'n ddim o'ch busnes chi. Ond fedra i ddim credu be dwi'n ei weld o fy mlaen i fan hyn… Disgybl Blwyddyn 7 wedi taro aelod o staff? Mi fedrwn i'ch taflu chi'ch dwy o'r ysgol yr eiliad yma."

O na, meddyliais, cael fy ngwahardd o'r ysgol heb ddatrys dim! Cofiais eto eiriau ola Mrs Pi: mae ysbïwr da yn anweledig.

"Mr Bylbs, sut fedrech chi adael i ddwy ferch fach…? Wyt ti'n crio?"

Cododd Mr Bylbs ar ei draed. Roedd yn dal ei ben yn ôl i atal y gwaed rhag llifo dros bob man.

"Miss Glein... Dim ond mymryn o gamddealltwriaeth oedd y cyfan. Damwain. Na, sai'n llefen! Ym... Doeddwn i ddim yn ei ddisgwl e, 'na i gyd!"

Do'n i ddim yn gallu credu fy nghlustiau. Roedd Mr Bylbs yn fwy o lwfrgi nag o'n i'n feddwl, oedd yn lwcus iawn i ni.

"Poeni amdana i roedd Lleucu," ychwanegodd Twm mewn llais undonog, diflas. "Mae tymor cynta mewn ysgol newydd yn anodd."

Roedd hi'n amlwg fod rhywbeth wedi digwydd iddo. Oedd Lleucu wedi sylwi hefyd?

Anfonwyd Twm i gael ei swper cyn i Lleucu na finnau allu gael gair ag o ac anfonwyd ni'n dwy i'n hystafell gyda rhybudd nad oedden ni i adael heblaw am i fynd i'r tŷ bach. Eisteddodd y ddwy ohonon ni ar ein gwelyau ein hunain yn gwbwl dawel. Erbyn hyn roedd golau'r lleuad yn sleifio i mewn ar flaenau'i draed drwy'r ffenest fach. Ymhen hir a hwyr, roedd yn rhaid i mi dorri'r tawelwch.

"Wel, do'n i ddim yn disgwyl hynna gen ti, Lleucu. Roedd Mr Bylbs yn troi yn ei unfan bron iawn!"

Edrychais arni ac edrychodd hithau arna i a chyn pen dim roedden ni'n dwy'n rholio chwerthin. Roedden ni ar ein cefnau, ac roedd hi fel petai'r chwerthin yn dod o fodiau'n traed. O, roedd hi'n braf cael chwerthin yn iawn a chlywed Lleucu'n chwerthin hefyd.

Ond roedd yn rhaid i'r hwyl ddod i ben. Roedd Lleucu'n dal i boeni am Twm, ac ro'n innau hefyd, ond llwyddais i berswadio Lleucu ei fod yn iawn ac y bydden ni'n cael sgwrs ag o drannoeth.

"Ma 'na rywbeth od yn mynd 'mlaen yn yr ysgol 'ma," meddai Lleucu.

Ro'n i'n gwybod bod ganddi hi a Twm eu hamheuon ond doedd hi ddim wedi cyfaddef fel hyn o'r blaen.

"Do'n i ddim yn credu Twm i ddechrau. Mae o wedi gwneud popeth i drio cael ei hel o'r ysgol 'ma. Roedd o wedi swnian a swnian ar Mam i beidio fy ngyrru i i'r un lle. Ond tydw i ddim yn meddwl bod Mam na Dad 'rioed wedi gwrando dim arnon ni." Ochneidiodd eto.

Do'n i ddim isio torri ar ei thraws. Roedd hi fel petai'n cael rhyddid i siarad yn iawn am rywbeth am y tro cynta.

"Mae Twm wastad wedi edrych ar f'ôl i a fedra i ddim gadael i rywun fel Miss Glein gael ei chrafangau dieflig arno fo... fy mrawd gwirion i!"

Cafodd Lleucu siarad y noson honno ac mi ges i wrando a sgwrsio. Ro'n i'n dechrau teimlo, am y tro cynta yn fy mywyd, bod gen i ffrind.

Ymhen hir a hwyr, llithrodd Lleucu i drwmgwsg. A diolch byth am hynny, achos roedd hi'n bum munud i un ar ddeg ac ro'n i'n gwybod y byddai Mam a Mrs Pi ar bigau'r drain yn disgwyl i mi gysylltu. Gafaelais yn fy mag ysgol a'r pecyn casglu data ac agor y drws. Golau gwan iawn oedd yn goleuo'r coridor, dim ond digon i mi weld y ffordd i'r ystafell ymolchi. Roedd honno'n oeraidd a moel, a phopeth yn wyn, hyd yn oed y golau. Caeais y drws a'i gloi, cyn eistedd i lawr gyda fy nodiadau i gyd er mwyn anfon neges. Roedd modd i mi eu ffonio, ond dim ond mewn argyfwng – roedd Mrs Pi wedi fy siarsio. Felly, teipiais yr holl bethau ro'n i wedi eu gweld a'u clywed ar y sgrin fach ac anfon y neges.

Ar ôl tri chwarter awr o aros am ymateb, penderfynais fynd yn ôl i fy ngwely a derbyn efallai na fyddwn i'n cael eu neges tan fory. Ro'n i bron â marw isio cysgu ac roedd hi'n andros o oer ac annifyr yn yr ystafell ymolchi. Wrth i mi godi fy mag ysgol, dechreuodd grynu a gwneud sŵn tawel fel pryfyn yn sownd yng nghornel ffenest. Edrychais ar y sgrin fach – roedd Mrs Pi yn fy ffonio. Rhoddais fy nghlustffonau dros fy nghlustiau a chodi meicroffon bach at fy ngheg cyn gwasgu botwm i ateb yr alwad.

Roedd Mrs Pi a Mam hefyd wedi bod yn brysur iawn yn casglu gwybodaeth, ac roedden nhw wedi darganfod cyfrinachau mawr am Miss Glein a Mr Bylbs. Roedd gan Mr Bylbs chwaer o'r enw Carys.

"Carys ydi Miss Glein..." meddwn i. "Carys Bylbs!"

Aeth Mrs Pi ymlaen i sôn nad oedden nhw wedi medru darganfod llawer mwy am eu teulu ac nad oedd sôn am rieni. Roedden nhw wedi cael eu magu gan ddwy hen fodryb iddyn nhw ond doedd neb yn gwybod dim amdanyn nhw bellach. Roedd Miss Glein hefyd wedi cael ei gweld yn treulio nosweithiau rhamantus gyda'r comedïwr enwog Rhodricês Llywethin ac, yn ôl gwaith ymchwil Mrs Pi, roedd Rhodricês Llywethin yn rhoi swm mawr iawn o arian yng nghyfrif banc Miss Glein unwaith y tymor.

"Rhods oedd ar y ffôn, mae'n rhaid," oedd fy ymateb. "Unrhyw syniad beth yw'r ffeiliau sain roedd Miss Glein yn sôn amdanyn nhw?"

Doedd Mrs Pi ddim yn siŵr beth oedd y ffeiliau sain ond roedd hi'n amau mai talu am y rheini yr oedd Rhodricês bob tymor. Ond am ba fath o ffeiliau sain y byddai comedïwr yn fodlon talu cymaint o arian?

"Mae gen ti dipyn o waith ysbïo i'w wneud eto. Rhaid darganfod beth mae Miss Glein yn ei werthu i Rhodricês Llywethin."

"Iawn," meddwn i, "a beth am y disgyblion sy'n

cael eu hypnoteiddio neu beth bynnag sy'n digwydd iddyn nhw?"

"Mae gen ti wers wyddoniaeth bore fory, yn does?"

"Oes, pam?"

"Wel," meddai Mrs Pi, "rydan ni wedi dod o hyd i un cyn-athro Gwyddoniaeth Ysgol Breifat Pen y Rhych – ac mae 'na lawer o gyn-athrawon Gwyddoniaeth Ysgol Breifat Pen y Rhych! Roedd o'n dweud bod y gwersi Gwyddoniaeth yn cynnwys gwaith arbrofol nad oedd o erioed wedi ei wneud o'r blaen. Ond roedd Miss Glein yn mynnu ei fod yn dilyn canllawiau gwyddonol arbennig yr ysgol. A phan ddechreuodd ei chwestiynu ac amau bod rhywbeth od yn mynd 'mlaen, fe gollodd ei waith a chafodd o fyth ddysgu mewn unrhyw ysgol eto."

Ffarweliais â Mrs Pi gan addo y byddwn i'n wyliadwrus iawn yn ystod fy ngwersi Gwyddoniaeth o hyn allan. Roedd gen i a Mrs Pi y teimlad ein bod ni'n agos iawn at ddatrys yr holl ddirgelwch. Ches i ddim siarad â Mam – doedd hi ddim yno ar y pryd.

"Gei di siarad â dy fam ddiwedd yr wythnos gobeithio. Hwyl rŵan... a chofia aros yn anweledig."

Rhoddodd Mrs Pi y ffôn i lawr gan fy ngadael yn nhawelwch rhyfedd yr ystafell ymolchi oeraidd.

Roedd hi'n ychydig funudau cyn hanner nos erbyn hyn ac ro'n i'n ysu am fy ngwely. Rhoddais fy mag ar fy nghefn, agor clo drws yr ystafell ymolchi a thynnu'r drws yn agored. Wrth i mi gerdded heibio ystafelloedd gwely pawb ym Mlwyddyn 7 ac anelu am fy ystafell i a Lleucu, roedd 'na sŵn gwynt yn sisial yn dawel. Ond roedd 'na sŵn rhywbeth arall hefyd – rhyw sŵn isel yn gymysg â sisial y gwynt. Arhosais yn fy unfan i wrando wrth ddrws ystafell rhif 66. Sylweddolais fod y sŵn yn dod o'r ystafell wely. Rhoddais fy nghlust yn erbyn y drws a gwrando'n astud. Roedd sŵn chwerthin yn dod o'r ystafell. Gwrandewais wrth ddrws 65, 64, 63 a 62 ac roedd 'na sŵn chwerthin yn dod o bob un ohonyn nhw. Rhedais i lawr y coridor a dewis drws arall ar hap i wrando. Roedd sŵn chwerthin yn dod o bob ystafell! Gwrandewais wrth ddrws 26, ystafell Celi a Ceri. Oedd – sŵn chwerthin. Cnociais ar y drws ond ddaeth neb i'w ateb. Es i wrando wrth ddrws rhif 25, ystafell Lleucu a finnau, ond doedd 'na ddim smic o'r fan honno. Agorais y drws a rhoi'r golau ymlaen. Roedd Lleucu'n cysgu'n drwm yn ei gwely, a doedd hi ddim yn chwerthin.

Beth ar wyneb y ddaear oedd yn digwydd? Pam nad o'n i wedi clywed hyn o'r blaen? Ond do'n i ddim wedi mynd i'r gwely mor hwyr â hyn o'r blaen. Es yn ôl at ddrws Celi a Ceri a gwrando eto. Roedden nhw'n dal i chwerthin lond eu boliau – ac yn sgwrsio hefyd. Doedd dim amdani ond agor y drws. Roedd y tywyllwch fel triog. Roedd fy mag yn dal ar fy nghefn a chofiais fod gen i olau bach arno. Gafaelais yn y tortsh a'i droi ymlaen. Roedd yr hyn a welais ac a glywais i gydag un o'r pethau rhyfeddaf ro'n i erioed wedi eu gweld. Roedd Celi a Ceri yn gorwedd yn eu gwlâu yn cysgu'n sownd, a'u llygaid ar gau, ond roedden nhw'n rholio chwerthin. Yna gofynnodd Celi:

"Be ti'n galw merch sy'n casáu mwstashis?!"

"Na-tash-a!" atebodd Ceri, cyn chwerthin nerth ei phen ac yna gofyn, "Be ti'n galw brechdan ffa pob?"

"Rhechdan!" atebodd Celi wedyn.

Roedd y ddwy yn cysgu'n sownd ond yn chwerthin a rhannu jôcs!

Roedd eu chwerthin yn llenwi'r ystafell. Roedd hi'n ugain munud wedi hanner nos erbyn hyn. Gadewais eu hystafell a mynd i dair ystafell wely arall, a'r un oedd yr olygfa ym mhob man. Roedd pawb yn rhannu jôcs a straeon doniol ac yn rholio chwerthin yn eu cwsg. Ro'n i hyd yn oed yn chwerthin! Erbyn i mi gyrraedd y bedwaredd ystafell a sefyll yno am sbel, roedd hi bron yn hanner awr wedi hanner nos. Yn sydyn, dyma'r chwerthin yn stopio. Roedd y ddau ddisgybl yn dal i gysgu'n drwm, ond roedd y chwerthin wedi peidio. Ai dim ond pwl o hanner awr yr oedd pawb wedi'i gael? Wrth i mi benderfynu gadael a mynd yn ôl i fy ngwely, clywais sŵn blîp electronig a golau bach coch yn fflachio wrth droed un o'r gwelyau. Roedd rhywbeth wedi bod yn eu recordio nhw. Penderfynais ei heglu hi oddi yno'n reit handi.

Roedd y coridor yn dawel fel neuadd arholiad unwaith eto. Pan gyrhaeddais fy ystafell, fedrwn i ddim peidio â chwilio am ateb i'r holl beth. Pawb yn chwerthin a rhannu jôcs yn eu cwsg? Ai dyna'r ffeiliau sain? Ai o'r fan hyn yr oedd Rhodricês Llywethin yn cael ei jôcs? Ai dyna gynllun mawr Miss Glein? Roedd fy meddwl fel chwyrligwgan. Sut ar wyneb y ddaear yr o'n i'n mynd i fedru cysgu rŵan? Ond cysgu wnes i, mae'n rhaid, a diolch byth am hynny – fe fyddwn i angen fy holl egni.

8
YN Y BORE MAE 'I DAL HI!

Pan ddeffrais drannoeth doedd Lleucu ddim yn ei gwely. Wedi mynd i ymolchi, mae'n rhaid, meddyliais. Yna, cofiais yn sydyn am ddigwyddiadau'r noson cynt. Efallai nad oedd chwerthin o gwbwl yn ystod y dydd yn Ysgol Breifat Pen y Rhych, ond roedd y lle'n llawn chwerthin yn y nos. Ac yn rhyfeddach na hynny, ro'n i'n sicr fod rhywun yn recordio'r chwerthin a'r jôcs. Es ar fy mhengliniau i chwilio wrth droed y gwely am y golau coch ro'n i wedi ei weld neithiwr mewn ystafell arall. Doedd dim byd amlwg i'w weld ond wrth i mi redeg fy mysedd ar hyd rhychau'r pren teimlais wifren fach a phen arni. Tynnais hi i'r golwg a gweld mai meicroffon bach ydoedd. Dilynais y wifren, oedd yn arwain o dan y gwely ac i'r wal. Roedd yr un peth yn wir am wely Lleucu hefyd.

Wrth i mi guddio'r wifren yn ôl yn ei lle, sgrechiodd cloch yr ysgol fel petai rhywun wedi sefyll ar droed cath. Edrychais ar y cloc wrth fy ngwely a sylweddoli 'mod i wedi cysgu'n andros o hwyr a bod y gwasanaeth boreol ar fin dechrau. Neidiais i fy nillad ysgol a thaflu fy mag dros fy ysgwydd. Pam na fyddai Lleucu wedi fy neffro i? Ro'n i'n bytheirio wrth redeg tuag at y neuadd fawr.

Cyrhaeddais fy sedd heb golli 'ngwynt. Doedd dim golwg o Lleucu. Ceisiais edrych dros fy ysgwydd i chwilio am Twm, a gwelais y twmffat yn eistedd yn llonydd gyda'i ddwylo ar ei liniau fel pawb arall o'i gwmpas. Roedd o'n edrych fel delw, ac roedd pawb ym Mlwyddyn 7 yn edrych yr un mor ddiflas. Oni bai amdana i.

Daeth Miss Glein i mewn a sefyll wrth ei phulpud, ond doedd dim sôn am Mr Bylbs. Roedd y neuadd yn ddistaw. Dechreuodd Miss Glein ar ei haraith foreol ac yna'r cyhoeddiadau ychwanegol. Yna, cyn gorffen, aeth hi ymlaen i ddweud:

"Rhaid i mi'ch atgoffa chi o ambell reol hanfodol sydd gyda ni yma yn Ysgol Breifat Hynod Lewyrchus Pen y Rhych. Does DIM crwydro i fod yn ystod y nos. Mae hynny wedi ei wahardd yn llwyr. Rydyn ni'n disgwyl i chi ddefnyddio'r stafelloedd ymolchi cyn deg o'r gloch y nos a does gan neb hawl i adael eu stafelloedd rhwng hanner nos a phump o'r gloch y bore. Os bydda i neu Mr Bylbs yn darganfod UNRHYW blentyn yn torri'r rheolau yma, mi fydd y gosb yn llym iawn."

Wnaeth hi ddim dweud yn uniongyrchol bod rhywun wedi cael ei ddal yn crwydro neithiwr ond ro'n i'n teimlo ei bod hi'n syllu'n syth arna i ac yn rhoi rhybudd personol i mi. Llithrodd ias i lawr fy nghefn.

Fy ngwers gynta oedd Gwyddoniaeth – ein gwers ymarferol gynta yn y labordy – ac fel ro'n i wedi addo i Mrs Pi, roedd yn rhaid i mi fod yn wyliadwrus iawn. Ro'n i'n disgwyl i Lleucu ymddangos o rywle er mwyn dod i'r wers, ond wnaeth hi ddim. Eisteddais ar stôl bren giami ar ben fy hun yng nghefn y labordy. Doedd yr athro heb gyrraedd ond roedd y cymhorthydd yno, yn gosod offer o'n blaenau ni i gyd. Roedd y cymhorthydd yn edrych yn gyfarwydd.

Ymhen hir a hwyr daeth yr athro, Pritch Titch, i'r dosbarth gan gario pentwr o lyfrau a phapurau. Gosododd nhw ar y bwrdd o'i flaen.

"O. Rydych chi wedi gosod yr offer yn barod? O, da iawn. Ar gyfer y wers gynta yn y llyfryn, rwy'n cymryd?" gofynnodd Pritch Titch yn betrusgar wrth y cymhorthydd – hogyn gweddol ifanc a'i wallt fel cynffonnau llygod mawr yn ffrâm am ei wyneb. Ro'n i wedi ei weld o'r blaen. Ond ble?

Atebodd y cymhorthydd gydag edrychiad arswydus a nòd araf. Am beth od, meddyliais. Roedd hi fel petai gan y cymhorthydd fwy o glem beth i'w wneud na'r athro.

"Iawn… ymmm… gadewch i ni ddechrau 'ta. 'Dan ni'n dechrau gydag… ymmm… arbrawf bach."

Daeth y cymhorthydd o'i gwpwrdd yng nghefn y labordy gyda bocsys plastig yn llawn cemegion nad o'n i erioed wedi eu gweld na chlywed amdanyn nhw.

Roedd y wers yn un od iawn. Yn hytrach na thrafod beth oedd yn digwydd wrth gymysgu'r cemegion, roedd Mr Pritch yn darllen rhyw fath o gyfarwyddiadau a ninnau'n gwneud yr hyn roedd o'n ei ddweud. Ceisiais nodi enwau'r cemegion a'r broses o'u cymysgu a'u cynhesu, er mwyn gwneud ychydig o waith ymchwil fy hun arnyn nhw. Ar ddiwedd y wers, roedd gan bob un ohonon ni botyn jam yr un o hylif gwyrdd.

"Wel, dyna ni, da iawn. Dim ond rhyw arbrawf bach i weld oeddech chi'n medru ymdopi'n iawn. Tro nesa, fe fyddwn ni'n dechrau ar waith arall…"

Wrth iddo ddweud hyn, rhoddodd y cymhorthydd ddarn o bapur o'i flaen.

"O, diolch. Ymm… o. Mi fyddwn ni'n dod 'nôl i geisio ail-greu'r hylif yma eto yn ystod y gwersi. Efallai y tro nesa y gallwn greu mwy ohono, gawn ni weld. Diolch yn fawr. Ewch am doriad bach rŵan."

Eisteddodd Mr Pritch gan afael yn ei lyfr a'i bapur a dechrau darllen popeth yn llawer mwy manwl.

Roedd pawb arall wedi cadw eu pethau ac ar eu ffordd allan cyn i mi gau fy llyfr hyd yn oed. Cymerais fy amser i gadw fy llyfrau a chlirio'r offer oddi ar fy nesg, gan gadw un llygad ar y cymhorthydd. Roedd yn rhoi caead ar bob un o'r potiau llawn hylif gwyrdd ac yn eu cadw'n ofalus mewn bocsys plastig glas. Yna, roedd yn rhoi rhyw fath o label arnyn nhw. Rhoddais fy mag ar fy nghefn a gadael y labordy, ond cyn i mi fynd draw i'r ffreutur i gael rhywbeth i'w fwyta pwysais fy nghefn ar wal y coridor, tynnu fy llyfr nodiadau o'r bag a nodi popeth oedd wedi digwydd yn y wers. Wrth i mi wneud hyn, agorodd rhywun ddrws y labordy. Daeth y cymhorthydd allan, yn gwthio troli bach â dau o'r bocsys plastig glas arno. Wnaeth o ddim fy ngweld i, felly penderfynais ei ddilyn.

Aeth â'r bocsys yr holl ffordd i ochr arall yr adeilad a thrwy'r brif fynedfa. Roedd hi'n anoddach ei ddilyn yn yr awyr agored gan nad oedd neb arall o gwmpas ac roedd yntau fel petai'n fwy gwyliadwrus. Aeth â'r troli o gwmpas ochr yr adeilad, a dyna pryd y daeth fy sgiliau dringo i'n werthfawr. Ro'n i'n gallu ei ddilyn yn weddol agos drwy neidio a dringo ar hyd waliau ochr yr ysgol heb iddo 'ngweld i. Daeth y cymhorthydd at ddrws cefn cegin yr ysgol. Ro'n i erbyn hyn ar y to uwch ei ben yn edrych i lawr arno a'r drws. Cnociodd y drws ddwywaith yn araf a dwywaith yn gyflym. Agorodd rhywun y drws ac aeth y cymhorthydd, y troli, y bocsys glas a'r jariau o hylif gwyrdd i mewn i'r gegin. Yna, fflachiodd atgof o flaen fy llygaid. Dyna lle'r o'n i wedi gweld y cymhorthydd o'r blaen... yn y gegin, yn golchi llestri amser cinio ar fy niwrnod cynta!

Neidiais i lawr yn ddidrafferth a rhedeg yr holl ffordd yn ôl i mewn i'r ysgol. Roedd yn rhaid i mi ddod o hyd i Lleucu a dweud wrthi beth oedd wedi digwydd. Ond wrth i mi redeg rownd y gornel tuag at y ffreutur, trawais yn syth i mewn i fol trampoliniog. Ro'n i ar fy hyd ar y llawr cyn i mi fedru gweld dim. Edrychais i fyny a dyna lle roedd Twm.

"Twm! Be ti'n neud?"

"Aros i fynd i weld Miss Glein."

"Y? Pryd? Hei... Wyt ti wedi gweld Lleucu?" gofynnais wrth godi ar fy nhraed.

Roedd Twm yn dal i edrych yn eitha robotaidd, ond roedd o'n blincio tipyn mwy erbyn hyn.

"Lleucu?" gofynnodd, heb lawer o emosiwn.

"Ia, Lleucu... dy chwaer!"

"Lleucu?" Daeth ychydig o liw i'w wyneb. "Lleucu? Naddo, pam lle mae hi?"

"Wel, dwi ddim yn gwybod. Dyna pam dwi'n gofyn i chdi'r twmffat!"

Gyda hyn, agorodd y drws oedd wrth ein hymyl – drws swyddfa Mr Bylbs.

"A! Twm Ffrancs, 'co ti. Ac Alys Phillips… beth y't ti'n neud nawr, ferch? O, mam bach…" meddai Mr Bylbs gan ein hyrddio ni'n dau i mewn i'w swyddfa. "Eisteddwch fan hyn am nawr. Rwy'n mynd i siarad â Miss Glein. Mae hi moyn eich gweld chi'ch dau, fel mae'n digwydd."

Gadawodd Mr Bylbs yr ystafell.

Roedd gen i boen yng ngwaelod fy stumog. Roedd rhywbeth yn bod. Pam ar wyneb y ddaear roedd y cymhorthydd yn mynd â'r hylif gwyrdd i'r gegin? Beth oedd yr hylif gwyrdd? Ble oedd Lleucu? Oedd Miss Glein wedi fy ngweld i ganol nos neithiwr?

"Twm, fedri di wenu?"

"Gwenu?" gofynnodd.

"Ia, fedri di wenu?"

Tynnodd Twm anadl ddofn a gwenodd am un eiliad, dyna i gyd.

"Medra, ond dwi ddim yn cofio sut i neud yn iawn."

"Be ddigwyddodd i chdi ddoe, Twm? Wyt ti'n cofio? Fuest ti yn swyddfa Miss Glein?"

"Pam?"

"Mae'n bwysig. Er mwyn Lleucu," meddwn i wrtho, yn y gobaith y byddai'n cofio'r hyn 'ddigwyddodd iddo. Ond wrth i mi ddweud yr enw 'Lleucu', dechreuodd flincio'n aml a phesychu.

"Lleucu? Lle mae hi?"

"Dwi'n meddwl ei bod hi yn swyddfa Miss Glein… tu ôl i'r wal. Wyt ti wedi bod tu ôl i'r wal?"

Roedd siarad am Lleucu fel petai'n dod â Twm yn ôl ato'i hun.

"Dwi'n cofio bod yn swyddfa Miss Glein. A dwi'n cofio…"

"Be?"

Ro'n i ar dân isio iddo fo gofio, cyn i Mr Bylbs ddod yn ei ôl.

"Dwi'n cofio… cwstard!"

"Cwstard?!"

Wrth i mi ddweud y gair, agorodd drws swyddfa Miss Glein ac roedd hi a Mr Bylbs yn sefyll yno'n edrych arnon ni.

"Chi'ch dau. Dewch gyda ni," meddai Miss Glein wrth i Mr Bylbs afael ynddon ni a'n gwthio i mewn i'r swyddfa.

9
MAE'N GAS GEN I GWSTARD!

Baglodd Twm a finnau i mewn i swyddfa Miss Glein, a chamodd hithau y tu ôl i'w desg. Gafaelodd Mr Bylbs yn ein bagiau a'u taflu ar lawr. Roedd ei gyrls melyn wedi stopio bownsio erbyn hyn.

"Dau sy'n ddim ond trwbwl, Miss Glein. Dyw hon ddim hyd yn oed yn lico cwstard!" meddai Mr Bylbs.

"Twm," dechreuodd Miss Glein yn araf, "dim ond trafferth wyt ti wedi bod ers i ti gyrraedd. Rwyt ti'n fwli, yn ddrygionus, yn pallu cadw at reolau, yn dwp. A tan ddoe, doeddwn i ddim yn credu y byddwn i'n medru dy reoli di chwaith. Oni bai am dy rieni fe fyddwn i wedi dy daflu di o'r ysgol ymhell cyn heddiw, heb sôn am adael i'r chwaer fach wyllt 'na sydd gen ti ddod yn agos i'r lle."

Roedd Twm yn sefyll yn hollol lonydd. Doedd o ddim yn ymateb o gwbwl. Do'n i ddim yn siŵr oedd o'n medru ei chlywed hi hyd yn oed. Roedd Miss Glein yn dal i draethu a Mr Bylbs yn cydio'n dynnach yn fy mraich wrth i mi geisio gwingo'n rhydd.

"Ond rydw i'n falch iawn o weld bod yr arbrawf

diweddaraf wedi gweithio a'n bod ni, o'r diwedd, wedi concro Twm Ffrancs. Dim ond gwneud yn siŵr ein bod ni'n rhoi'r un ddos i dy chwaer fach di ac mi fydd pob dim yn ei le. Wel, dyna oedd y cynllun tan i ti, Alys Phillips, gyrraedd, fel petaet ti wedi disgyn o'r awyr. Wel, dos ddigon cryf i ti hefyd dwi'n meddwl."

Edrychodd arna i. Roedd ei llygaid hi'n fawr a'i ffroenau'n fflapio, ac mi faswn i'n taeru bod ei gwallt hi wedi mynd yn gochach.

"Lle mae Lleucu? Be sy'n mynd 'mlaen?" Taflais y cwestiynau tuag ati.

Dechreuodd Miss Glein sgrechian: "PWY TI'N FEDDWL WYT TI? Dim ond merch fach wirion wyt ti! Wyt ti'n meddwl y galli di fy herio *i*?"

Roedd arna i ofn, ond doedd gen i ddim dewis ond ei herio hi. Fi oedd yr unig obaith bellach.

"Wel, tydw i ddim gwaeth na thrio, ydw i?"

Trodd ei hwyneb yn biws. Clywais Mr Bylbs yn llyncu ei boer y tu ôl i mi. Yna plygodd Miss Glein a rhoi ei hwyneb o 'mlaen gan sibrwd yn filain,

"Gei di weld, fy merch i." Yna sythodd yn sydyn a gweiddi, "Barri, i lawr â nhw!"

Tarodd y botwm coch o dan ei desg a llithrodd y wal yn agored. Y tu ôl iddi roedd 'na ddegau o sgriniau teledu, yn dangos llygaid pob camera yn yr ysgol. Ond yn y canol roedd 'na ddrws. Ciciodd Miss Glein y drws yn agored, yna cafodd Twm ei wthio drwyddo a chefais innau fy llusgo gan Mr Bylbs.

Yr ochr arall i'r drws roedd 'na risiau yn arwain i lawr i'r tywyllwch. Ar waelod y grisiau roedd drws arall. Agorodd Miss Glein y drws ac yno roedd Lleucu.

"Lleucu!"

Rhedais ati. Roedd hi'n eistedd mewn rhyw fath o beiriant ac roedd ganddi lond ceg o rywbeth. Gafaelais ynddi a phoerodd Lleucu beth bynnag oedd yn ei cheg drosta i.

"Lle dach chi wedi booooood?!"

"Ych a fi… be 'di'r stwff 'ma?" Roedd yn codi pwys arna i.

"Cwstard," meddai Lleucu.

"Cwstard," meddai Miss Glein.

"Cwstard? Mae'n gas gen i gwstard!" meddwn i.

Fflachiodd popeth drwy fy meddwl. Cwstard… cinio… cymhorthydd… hylif gwyrdd i'r gegin… CWSTARD!

"Barri… sortia'r rhain. Mae'n rhaid i mi drefnu'r ffeiliau sain i Rhodricês," meddai Miss Glein, gan ein gadael a chau'r drws yn glep y tu ôl iddi.

"Alys Phillips, plis paid gwneud unrhyw beth twp

nawr. Dere, mae 'na sedd i ti fan hyn. Twm, helpa fi, 'nei di?" meddai Mr Bylbs a'i lais yn gryndod.

Roedd hi'n ymddangos ei fod yn dal i gredu bod Twm dan ddylanwad Miss Glein.

"Na, Alys, paid â gadael iddo dy roi di yn y peiriant!" gwaeddodd Lleucu.

Dychrynodd Mr Bylbs a gafael yn fy mraich, ond gafaelais yn ei arddwrn a'i droi. Yna llwyddais i ddefnyddio fy nghorff i wthio yn erbyn ei gorff yntau a'i daflu dros fy ysgwydd nes iddo lanio ar ei gefn ar lawr. Sgrechiodd Mr Bylbs fel hen nain.

Rhedodd Twm ata i mewn syndod. Roedd y ddau ohonon ni'n sefyll uwchben Mr Bylbs ac roedd llygaid hwnnw'n rholio yn ei ben, fel petaen nhw'n ceisio dilyn ei gyrls rownd a rownd.

"Be 'dan ni am neud efo fo rŵan?" gofynnodd Twm.

"Dwn i'm, ond dwi'n falch o weld dy fod ti 'nôl hefo ni, 'de Twm! Fedri di wenu?"

Ond cyn i Twm fedru ateb, daeth llais o'r tu ôl i ni.

"Ymmmm, heloooo?! Ydi hi'n bosib i fi gael chydig o help os gwelwch yn dda?!"

"Lleucu!" meddai'r ddau ohonon ni gan droi a rhedeg ati.

Roedd hi wedi ei chlymu i'r peiriant ac fe gawson ni dipyn o drafferth i'w chael hi'n rhydd.

"Be ar wynab y ddaear ydi'r peiriant 'ma?" gofynnais wrth i Lleucu gamu oddi arno.

"Maen nhw'n dy orfodi di i fwyta bwceidiau o gwstard," atebodd Twm. "Fues i fan hyn ddoe… dwi'n cofio!"

"Y cwstard sy'n stopio pawb rhag chwerthin!" meddai Lleucu. "Ond sut? Dwi ddim yn dallt."

"Ydach chi wedi bod yn creu hylif gwyrdd yn eich gwersi Gwyddoniaeth, Twm?" holais.

"Mae pob gwers Wyddoniaeth yn gorffen â rhyw fath o arbrawf lle 'dan ni'n creu hylif melyn, nid gwyrdd," atebodd Twm.

"Wel, welais i'r cymhorthydd yn mynd â'r hylif gwyrdd 'naethon ni yn ein gwers bore 'ma i'r gegin."

"Be ti'n trio'i ddeud, Alys?" Roedd Lleucu'n fwy llwyd nag arfer, heblaw am y cwstard oedd wedi sychu'n felyn rownd ei cheg.

Yn sydyn, atebodd Mr Bylbs ar ei rhan.

"Beth mae hi'n drio'i ddweud yw eich bod chi'n rhy hwyr. Ry'n ni wedi llwyddo i greu'r cymysgedd perffaith o'r diwedd, sy'n mynd i wneud yn siŵr fod pob plentyn yn stopio chwerthin am byth ar ôl un ddos yn unig. Heb eithriadau fel CHI'CH DAU."

Pwyntiodd Mr Bylbs tuag at Twm a Lleucu. A oedd wedi colli ei farblis yn llwyr?

"A fydd 'na ddim angen i bawb fwyta cwstard bob diwrnod chwaith. Dim ond un dropyn bach ac fe fydd yr ysgol yma'n dyblu yn ei gwerth. Heb sgileffeithiau gwirion fel dweud jôcs! Pa! Pwy glywodd am y ffasiwn beth?! Chi'n rhy hwyr... chi'n clywed fi?! Chi'n rhy hwyr, mae Carys wedi ennill!"

"Wel... Barri..." meddwn i, "heb y sgileffeithiau hynny fydd ganddoch chi ddim ffeiliau sain i'w gwerthu i Rhodricês Llywethin!"

"Be?!" Roedd Lleucu a Twm yn edrych arna i fel petawn i'n hurt.

"Shwd wyt ti'n gwybod am 'ny?" Doedd Mr Bylbs ddim yn edrych yn gymaint o glown erbyn hyn.

"Mae o i gyd yn neud synnwyr. Mae Miss Glein a Barri fan hyn – neu ddylswn i ddeud Carys Bylbs a'i brawd – wedi darganfod ffordd o wneud arian. Maen nhw'n recordio pawb yn dweud jôcs yn y nos ac yn gwerthu'r ffeiliau i Rhodricês Llywethin, sy'n defnyddio'r jôcs a'r straeon yn ei raglenni teledu ac yn gwneud miloedd o bunnoedd."

Roedd wynebau Lleucu a Twm yn bictiwr wrth iddyn nhw geisio prosesu'r hyn ro'n i newydd ei ddweud.

"O, Alys, sda ti ddim syniad!" meddai Mr Bylbs, a gwyn ei lygaid yn fflachio. "Rhywbeth ar yr ochr i wneud arian oedd hynny. Digon o arian i ddatblygu'r cwstard newydd. Ac mae'r cwstard newydd yn fwy pwerus o lawer nag arian. Nid yn unig y byddwn ni'n stopio pawb rhag chwerthin ac yn creu plant anarferol o glyfar, ond fe fyddwn ni hefyd yn rheoli'r plant a, thrwy hynny, fe fyddwn ni'n rheoli'r byd. A fydd 'na ddim chwerthin yn ein byd ni!"

Erbyn hyn roedd Mr Bylbs ei hun yn chwerthin, a chwys afiach yn sboncian oddi arno wrth iddo ysgwyd.

"Chi'n rhy hwyr… bydd y plant yn dod am eu cinio nawr!" meddai Mr Bylbs.

"Owff… dwi 'di cael digon!" meddai Lleucu a tharo Mr Bylbs yn ei wyneb nes ei fod yn hedfan ar ei gefn ar lawr.

"Brysia!" meddai Twm wrth Lleucu a rhedeg tuag at Mr Bylbs. "Rown ni o yn un o'r peiriannau 'ma."

Roedd y ddau'n straffaglu i'w godi ond doedd gen i ddim amser i'w helpu – roedd yn rhaid mynd i rybuddio Meri Grefi a Blod Sglods.

"Rhaid i mi stopio Grefi a Sglods rhag rhannu'r cwstard!" meddwn i.

"Ia… dos, fyddwn ni'n iawn," atebodd Twm.

Gadewais yr ystafell a rhedeg i fyny'r grisiau. Roedd drewdod cwstard melys yn dawnsio o 'nghwmpas. Ro'n i isio chwydu – mae'n gas gen i gwstard!

Cyrhaeddais swyddfa Miss Glein a rhedeg at y

drws, ond roedd o wedi ei gloi. Ceisiais bopeth i'w agor ond roedd yn rhaid cael cod arbennig. Yn sydyn, gwelais fy mag ysgol. Gafaelais yn y pecyn casglu data a gyrru neges frys i Mrs Pi:

ANGEN CYMORTH RŴAN! CEGIN!

Roedd ffenest uchel yn y nenfwd. Llusgais y ddesg tuag ati a rhoi dwy gadair ar ben ei gilydd i'w chyrraedd. Doedd y twr cadeiriau ddim yn saff iawn ond roedd hyn yn fater o frys. Gafaelais yn y saeth a'r wifren oedd yn sownd wrth fy mag a'i saethu drwy'r ffenest i lawr at ddrws y gegin. Sbydodd y gwydr i bob man, a glaniodd y saeth yn y ddaear. Gwthiais fy hun yn ofalus drwy'r ffenest, gan geisio osgoi gweddillion y gwydr, ac eistedd ar y to. Yna, tynnais ben arall y wifren oddi ar y bag a'i glymu'n dynn i'r gadair uchaf yn y twr, a fyddai'n rhy fawr i ddod drwy'r ffenest ac felly'n dal yn sownd yn erbyn y wal. Rhoddais y bag dros y wifren a gafael yn dynn ynddo cyn neidio oddi ar y to. Gwibiais i lawr y wifren a chyrraedd y llawr ar fy nhraed. Yna rhoddais y bag ar fy nghefn a sleifio at ddrws cefn y gegin.

Ro'n i'n gallu clywed Meri a Blod yn sgwrsio, yn chwerthin a chanu gyda'i gilydd. Do'n i ddim yn gallu gweld neb, ddim hyd yn oed y cymhorthydd, ond clywais sŵn plant yn cyrraedd y ffreutur. Roedd yn rhaid i mi eu stopio nhw rhag dechrau ciwio am ginio nes y byddwn i wedi darganfod y cwstard. Yn sydyn, cofiais am y potyn drewllyd yn fy mag. Roedd o i fod yn arf pwerus iawn, yn ddigon drewllyd i wagio ystafell.

Llithrais drwy'r gegin heb i neb fy ngweld, ac agor un o'r drysau oedd yn arwain i'r ffreutur. Daliais fy nhrwyn, agor y potyn a'i daflu ar lawr y ffreutur cyn cau'r drws ar fy ôl. Yna, llithrais yn ôl i fy nghuddfan yn y gegin. Mae'n rhaid bod y potyn bach yn rhyfeddol o gryf gan i mi glywed pob math o sŵn cyfogi a phoeri, ac ychydig o grio hefyd dwi'n amau. O fewn munud, roedd y ffreutur yn dawel. Pawb wedi gadael… neu lewygu efallai!

Yn sydyn, gwelais y cymhorthydd yn sefyll wrth un o'r sincs gyferbyn â sosbennaid fawr o gwstard. Yn ei law roedd potyn o hylif gwyrdd ac roedd o wrthi'n agor y caead…

Roedd yn rhaid i mi wneud rhywbeth cyn iddi fynd yn rhy hwyr.

"NAAAAA! PAID!"

Neidiais o fy nghuddfan a hedfan drwy'r awyr gan gicio'r potyn o'i law.

"Be ti'n feddwl ti'n neud?" meddai'r cymhorthydd â'r gwallt afiach.

"Be sy'n mynd 'mlân?" Daeth llais Meri neu Blod o ochr arall y gegin.

"Dim byd!" meddai'r hogyn gan afael mewn potyn arall o'r bocs a'i agor.

"Paid â meiddio gwneud dim efo'r hylif 'na," meddwn i gan sefyll ar fy nhraed yn barod am ornest karate. Ond daeth llais hufennog, iasol o'r tu ôl i mi.

"Pam? Be ma rhyw lipryn o ferch fach fel ti'n mynd i neud am y peth?"

Miss Glein oedd yn sefyll yno, mor ddychrynllyd ag erioed.

"Dwi'n gwybod pob dim," meddwn i wrthi. Doedd arna i mo'i hofn hi bellach. "Ac mae'r heddlu ar eu ffordd yma."

"Ti'n rhy hwyr, mae'r hylif yn y cwstard yn barod."

"Nadi," meddai'r cymhorthydd, "tydi o ddim. *Ti* sy'n rhy hwyr, Carys Bylbs."

"Be?" meddwn i a Miss Glein fel deuawd.

Yna, tywalltodd y cymhorthydd yr hylif oedd yn ei law i lawr y sinc.

"NAAAA...! Be ti 'di neud? Mi wna i dy ddinistrio di am hyn. Ti'n meddwl y galli di ddianc nawr?"

Gafaelodd Miss Glein yn ei goler.

"Sdim ots gen i ddim mwy," sibrydodd y cymhorthydd wrthi.

Do'n i ddim yn dallt beth oedd yn digwydd. Pwy oedd y cymhorthydd yma?

Yn sydyn, dyma bob drws yn y gegin, gan gynnwys drysau'r cypyrddau a'r biniau mawr a phopeth arall oedd â drws iddo, yn agor. Rhedodd degau o bobol mewn du gyda masgiau dros eu hwynebau a gynnau yn eu dwylo i mewn i'r gegin gan weiddi a sgrechian. Taflais fy hun ar y llawr. Disgynnodd y cymhorthydd hefyd. Ond roedd Miss Glein yn sefyll yno'n stond. Tawelodd y bobol mewn du. Edrychais i fyny'n ara deg a phwy welwn i'n cerdded drwy'r cyfan gyda gwn yn ei llaw ond Mam.

"Mam!"

Cododd y cymhorthydd ei ben.

"Lynwen!" meddai.

Edrychais arno fel petai ganddo gynffon yn tyfu ar ei dalcen.

"Oi, sut wyt ti'n nabod...?" dechreuais.

"Wel, wel, wel, Lynwen... Dylwn i fod wedi ame y byddet ti yn y potes yn rhywle," meddai Miss Glein.

"Pam, Carys? Pam hyn i gyd?"

"Oherwydd bod rhai ohonon ni isie gwneud y byd 'ma'n lle gwell. Llai o'r sŵn chwerthin annifyr 'na, mwy o arian a mwy o bŵer. Meddylia, rheoli'r holl blant clyfar 'ma. Yn yr ysgol yma mae prif weinidogion y dyfodol, prif wyddonwyr y dyfodol, cyfreithwyr y dyfodol, doctoriaid, dyfeiswyr, arbenigwyr ar bopeth, a fi fydd yn rheoli'r CYFAAAAAN!"

Roedd ei gwallt coch yn fflachio dros y lle, yn union fel petai ei phen ar dân. Gafaelodd mewn jar o'r hylif gwyrdd a'i hagor. Neidiodd dau o'r bobol mewn du arni a'i dal i lawr. Roedd hi'n sgrechian a nadu ac yn gweiddi pob math o bethau:

"Na... na... na! Fedra i ddim diodde mwy... Dim mwy o chwerthin! Na! Modryb Meri...?! Modryb Blod...?! BARRIIIII?! Gadewch fi fynd! BARRI?!"

Daeth Barri i mewn, wedi ei ddal rhwng dau o'r dynion mewn du. Y tu ôl iddyn nhw roedd Twm a Lleucu yn gwstard drostyn nhw i gyd a'u hwynebau'n methu credu'r olygfa. Ro'n i'n dal ar y llawr nes i mi glywed Miss Glein yn dweud "Modryb Meri" a "Modryb Blod"... Meri Grefi a Blod Sglods!

"Y merched cinio!" meddwn i gan neidio ar fy nhraed.

"Chi'ch tri," meddai Mam gan siarad â thri o'r dynion mewn du, "dewch o hyd i'r ddwy ddynes ginio, yn gyflym. Mae hi bron yn amser i ni glirio'r lle a gadael i'r heddlu lleol ddod i wneud eu gwaith."

Yna cerddodd tuag ata i a'r cymhorthydd, oedd yn dal ar lawr.

"Alys, ti'n iawn?"

"Yndw. Dwi'n meddwl."

"Asiant C, mae hi'n dda iawn dy weld di," meddai Mam wrth y cymhorthydd.

"Pwy?" gofynnais mewn syndod gan droi at y cymhorthydd.

"Alys, dyma Asiant C. Yr asiant cynta ddaeth i mewn."

"Ond nest ti ddiflannu!" meddwn i, wrth gofio'r stori fod asiant wedi cael ei anfon i osod meicroffonau yn yr ysgol ond ei fod wedi diflannu.

"Ti'n iawn, ro'n i yma dros yr haf. Ro'n nhw wrthi'n datblygu'r hylif newydd yma, ond fe wnaeth Miss Glein ddarganfod fy mod i'n ysbïwr. Ond roedd hi'n meddwl mai ysbïwr Rhodricês Llywethin o'n i, felly cynigiodd hi arian mawr i mi aros i'w helpu hi a dweud dim wrth Mr Llywethin. Doedd fiw i mi gysylltu efo Mrs Pi rhag ofn i mi gael fy nal unwaith eto."

"Ond neithiwr," meddai Mam, "fe wnaeth Asiant C gysylltu hefo fi tua'r un pryd ag y gwnest ti gysylltu efo Mrs Pi, a dweud y cyfan. Rydach chi'ch dau wedi achub bywydau cannoedd o blant heddiw," ychwanegodd, cyn troi'n ôl at y tri oedd wedi bod yn chwilio am Blod Sglods a Meri Grefi.

Trodd Asiant C ata i.

"Gyda llaw, dwi'n cymryd dy fod ti wedi 'nilyn i'r bora 'ma, ond 'nes i ddim amau hynny am eiliad. Mae'n rhaid dy fod ti'n un dda!" meddai, a rhoi winc fach i mi.

Toc daeth Mam yn ôl gyda newyddion drwg.

"Mae Meri a Blod wedi dianc. Does neb yn medru dod o hyd iddyn nhw. Mae tri thîm wedi mynd allan ar eu holau. Alys, mae'n bryd i ni fynd. Asiant C, arhosa di i egluro wrth yr heddlu lleol – maen nhw ar eu ffordd. Bydd Carys a Barri Bylbs yn mynd i'r carchar am amser hir iawn."

"Beth am Rhodricês Llywethin?" gofynnais, gan obeithio na fyddwn i byth yn gorfod gweld ei wyneb gwirion ar fy nheledu byth eto.

"Paid â phoeni, mae Mrs Pi ei hun wedi mynd i'w sortio fo!" meddai Mam gan wenu. "Tyrd… amser i ni fynd."

Gafaelodd Mam yn fy llaw ond fedrwn i ddim mynd.

"Mam! Twm a Lleucu. Rhaid i mi egluro popeth. Faswn i ddim wedi medru gwneud hyn hebddyn nhw."

Dechreuais gamu tuag at y ddau, oedd yn edrych fel dau bwdin yn nrws y gegin.

"Na, Alys, fedri di ddim dweud wrthyn nhw. Rhaid i ni fynd. Cofia, mae ysbïwr da yn anweledig."

"Ond, Mam…" Edrychais arni. Do'n i erioed wedi mynd yn groes iddi o'r blaen, ond y tro hwn gollyngais ei llaw. "Rhaid i mi ddweud ta-ta ne' rwbath… plis."

Ddywedodd Mam ddim byd, ond wnaeth hi ddim fy stopio rhag mynd atyn nhw chwaith.

"Alys!" meddai Lleucu. "Be sy'n digwydd? Pwy ydi'r rhein?"

"Ydan ni wedi dal Miss Glein?" gofynnodd Twm, yr un mor eiddgar â Lleucu.

"Do. 'Dan ni wedi. Dach *chi* wedi."

Roedd 'na ddistawrwydd. Do'n i ddim isio ffarwelio â nhw, ddim hyd yn oed Twm Ffrancs y twmffat.

"Dwi'n gorfod mynd rŵan. Ond dwi'n meddwl y bydd ysgol Pen y Rhych yn ysgol arferol unwaith eto cyn bo hir... ysgol dipyn hapusach, gobeithio."

"Dwi'n edrych 'mlaen," meddai Lleucu. "Meddylia, Alys, gawn ni chwerthin go iawn!"

"Cewch. Ond fydda i ddim yma."

"Pam?" gofynnodd y ddau.

Roedd hyn yn torri fy nghalon. Am y tro cynta yn fy mywyd, roedd gen i ffrindiau – ffrindiau da – ond roedd yn rhaid i mi fynd â'u gadael nhw ac, am wn i, fyddwn i ddim yn eu gweld nhw byth eto.

"Mi sgwennu i lythyr atoch chi. Diolch am bob dim."

Ro'n i'n dweud celwydd fel petawn i'n dweud y gwir. Ro'n i'n gwybod na chawn i sgwennu llythyr atyn nhw. Ond rhoddais andros o garu mawr i'r ddau a throi ar fy sawdl.

Yna rhedais allan o Ysgol Breifat Pen y Rhych, gan frysio i afael yn llaw Mam.

10
HEDDIW

'Dan ni'n dal i chwilio am Meri Grefi a Blod Sglods.
Mae'n bosib eu bod nhw'n gweithio fel merched cinio
rywle yn ne Cymru. Mi ges i weld Lleucu a Twm
eto. Penderfynodd Mrs Pi bod y ddau'n addas iawn
ar gyfer y byd ysbïo ar ôl i mi ddweud wrthi beth
roedden nhw wedi'i wneud i geisio stopio Miss Glein.
Mae'r ddau'n gweithio fel finnau rŵan, yn cadw llygad
ar unrhyw beth amheus yn ysgolion Cymru. A 'dan
ni'n tri'n ffrindiau gorau... er 'mod i'n dal i feddwl
mai twmffat ydi Twm. Tydw i ddim yn gwybod lle
mae Twm na Lleucu yn gweithio heddiw. Cha i ddim
gwybod, wrth gwrs, a chân nhw ddim gwybod lle
ydw i. Ac er 'mod i wedi rhannu cyfrinach fawr yn y
llyfr yma, cha i ddim dweud wrthat ti chwaith lle ydw
i erbyn heddiw. Ella 'mod i yn dy ysgol di, pwy a ŵyr.
Cofia, mae Asiant A yn ysbïwr da... ac mae ysbïwr da
yn anweledig.

CHAPTER ONE

THERE were some days when it just didn't pay to get out of bed, Rebekah groaned as she lifted her head from the pillow and caught sight of the digital clock.

It was blinking, indicating a power failure through the night had disrupted the alarm mechanism.

She fumbled for her watch, checked the time and uttered a muffled oath as she slid from the bed, then cursed out loud as she stubbed her toe on her way to the *en suite*.

The icy blast of water ensured the quickest shower on record, and, dressed, she raced into the kitchen, dished out fresh food for the cat, snatched a container of orange juice from the refrigerator, gulped a mouthful, then she collected her bag and took the lift down to the underground car park.

Seconds later she slid in behind the wheel of the Blooms and Bouquets van, inserted the key into the ignition…and nothing.

Don't do this to me, she begged as the engine refused to kick over. *Please* don't do this to me! During the ensuing minutes she coaxed, cajoled, promised, and still it remained as dead as a doornail.

She restrained the urge to scream in frustration. Talk about having Friday the thirteenth on a Tuesday!

thanks to a bequest from her late mother the business was free from any loan encumbrances.

It was six-thirty when she unlocked the outer door and she tripped the lights, filled the coffee percolator, then set to work.

While the percolator took its time, she booted up the computer and downloaded email orders, then she checked the fax machine.

They were in for a busy day, and there was a need to adjust her order. She crossed to the phone, made the call, then she rang a mechanic to go check the van.

Hot, sweet black coffee boosted her energy levels, and she was on her third and last cup for the day when Ana arrived.

Looking at her sister was akin to seeing a mirror image of herself...almost. They shared the same petite height, fine-boned features, slender curves and naturally blonde hair. Two years separated them in age, with Ana the eldest and twenty-seven. Their natural personalities were similar, although Rebekah felt she held an edge when it came to determined resolve.

The necessity for self-survival in an abusive relationship had provided a strength of will she hadn't been aware she possessed. It had also implanted an ingrained distrust of men.

A year's engagement to Brad Somerville, a beautiful wedding, embarking on a dream honeymoon...nothing prepared her for the sudden change in the man she'd vowed to love and honour less than ten hours before.

At first she'd thought it was something she'd done or said. Verbal abuse was bad enough; physical abuse was something else. Jealous, possessive to the point of obsessiveness, he soon killed any feelings she had for him, and after three months of living in a hellish marriage she'd simply packed a bag and walked out of his life.

Following the divorce she'd legally reverted to her maiden name, bought an apartment, adopted a beautiful Burmilla kitten whom she'd named Millie, and lived to work.

'Hi.' Rebekah summoned a sympathetic smile as she glimpsed the slight air of fatigue evident in Ana's expression. 'Late night? Morning sickness?'

'That bad, huh?' her sister queried as she crossed to the computer and began cross-checking the day's orders.

'Maybe you should listen to Luc and cut down your hours.'

Ana shot her a telling glance. 'You're supposed to be on my side.'

Rebekah wrinkled her nose in humour. 'I am, believe me.'

'What would I do in that great house all day? Petros is the ultimate manservant.'

The phone rang, and Ana picked up, listened, then handed over the cordless receiver. 'For you.'

It was the mechanic with word all the van needed was a new battery, which he'd install, and mail her the account.

'Problems?'

'The van wouldn't start.' She relayed the repercussions, then took the next phone call.

It didn't get better as the morning wore on. A difficult customer took most of her patience, and another complained bitterly about the cost of florists' delivery charges.

Food, she needed food. It was almost midday, and the energy boost from juice, coffee and a cereal bar had clearly dissipated.

'I'll go pick up a salad sandwich. Then you can take a lunch break.'

Ana glanced up from the computer. 'I can eat lunch on the run just as well as you.'

'But you won't,' Rebekah said firmly. 'You'll buy a magazine, seat yourself at any one of the nearby café's, and take your time over a latte and something sensible to eat.'

Ana rolled her eyes. 'Tea,' she amended with a grimace. 'And if you begin treating me like a precious pregnant princess, I'll hit you!'

She laughed, a low, throaty chuckle, and her eyes held a mischievous gleam. 'Petros?' she hazarded. The middle-aged manservant had been part of Luc's household for years, well before she'd first met Ana's inimitable husband. 'Does he still refer to you as Ms Dimitriades?'

Ana's laughter was infectious. 'He considers anything less would be regarded as undignified.'

She adored her sister, and they'd been the best of friends since she could remember, sharing, caring, *close*. Ana's marriage to Luc Dimitriades a year ago had been one of the happiest moments of her life.

'Luc has made a booking for dinner this evening.'

Ana named the restaurant, and Rebekah's eyebrows rose a fraction. It numbered as one of the ritziest places in town. 'We'd like you to join us. Please,' she added. '*Two* Dimitriades men are too much for one woman to handle.'

Rebekah felt an icy shiver slither the length of her spine, and the nerves in her stomach tightened into a painful ball. Please let her voice give no hint to her inner turmoil. 'One of Luc's cousins is in town?' Amazing she could sound so calm, when her defence mechanism had already moved to *alert*, and her mind issued the silent scream *Please don't let it be Jace*.

'Yes. Jace arrived yesterday from the States.'

No. The silent scream rose and died in her throat as Jace Dimitriades' image rose to the fore to taunt her.

Tall, broad shoulders, chiselled features, piercing dark grey eyes, and a mouth to die for.

She had reason to know how it felt to have that mouth possess her own. Even now, a year later, she still retained a vivid memory of Luc and Ana's wedding, partnered as her sister's maid of honour with Jace as Luc's best man. How for several hours she'd been aware of Jace's close proximity, the touch of his hand at her waist, the brush of his body against her own as they assembled for bridal group photos.

Dancing with him had been a nightmare. Sensual

heat spiked her blood and sent it racing through her veins. Sexual chemistry at its most base level.

Hadn't that been the real reason for her momentary escape onto the terrace within minutes of Luc and Ana taking their leave?

Yet Jace was there, standing close, almost caging her against the terrace railing as she turned to move away.

That had been her mistake, for it brought her much too close to him. The next instant his lips brushed her cheek, then slid to savour her mouth, and in a moment of sheer madness she angled her mouth to his own.

His instant response was devastating.

Shocked didn't cover it. No one had kissed her quite like that. As if somehow he'd reached down into the depths of her soul, tasted, savoured, with intent to conquer. It left her feeling as if she'd leapt off a high cliff and was in dangerous free fall. Exhilarated by the instinctive knowledge he would catch her…before she hit the ground.

Who was the first to break contact? To this day she couldn't be sure. All she remembered was something inexplicable in those dark grey eyes, a stillness that held a waiting, *watching* quality as she went from shock to dismay in a few seconds flat.

Anger kicked in, and she slapped him…hard. Then she walked away, aware that he made no effort to stop her. She rejoined the wedding guests, and smiled until her facial muscles ached.

Afterwards had come the rage…with herself for initiating something so foolish, and with him for indulging it.

Now Jace Dimitriades was back in town, and Ana and Luc expected her to make up a foursome for dinner?

'*No,*' she reiterated aloud.

'No…you don't want to.' Ana's gaze narrowed as she attempted to analyse her sister's expression. 'Or no, you can't?'

'Choose whichever one you like.'

Ana appeared to take a deep breath. 'OK. Are you going to tell me about it, or do I have to drag it out of you?'

'Neither. Simply accept I decline your invitation.'

'That won't wash, and you know it. You haven't seen Jace since the wedding.' Her sister's eyes assumed a speculative gleam. 'What did he do? Kiss you?'

Oh, my. 'On what do you base that assumption?' she managed calmly, and saw Ana's gaze narrow.

There was a telling silence. 'It's not like you to wimp out,' her sister said at last.

Wimp? 'Forgive me, but I'm not in the mood to embark on a verbal fencing match with a man who'd enjoy every thrust and parry!'

'Think of the fun you'll have in besting him,' Ana offered persuasively.

Rebekah glimpsed the mischievous challenge in those guileless blue eyes, and her lips curved into a slow smile. 'You're wicked.'

Ana grinned. 'The black Versace halter-neck will be fine.'

A backless creation which didn't allow for wearing a bra? 'I haven't said *yes*.'

'We'll come by and collect you. And drop you home again.'

She could imagine how easily, *smoothly* Jace could intercede and insist he escort her home in a taxi.

'*If* I agree,' she qualified, shooting Ana a warning glance. 'I'll drive my own car.'

'*Brava.*' Ana's eyes gleamed with humour, and Rebekah shook her head in mock-despair as her sister executed the *victory* sign.

It was almost seven when Rebekah slid from behind the wheel of her MG and allowed the uniformed attendant tend to valet parking.

For the umpteenth time she silently questioned her sanity. Except *retreat* at this late stage wasn't part of her agenda.

How had the past year affected Jace Dimitriades?

Did he have a lover? Was he between relationships?

Fool, she mentally derided as she entered the restaurant foyer. Men of Jace Dimitriades' calibre were never without a woman for long. She recollected Ana relaying Jace regularly commuted between London, Paris and Athens. He probably had a mistress in each major city.

The *maître d'* greeted her with polite regard, elicited her name, the booking, and directed her to the lounge bar, where patrons lingered over drinks.

The ambience spelt *money*…serious money. The floral displays were real, not silk imitation. The carpet thick-piled and luxurious, the furniture expensive.

A pianist was seated at a baby grand, effortlessly providing muted background music, and the drinks stewards were groomed to the nth degree.

Refined class, Rebekah conceded as a steward enquired if he could assist locating her friends.

He succeeded with smooth efficiency, and she followed in his wake.

'Mr Dimitriades.' His acknowledgement held deferential respect, and she had a ready smile in place, polite words of gratitude on her lips as she tilted her head.

Only to have the smile freeze as she saw it was Jace, not Luc, who had moved forward to greet her.

'Rebekah.'

In one fluid movement he came close, lowered his head and brushed his lips to her cheek. The contact was stunningly brief, but it robbed the breath from her throat for all of five seconds before anger hit.

'How dare you?' The words escaped as little more than a vehement whisper.

One dark eyebrow slanted, although his eyes held a watchful expression. 'You expected formality?'

She didn't trust herself to respond. Her attention was held, *trapped,* by the man standing within touching distance.

Tall, so tall her eyes were on a level with the loop of his impeccably knotted silk tie, and his breadth of shoulder was impressive sheathed in exclusive tailoring.

In his mid-thirties, his broad, chiselled facial bone structure gave hint to his Grecian ancestry, and there was an inherent quality in those dark grey, almost black eyes that took hold of her equilibrium and tore it to shreds.

No one man deserved to exude quite this degree of power...nor possess such riveting physical magnetism.

Sexual alchemy at its zenith, she acknowledged shakily as she attempted to gain a measure of control over her rioting emotions.

One look at him was all it took for her to remember how it felt to have that mouth close over her own with diabolical finesse. Exploring, coaxing...and staking a claim.

She was suddenly aware of every breath she took, every heightened pulse-beat, and the way her heart seemed to thud against her ribcage.

It was crazy, *insane* to feel like this. In the name of heaven, *get a grip.* To allow him to see just how deeply he affected her was impossible.

Why, suddenly, did she feel as if she'd walked into a danger zone? And that it was *he*, and not she, in command of the situation?

Dammit, she'd accepted Ana's invitation, and she owed it to her sister and Luc to be a pleasant guest. Hadn't she dressed accordingly, and given a promise to sparkle?

CHAPTER TWO

PROJECTING *joie de vivre* required effort, and there was a very real danger she'd verge towards overkill.

A glass of wine would help dull the edges, but she'd had nothing to eat since lunch. Consequently iced water seemed a wise choice, especially as she'd need all her wits to parry words with Luc's inimitable cousin.

The restaurant's chef was reputed to be one of the city's best, and numbered among the country's finest. Hence, the selection offered was meant to tempt a gourmand's palate.

Rebekah ordered soup as a starter, requested an entrée-size meal as a main, and deferred a decision on dessert.

She settled back in her chair and glanced towards Jace. 'You're in Sydney on business, I believe?'

There was nothing like taking control and initiating conversation.

'Yes.' He met her level gaze, held it, and wondered if she had any idea how well he could read her. 'Also Melbourne, Cairns, Brisbane and the Gold Coast.'

'Interesting. Presumably matters which require your personal attention?'

How would she react if he revealed *she* was one

16

of them? He inclined his head. 'I'm unable to delegate in this instance.'

Property he wanted to sight? Yet in a high-tech age, it was possible to scan digital images at the speed of light, and as he shared some investment interests with Luc, why couldn't Luc act on his cousin's behalf?

The waiter delivered their starters, and Rebekah toyed with the soup, spooning the contents automatically without affording it the appreciation it truly deserved.

'Tell me something about floristry.' Jace's voice was pure New York, and she waited a beat before countering,

'An idle query, or genuine interest?'

His eyes held a humorous gleam. 'The latter.'

'The art, or a day in the life of…?'

'Both.'

'Floral artistry comprises a good eye for colour and design, shapes appealing to the customer's wants and needs, the specific occasion.' If he wanted facts, she'd supply them. 'Which blooms suit, room temperature, the effect the customer wants to achieve.'

She lifted her shoulders and effected a light shrug. 'Knowledge where exotic out-of-season stock can be bought and how long it takes to air-freight it in. And the expense involved. Unfortunately there are always those who want the best at minimum cost.'

'I'm sure you manage to apprise them that quality comes with a price?'

'Don't be fooled by Ana and Rebekah's petite stature,' Luc drawled. His mouth curved into a warm smile. 'I can assure both sisters pack a powerful verbal punch.' He turned towards Ana and brushed light fingers down her cheek. 'My wife, especially.'

'It's a defence mechanism,' Ana responded sweetly. The waiter removed their plates, and Rebekah's gaze shifted to Jace in a deliberate attempt at dispassionate appraisal.

Superb tailoring emphasised an impressive breadth of shoulder, and the deep blue shirt with its impeccably knotted silk tie accented his olive textured skin.

All she had to do was look at him, and warmth flared to uncomfortable heat as her mind spun into overdrive, remembering how it felt to have his mouth on hers. From there it was just a step away for her mind to spiral out of control, imagining what lay beneath the trappings of his conventional attire.

Don't go there. Dear heaven, what was *wrong* with her? No one, not even her ex-husband in the heightened throes of pre-marital passion, had been able to arouse such an intense reaction.

She was conscious of every breath she took, and co-ordinating cutlery with morsels of food and the actual eating process was fraught with nervous tension.

Was Jace aware of her inner turmoil? Dear God, she hoped not.

Oh, for heaven's sake, she mentally chastised. You're only sharing dinner with him, and acute vulnerability could be conquered…couldn't it? Or at least successfully masked. Besides, Jace Dimitriades was only a man like any other man, and hadn't Brad been charm personified in the beginning? Only to turn into a wolf in sheep's clothing.

Except instinct warned comparing her ex-husband to Jace Dimitriades was akin to associating an ill-bred canine with a powerful panther.

There was a part of her that wanted to replace her cutlery, stand to her feet, and leave. Retreat to the safety of her car, return to her apartment with her sanity intact.

Except such an action was a cop-out, and besides, what excuse could she present? *Act,* she commanded silently. You deal with people every day in the shop and utilise psychological skill to handle difficult customers. How difficult could it be to deal with Jace Dimitriades for a few hours? There was the added advantage of Ana and Luc's presence to provide a buffer. It should be a breeze.

Fat chance! She felt about as relaxed as a cat on hot bricks!

Why hadn't she listened to her initial instinct and remained adamant at not doing this? Because she cared for her sister. At least, that was the simple answer. The more complex one didn't bear contemplating.

Maybe some wine would loosen her nerves a little, and she indicated the wine steward could fill her glass. Seconds later she took an appreciative sip, and felt the grape's delicate bouquet slip into her bloodstream.

It was a relief when the waiter presented the next course. Her appetite was non-existent, and although her meal was a decorative vision in cuisine artistry, her tastebuds appeared to be on strike.

Travelled south for the duration, she accorded with silent wry humour, aware to an alarming degree just where they'd chosen to settle.

Eat, she commanded silently. Focus on the food. The evening would eventually come to a close, and she'd never have to place herself in this position again.

She may as well have told herself to go jump over the moon for all the good it did, for she was supremely conscious of every movement he made. The economical use of his hands as he apportioned each morsel of food. The way the muscles at the edge of his jaw bunched as he ate. His hands were broad, tanned with a sprinkling of hair, the fingers tapered with neatly shaped nails.

How would those hands caress a woman's skin? Lightly skim the silken surface, discover each pleasure pulse and linger there?

Her mind came to a screeching halt. What was the matter with her? She couldn't blame the wine, for she'd only consumed a few sips, and alternated it with chilled water.

'You have an early start in the morning?' Luc queried solicitously.

Could she conceivably use that as an excuse to slip away soon? 'I have to be at the flower market around four-thirty.'

Jace's gaze narrowed. 'Every day?'

'Six out of seven.' It didn't bother her. Never had,

for she was a morning person. However, after a four-teen-hour day on her feet anything less than six hours' sleep and she was wrecked.

'I'll order coffee.' Luc signalled the waiter, and she joined Ana in choosing tea, all too aware coffee would keep her awake. How long had they been here? Two hours? Three?

They were almost done, and within half an hour she'd be free to slip behind the wheel of her car and drive home.

Wonderful, she determined as Luc fixed the bill, and she stood to her feet, collected her evening purse, and followed Ana to the foyer.

Her skin prickled in awareness of Jace's close proximity, and it took considerable effort to move at a leisurely pace. She could almost feel the warmth of his body, and her own stiffened at the light touch of his hand at the back of her waist as they gained the pavement.

'I'll see you to your car.'

'I had a valet attendant park it for me.'

Ana tilted her face as Jace leant down to brush his lips to her cheek. 'Luc and I can give you a lift back to the hotel.'

'I'm sure Rebekah won't mind.' Jace straightened and shot his cousin a measured look. 'I'll be in touch tomorrow.'

Rebekah uttered a silent prayer that Luc would in-tercede, only the deity wasn't listening. Ana leant for-ward and brushed her lips to her sister's cheek, accepted Jace's affectionate 'Goodnight', then she moved with Luc towards their car.

It was so smoothly effected, she could hardly believe she'd been cleverly manipulated. His hotel *was en route* to her apartment. Given she had to pass right by the main entrance, it would be churlish to refuse.

However, her mind screamed in silent denial as she waited for the attendant to fetch her car. She didn't want to be alone with him, ever, and especially not in the close confines of her MG sports car.

What had prompted him to suggest it when she'd been so painstakingly polite all evening? She hadn't flirted, or given him any reason to think she coveted his attention.

Dammit, just get in the car, drop him off at the hotel, then that'll be the end of it. Ten, fifteen minutes was all it would take.

There wasn't a lot of leg-room, and it gave her a degree of satisfaction as he folded his lengthy frame into the front passenger seat.

Rebekah didn't waste a second, and she gained the street, then headed towards Double Bay. Idle conversation, simply for the sake of it, wasn't on her agenda, and she didn't offer a word as she took liberties with the speed limit.

Ten minutes and counting.

It was a beautiful late-spring evening, the dark sky a clear indigo sprinkled with stars. Cool, sharp temperatures promised another fine day, and she directed her mind to the shop's orders and the stock she'd need to purchase from the markets.

It didn't work, for she was supremely conscious of the man seated beside her. In the close confines of the car she was aware of the subtle tones of his cologne, the clean smell of his clothes...and the faint male muskiness that was his alone.

Rebekah felt the tell-tale prickle of her skin as her body began an unbidden response. There was warmth, and heat pooled deep inside, intensifying with damning speed as her pulse accelerated to a crazy beat.

His hand rested on one knee, which was close, much too close to the gear-shift, making it impossible not to touch him whenever she changed gears. Avoiding contact without appearing to do so required care, and she wondered if he sensed her disquiet.

What if he did, and he was silently amused? Oh, dammit, just *drive*. In another five minutes she'd be free of his disturbing presence.

One more set of traffic lights and she'd enter the outer fringes of suburban Double Bay. A sense of intense relief began to descend as she turned into the street housing the main entrance to his hotel, and she drew to a halt in the impressive forecourt.

A uniformed bellboy moved towards the car, and Rebekah turned towards Jace. 'Goodnight.'

In one fluid movement he captured her face with his hands, then lowered his mouth to hers in an evocative kiss that invaded and seduced. All too brief, it held the promise of *more*.

Shocked surprise encompassed her features as he lifted his head, and her mouth parted, only to close again as he offered a huskily voiced *au revoir* before sliding out from the low-slung seat.

She caught the faint gleam in those dark eyes before he turned and walked towards the main entrance.

Damn him. What did he think he was playing at?

She moved the gear-stick with unnecessary force, then sent the car into the street. Her apartment was situated two blocks distant, and she reached it in record time, easing the MG down into the underground car park.

In the lift she castigated herself for not predicting Jace's move. He'd bargained on the element of surprise, and had won.

So what did it matter? She was unlikely to see him again. But it irked unbearably he'd caught her unawares, and provided a not so subtle reminder that he was aware of her vulnerability, and, even more galling, susceptible to him.

She should have slapped his face. Would have, if his action hadn't rendered her momentarily speechless.

Ten o'clock wasn't *late*, and with only six hours' sleep ahead of her she should go straight to bed. Instead, she slid off her stilettos and roamed the apartment, too emotionally wound up to settle to an easy sleep.

Nothing on television held her interest for long, and after utilising the remote to flick through every channel she simply switched off the set, collected a magazine and flipped through the pages with equal uninterest before discarding it in disgust.

A derisive sound emerged from her throat as she doused the lights and made for her bedroom.

She could still *feel* Jace Dimitriades' touch when she began removing her clothes. As she cleansed her face of make-up she was positive she could still *taste* him, and she took up her toothbrush and cleaned her teeth, twice.

So vivid was his powerful image, she was prepared to swear he was there with her as she lay in bed staring into the room's darkness.

Over and over the evening replayed itself, and the memory of his kiss taunted her, awakening her imagination to such a level it became impossible to sleep.

Jace Dimitriades drained the last of his coffee, reached for his suit jacket and shrugged it on, collected his wallet and cellphone, then he exited his hotel suite, took the lift down to ground level and walked out into the sunshine.

He had an hour before he was due to join Luc at a business meeting in the city. Time enough to achieve his objective, he determined as he crossed the street and walked the block and a half to his intended destination.

Blooms and Bouquets was ideally sited, the window display colourful with expertly arranged blooms in numerous vases on stands of varying heights. A background wall held a similar display, and the overall look from outside was a mass of floor-to-ceiling flowers.

The result was visually stunning, and a testament to the two sisters who owned the boutique.

He pushed open the door, registered the electronic buzzer, and offered a greeting to Ana, swivelled his head to include Rebekah, who was deftly assembling a bouquet of orchids at the work table.

'Jace, how wonderful to see you.' Ana slid off her chair behind the computer and joined him. 'Is this a social call?'

He leant down and brushed his lips to her temple. 'How are you?' His smile held affectionate warmth. 'In answer to your question…social and business.'

'Then let's get business out of the way first.'

The phone rang, providing a convenient interruption. Not that he really needed one, but it helped. 'Answer that. Rebekah can organise the order.'

Could she, indeed? From the moment he stepped into the boutique all her senses had snapped into full alert. It was crazy the way her body reacted to the sight of him. Amend that to just *thinking* about him, she admitted wryly. Hadn't that very thing kept her awake last night?

Any hope of having Ana deal with him was shot, leaving her with little option but to place the bouquet taking shape onto the work table and move forward to assist him.

He looked…incredible, the dark grey business suit fashioned by a master tailor, fine cotton shirt, impeccably knotted silk tie. But it was the man himself who took hold of her composure and tore it to shreds.

She didn't like the feeling at all. It had taken two

years to repair the damage Brad had wrought and restore a measure of confidence. To have it undermined in any way was something she'd defend to the death.

Rebekah slipped into the polite, professional role with practised ease. 'Do you have anything particular in mind?'

Good, his presence rattled her. He'd caught the faint tremble in those capable hands, sighted a glimpse of her inner struggle as she geared herself to deal with him. Signs she wasn't anywhere near as calm as she'd have him believe.

'A journey is but a series of many steps.' The quote teased his brain, although he couldn't be sure of its accuracy or its origin, only that the words were pertinent.

Rebekah Stanford intrigued him. He admired the look of her, the strength of character apparent. The exigent sexual chemistry. But it was more than mere physical attraction. There was mystery surrounding her, something he couldn't quite pin down.

During the past year he hadn't been able to dismiss her from his mind. Her features teased his subconscious, the scent and feel of her. The way she'd responded to his touch haunted him…and destroyed anything he thought he could feel for another woman. Plural, he amended ruefully, aware of the few women he'd sought to fill a void.

Now he was back, intent on combining business with pleasure…or was it the other way round? Intent on determining if memory of an emotion still existed, and if it did, just what he intended to do about it.

'Roses.' Their velvety texture, exotic perfume, the exquisite petals so tightly budded just waiting to unfold.

'What colour do you have in mind?'

Rebekah moved towards the temperature-controlled cabinet and indicated several vases holding a variety of colours.

There was the perfection of white, glorious pinks and corals in their various shadings, and deep, dark red.

He didn't hesitate. 'The red.'

She opened the glass door, removed the vase and carried it to the work table. 'How many would you like? The cost—'

'Is immaterial,' Jace concluded. 'Three dozen.'

'Would you like them delivered? An extra charge applies.'

'I'll handle delivery.'

A woman undoubtedly. Hostess, friend, or lover?

If it was a lover, he must possess all the right moves. He'd only been in the country two days.

Rebekah gestured towards a stand containing cards for every occasion. 'Perhaps you'd like to choose a card and write on it while I fix these.' She was already reaching for Cellophane, and mentally selecting ribbon.

Within minutes the bouquet was ready, and she attached the card, accepted payment, then handed him the roses.

Jace took time to admire their assembled artistry, then he presented her with them. 'For you.' He observed a gamut of emotions chase across her expressive features, and saw her struggle with each and every one of them.

'Excuse me?'

'The roses are for you. I suggest you read the card.'

Rebekah read the words with a sense of mounting disbelief. *'Dinner tonight. Seven.'*

'I'll collect you.'

'You don't know where I live.' *What was she saying?* She had no intention of sharing dinner with him.

'Ana will give me the address.'

'No.'

One eyebrow slanted in mocking humour. 'No, Ana won't give me the address?'

'No, I won't accept your invitation.' The thought of spending time with him wasn't a good idea.

'I promise not to bite.'

'Thanks, but no, thanks.' She held out the magnificent sheaf of roses. 'Please take these. I can't accept them.'

'Can't, or won't?' His New York-accented drawl held humour, and something else she couldn't define.

Ana? Where was her sister when she needed her?

It took only a glance to determine Ana was still on the phone. 'I don't date.'

The stark admission appeared to have no effect at all. 'Seven, Rebekah.' He turned and walked from the shop, and her reiterated *no* fell on deaf ears.

She swore, and followed it with a husky litany that damned the male species in general and one of them in particular.

'Oh, my,' Ana declared as she replaced the receiver. 'What did he do? Issue an indecent proposal?'

'He asked me out.' Rebekah's voice came out as an impassioned hiss.

'And that's the extent of his crime?'

Rebekah tossed the bouquet of roses onto the work table. 'I'm not going.'

'Of course not.'

'How dare he come in here and order roses…?' She could hardly contain her anger. '*Three dozen* of them.' Her eyes flashed blue fire. 'Then give them to *me*?'

Ana clicked her tongue and shook her head. 'Very bad taste.'

Rebekah's mouth tightened. 'I'm not accepting them.' She pushed the bouquet into her sister's hands. 'You take them home.'

'Why not you?' Ana queried reasonably.

'I'll return them to stock.' She spared them a glance, and her artist's eye admired the blooms' beauty. Just for a moment she felt a twinge of remorse.

No man had gifted her anything in a while. And never flowers.

'Who does Jace Dimitriades think he is?' It was a question that required no answer, and she banked down a further tirade as a customer entered the boutique.

Rebekah was glad of the interruption, although she seethed in silence for the rest of the day. A number of scenarios as to how she'd deal with him crossed her mind. Some of which, should she put them into effect, would be sure to get her arrested for causing grievous bodily harm.

'Do you have a number where I can contact him?'

It was late afternoon, and Ana was about to leave.

'Jace?'

'Of course, *Jace*.'

Ana's features assumed a thoughtful expression.

'It's been two years since your divorce. Don't you think it's time you emerged into the real world again?'

'You're advocating I have an affair?'

'Who are you afraid of?' Ana queried gently. 'Jace or yourself?' She walked to the door, paused and turned to give her sister a warm smile. 'Think about it.'

Rebekah opened her mouth, then closed it again.

As an exit line, it was without equal.

CHAPTER THREE

IT WAS after six when Rebekah eased the MG into the underground car park and rode the lift to the seventh floor.

Indecisiveness was not one of her traits, yet for the past hour she'd changed her mind at least a dozen times.

On entering her apartment she crossed to the phone, looked up the number for Jace's hotel, punched in the digits, only to replace the receiver minutes later. Jace Dimitriades didn't appear to be in his room, and a request for his cellphone number was politely declined.

Damn. Failure to contact him meant she had little option but to shower and dress in record time. Or stand him up.

Oh, for heaven's sake, she chided silently. A few hours, good food, pleasant conversation... What did she have to lose?

Her sanity, she conceded half an hour later as she replaced the in-house phone, gathered up her evening purse, car keys, then rode the lift down to the lobby.

He stood tall, the image of masculine strength, emanating a sense of power only those totally at ease with themselves were able to exude.

Rebekah met his probing gaze, caught his warm smile, and felt her stomach execute a slow somersault.

Any mental assurance she could survive the evening began to dissipate. Was it too late to change her mind? *Way too late,* an inner voice mocked with derision.

Jace watched the fleeting emotions evident, defined each and every one of them, and felt a sense of male satisfaction in knowing he affected her.

'Rebekah.' He moved forward, appreciating the cut and style of her clothes. The slim black skirt and matching jacket highlighted the creamy texture of her skin, and her make-up was minimal. A touch of gold at her ears and her throat added a pleasing addition. Her hair was drawn into a smooth twist, and his fingers itched to remove the pins and let it fall free.

What would she do if he drew her into his arms and covered that pretty mouth with his own? Undoubtedly she'd react like a frightened gazelle, he decided grimly.

What damage had her ex-husband done to kill her natural spontaneity? Something hardened inside him at the array of possibilities, resulting in a surge of anger against a man he'd never met.

'We'll take my car.'

'I've hired a vehicle for the duration of my stay,' Jace said smoothly, and glimpsed her faint disconcerted glance before it was quickly masked.

She wanted to retain control. It made her feel secure, and she suppressed the momentary uneasiness at Jace's increasing ability to undermine her confidence.

Together they walked through the entrance doors, and Jace led her towards a gleaming Jaguar, unlocked the passenger door and saw her seated, then he crossed in front of the car and slid in behind the wheel.

Rebekah's awareness of him became more pronounced within the close confines of the car, and she banked down the onset of nervous tension. Difficult, when her pulse had already increased its beat and she could feel the thud of her heart.

This was madness. She should have said an emphatic *no*, and, failing that, not left it until the last minute to rescind his invitation.

Except on reflection, his inaccessibility hadn't really given her much choice.

In the restaurant, Jace deferred to her preference in wine, ordered, then requested the menu.

Rebekah wasn't sure she could eat a thing, for her digestive system seemed to be in a mildly chaotic state. And it wasn't just her digestive system!

Oh, *move along,* an inner voice prompted. You're here with him. At least try to enjoy the evening. *Pretend.* Surely it can't be too difficult. You managed OK last night.

Yes, but then Luc and Ana had been present. Now she was on her own, and she'd been out of the social scene for too long. It was two years since she'd exercised her social skills to any great degree. One date soon after her divorce had proven to be disastrous, and at the time she'd vowed not to repeat it.

'Tell me what made you choose to be a florist.'

She took a sip of superb chardonnay, and replaced the goblet onto the table. Blooms and Bouquets…she could do shop-talk. 'The perfection of professionally grown blooms, their textures, colours and scents. The skill in assembling them together so the image conveys something special to the person to whom they're gifted.'

Jace watched her features become animated, her blue eyes deepen and gleam like blue topaz as she elaborated on her craft. Did she know how attractive she was? Or how deeply she appealed to him?

On every level, not just the physical.

'The pleasure, comfort and solace they provide for every occasion,' she continued, smiling in reflection of the many memories she'd shared where warmth and the sheer joy of making someone's day a little brighter became paramount.

'One imagines there's a downside?' he probed, and watched as she wrinkled her nose.

'Early starts, long days on your feet, dish-pan hands from having them constantly in and out of water.' She offered him a wry smile. 'Difficult customers who are impossible to please. The rush to get orders out on time. Incorrect addresses, mistakes made with deliveries by the courier.' She effected a negligible shrug. 'Like any business, there are the accompanying problems.'

The waiter delivered their starters, and they each

began eating. The prawn cocktail was succulent with a delicate sauce on a bed of shredded lettuce, and Jace forked his with evident enjoyment.

Did he enjoy women as much as he enjoyed food? She almost choked at the thought. *Where had that come from?*

She lifted her goblet and took a sip of wine. 'Your turn, I think.'

He set his empty dish aside and regarded her with a thoughtful gaze. 'New York-born to Greek immigrant parents. Graduated from university with a degree in business management.'

Rebekah held his gaze and attempted to define what lay beneath his composed exterior. 'The condensed version,' she acknowledged. '*Business management* covers a broad spectrum.'

'I specialise in takeovers and buy-outs.'

'Large companies with their backs against the wall?'

'Something like that.'

'It fits,' she said simply.

'On what do you base that assumption?'

'You have a ruthless streak,' she inclined with thoughtful contemplation, aware it was more than that. Leashed strength meshed with an animalistic sense of power, a combination which boded ill for any adversary.

'I imagine you wheel and deal with cut-throat determination.' She paused a beat. 'Mostly you win.' She doubted he ever lost…unless it was a deliberate tactical manoeuvre.

'An interesting character analysis,' Jace accorded with musing cynicism.

The waiter removed dishes, and the wine steward refilled their goblets.

Soft piano music provided a pleasant background for the muted buzz of conversation.

'You have family in New York?'

'Parents, one brother, two sisters, and several nieces and nephews.'

Was he removed from them, too caught up being a high-flying entrepreneur and too involved in his own life?

'My mother insists we all get together once a fortnight for a family dinner,' Jace drawled. 'Madness and mayhem would be an accurate description.'

'But fun?' She had a mental image of adults laughing, chiding children, noisy chatter and a table groaning with food and wine.

'Very much so.'

Did he take his women...it had to be plural, although presumably he was discriminative...to visit?

'Not often, no.'

Rebekah endeavoured to still her surprise, and failed. 'You read minds?'

'It's an acquired skill.'

'One in which you excel.'

Jace inclined his head, but there was no arrogance apparent, just the assurance of a man well-versed in the vagaries of human nature and possessed of the ability to deal with them.

It was during dessert that Rebekah happened to

glance towards the restaurant entrance. Afterwards she couldn't say what drew her attention there. Instinct, perhaps? Some deep, inner, protective element alerting her to danger?

For a few heart-stopping seconds she prayed she was mistaken, but she'd have known that profile anywhere, the angle of his head…

'What is it?'

She registered Jace's voice, and tried to tamp down the sick feeling that filled her stomach.

'Rebekah?'

Oh, God. *Think,* she bade silently. There's a good chance he won't see you, and if he does, what can he do?

Plenty.

Jace witnessed her pale features as the colour leeched from her cheeks, and her eyes had dulled an instant before she veiled them with her lashes. What, more relevantly *who* was responsible for rendering her as still as stone?

'Do you want to leave?' His voice was quiet, but serious in its intent.

She wanted to say *yes.* Now, quickly, quietly.

Except that was a coward's way out, and she'd vowed the day she legally severed all ties with him she'd never allow Brad Somerville to intimidate her again. Ever.

'My ex-husband has just walked in the door.'

Was she aware that with so few words she'd conveyed so much? Somehow he doubted it.

'Is it a problem?'

If she stuck with the truth, how would Jace Dimitriades deal with it? A hollow laugh rose and died in her throat. Why in hell would he *want* to?

'No,' she denied, and knew she lied.

Jace's eyes narrowed as he observed her monitor her ex-husband's progress towards a reserved table, and witnessed her fleeting expression the moment the man recognised her presence. It was neither embarrassment nor awkwardness...but fear.

'Well, *hello.*'

Rebekah kept her head erect, her eyes wide and steady. The action was a well-practised one, for she could never be sure what Brad's next move might be.

'Brad.' The acknowledgement was stilted, remote.

'Introduce me to your...companion.'

'Jace Dimitriades.' Jace's voice held a faintly inflected drawl and was dangerously quiet, almost lethal. He made no effort to rise to his feet or take Brad's extended hand.

Rebekah saw something move in Brad's gleaming gaze, recognised the early-warning sign of his temper, and felt her apprehension accelerate.

Brad focused his attention on Rebekah. 'Keeping it all in the family, darling?'

'The *maître d'* is waiting to show you to your table,' Jace intimated with deceptive mildness. Although anyone with any nous would see it as a dismissal. Those who knew him would have quailed at the leashed savagery lurking just beneath the surface.

Brad inclined his head. 'Of course.' His voice softened with silky threat. 'Take care, Rebekah.'

She hadn't realised she'd been holding her breath until she released it, and she forced herself to pick up her spoon and scoop a small serving of fruit, then eat it.

Calm? She felt the antithesis of *calm*. Yet she'd learned her lessons well, and it was far better to attempt normality. In the beginning, after the shock of discovering Brad's dual personality, she'd gone through an entire gamut of emotions…from heartbreaking tears, to anger, remorse, dislike, only to discover it made things worse.

'We can go somewhere else for coffee.'

Rebekah picked up her water glass with a steady hand. 'It's OK.'

Not, Jace determined as he surveyed her features. She was far too pale, and her actions were too rigidly controlled for his liking.

Almost as if she guessed his intention to summon the waiter and request the bill, she voiced quietly, 'Please, don't.'

'His presence here is making you feel uncomfortable.'

Now, that had to be the understatement of the year. 'You don't understand.'

His eyes narrowed, and she sensed a watchful quality evident. 'You think if we leave, he'll have won?'

He was too astute for her peace of mind. 'Yes.'

'Meanwhile you eat food you no longer taste, sip water or wine while we wait for coffee,' he pursued in a silky voice. 'And tie your stomach in knots during the process.'

She knew Brad's *modus operandi* only too well. Interpretation of her ex-husband's wild mood swings, anticipating his reactions had become an integral part of her survival.

'It's better this way,' she said coolly.

'Not for you,' Jace declared with certainty, and saw the slight lift of her chin as she met his gaze.

His own didn't waver from hers as he ordered coffee from a hovering waiter, and he settled the bill, waited patiently for her to finish, then he led her from the restaurant.

'I'll take a taxi,' Rebekah said stiffly, and incurred his swift dark glance.

'The hell you will.'

She didn't say a word, couldn't, for her throat was tight with nerves, and she walked at his side in silence, then slid into the passenger seat the instant he unlocked the car.

It didn't take long to reach her apartment building, and during the short drive she stared sightlessly out the window, unaware of the familiar scenery, the traffic.

Her mind was filled with the scene in the restaurant, Brad, and the electric presence of the man seated within touching distance.

'Thanks for dinner.' Politeness had been ingrained from a young age. She reached for the door-clasp, and froze as his hand captured her wrist.

'Is your ex-husband likely to confront you?'

She paused a few seconds too long. 'Why would he do that? He has no control over my life.'

Jace had questions he wanted to ask, but now was not the right time to get answers...even if she'd be willing to give them to him. 'I'll be in Melbourne for a few days with Luc. I'll ring you.'

'There's no need.'

He leaned closer and slid a hand to capture her nape, tilting her head so she had to look at him. 'Yes,' he said quietly. 'There is.'

For a heart-stopping second she thought he was going to kiss her, and she unconsciously held her breath, aware that a part of her craved the feel of his mouth on her own.

There was a hunger she couldn't quite control, and she trembled with it, wanting in that moment to be absorbed by this man. To have him take her to a place where she could temporarily forget the vindictiveness that lived inside Brad Somerville, and begin to repair the damage caused to her emotional heart.

She heard a faint sound emerge from his throat, and she swallowed painfully as he brushed his thumb over the curve of her lower lip, tracing its fullness.

His eyes were dark, too dark to determine his intent, and she felt the tension in him, the restraint, and knew instinctively the next move was hers.

All she had to do was use the edge of her teeth, the tip of her tongue on the tip of this finger to offer an unspoken invitation.

Dear God, she wanted to, she wanted *him*. Except she hesitated too long, and she thought she glimpsed the gleam of a faint smile, sensed the slight edge of his regret as she pulled back.

Then he did smile, and the hand holding her nape gentled and soothed the tension there for a few seconds, then he released her and eased back in his seat.

She felt as if her limbs were fused together, restricting mobility, and she was intensely aware of the sensual electricity apparent. Explosive and primitive, it shimmered as an elusive force, poised to shatter the shell she'd painstakingly erected around her fragile heart.

'Goodnight.' The word emerged as little more than a strangled sound, and she fumbled for the door-clasp, almost breathless in the need to escape.

Except the constraint of the seat belt stopped her, and she uttered a silent cry as his fingers sought the safety clip and unfastened it.

Within seconds she slid from the car and she almost ran the few steps to the haven offered by the entrance to her apartment building. The keys were plucked free from her purse and she selected the appropriate one as she punched the security code freeing the external door into the lobby.

From there it took only a moment to use her key to gain the area leading to the triple bank of lifts.

She was trembling by the time she reached her apartment, and inside she made for the kitchen, extracted bottled water from the refrigerator and gulped several mouthfuls before seeking a chair.

The evening was over. Although instinct warned whatever she shared with Jace was far from done.

It was as if something deep and primal was being resurrected from her soul, *his*. The sane, sensible part of her brain questioned any metaphysical connection, but the illogical part queried if they hadn't been joined together in a previous life, and their souls were forcing recognition.

Then there was Brad. She tamped down the memories and the pain. A few years was but a small window in the picture of her life. Hadn't that been the professional advice given at the time?

The sudden peal of the phone startled her, and she stood to her feet to take the call, except she was unable to reach the handset and pick up before the answering machine cut in.

Her automated greeting was brief, and she hesitated, wary as to who would be calling at this time of night.

'Having fun with your new man, sweetheart?'

It was followed by a click as the caller replaced the receiver.

Rebekah felt the blood drain from her face.

Brad. There was no mistaking his voice.

Shock jolted her senses and was quickly replaced by a sickening fear.

Her telephone number was unlisted. What ruse had he used to gain it? Had he also gained access to her cell-net number?

She crossed her arms and hugged them together across her midriff as her mind whirled with facts and possibilities.

The restraining order she'd had to take out against

him was still in place. If he chose to violate it he'd face the legal consequences.

Her body began to rock a little until she stilled the movements and crossed to sink down into a chair.

Please, *please*, she begged silently. Don't let the nuisance calls begin again.

Once, only *once* following her divorce had she dated another man. Immediately afterwards Brad had begun a series of phone calls. It had taken complaints to the police, written reports, warnings, and finally the filing of a restraining order to get him to stop.

Now, tonight, a chance meeting had started it all over again.

Thank God she was safe in her apartment. She'd chosen it deliberately for its high-tech security measures, and had installed double locks on her door as well as a safety chain.

She wrapped her arms around her knees and hugged hard. It was *coincidence*...wasn't it? Brad couldn't be having her followed? Even more frightening, monitoring her every move away from Blooms and Bouquets?

CHAPTER FOUR

THE day began much as any other, with the usual pre-dawn visit to the flower market, followed by setting all the blooms into troughs of water at the boutique.

Rebekah booted up the computer, downloaded orders, printed out hard copies, then checked whether she needed to order more stock.

Ana arrived around nine, and together they dealt with orders, customers, and the many phone calls that made up a typical day.

'Are you going to tell me how dinner with Jace went last night, or must I prise it out of you?' Ana queried during a momentary lull.

Rebekah added another spray of baby's breath to the bouquet she was assembling, made a deft adjustment, then gathered in the sheet of Cellophane. 'It was OK.'

'Just...*OK*?' her sister teased.

'If you're asking whether it became deep and meaningful... No.'

Jace was far too astute to move too fast too soon, Ana approved, silently applauding his style as Rebekah anticipated the next query.

'He said he'll phone. Am I seeing him again? I don't think so.'

'Why not?'

Because it'll cause problems for which there's no solution. The very reason she'd scaled her life down to a simplistic level. 'Why?' she countered. 'He's only here for a brief stay, then he'll return to New York. What's the point of starting something that has nowhere to go?'

She desperately wanted to confide about Brad's appearance in the restaurant, his phone call, and the disturbing fact he'd somehow gained access to her private line.

Except something held her back. There was concern for Ana's pregnancy, and besides it was too soon to determine whether Brad was bent on a single nuisance call or if he intended to resort to a repeat of his former behaviour.

She could only pray it wasn't the latter.

At that moment a customer entered the shop, and within minutes everything went to hell in a handbasket.

Luc's former mistress, the glamorous, unpredictable Celine, confronted Ana verbally, then launched into a physical attack that happened so quickly Rebekah wasn't swift enough to prevent it.

It was akin to a horror scene in a movie as Celine swept a glass vase to the floor, where it shattered, and a hard shove sent Ana down among scattered countless shards.

Rebekah gave an involuntary cry and flew to her sister's side, at the same time castigating Celine with pithy, unladylike language. 'You *bitch*,' just didn't begin to cut it.

Everything after that became a blur as Rebekah phoned Petros, Luc's manservant, contacted Luc on his cellphone, then she closed the shop and drove to the hospital, where she paced the visiting-room floor with all the pent-up anger of the demented as she waited for a medical professional to appear and provide a lucid report on Ana's condition.

'Your sister is fine. The ultrasound shows no sign of foetal distress. She's being transferred to a room, and one of the nursing staff will take you to see her soon.'

Rebekah's relief was a palpable thing, and she uttered a silent prayer in thanks.

It took only seconds to punch in Luc's number, relay the update and learn he was about to board a flight back to Sydney.

There was time to call the owner of the boutique adjacent Blooms and Bouquets, explain and request she tape a notice detailing a family emergency to the door.

With that taken care of, she began to relax, and she crossed to the coffee machine, inserted coins and sugared the black brew.

Hot and sweet was the best compliment she could offer, but it served to soothe in the aftermath of the past traumatic hour.

With smooth efficiency she made a series of calls, arranged replacement staff during Ana's enforced absence and notified a few regular customers their orders would be delayed.

Tears filled her eyes the instant she saw her sister

sitting upright in bed with bandages covering her hand and forearm.

'Don't you *dare* cry,' Ana warned, tempering the threat with a warm smile. 'I'm OK.'

'You might very well not have been.' The hug was a very careful one, then she stood back and brought the shaky feeling under control. Just thinking about Celine's crazy attack made her impossibly angry.

'The shop—'

'Is shut, and Jana has taped an explanation to the door.' She met Ana's clear gaze. 'Don't even think of suggesting I go back and leave you here on your own.' A determined smile lightened her features. 'I'm here until they throw me out.' Or at least until Luc arrives, she added silently.

'Promise me you won't work late tonight.'

Rebekah crossed fingers behind her back. 'You've got it.' Did it matter her interpretation of *late* wouldn't match that of her sister? A small transgression from the truth shouldn't count.

She deliberately made no mention of Celine. If Ana wanted to talk about it, so be it. Otherwise the subject was best left alone…for now. Luc, no doubt, would take appropriate action.

Various members of the nursing staff moved in and out of the suite as they conducted routine checks, and a proffered tray of tea and biscuits proved welcome.

Not long afterwards Ana drifted into a light doze, and Rebekah slipped into the corridor to use her cellphone.

A tall, dark-suited figure strode towards her, and

for a split-second her heart stopped. The two Dimitriades men were alike in height and breadth of shoulder, with similar features. Except this was Ana's husband, not Jace.

'Rebekah.' Luc clasped a hand over her shoulder. 'How is she?'

The words were almost cursory in his urgency to see his wife, and she offered him an understanding smile. 'OK,' she assured, and her eyes hardened. 'You're going to deal with Celine?'

His expression became harsh, almost lethal. 'It's done.'

She didn't want to contemplate what action he'd taken, and didn't ask. Whatever it was, she could only be glad she wasn't the one on the receiving end of Luc's wrath. He had the look of a predator who'd staked the kill, and by the time he finished with his quarry all that would remain would be skeletal bones.

'Ana is asleep.' She touched a light hand to his. 'I'll check in later.'

'Thanks.' Momentary warmth lightened his eyes, then he turned and entered the suite.

Rebekah drove to Blooms and Bouquets, popped in quickly to thank Jana for her help, then she unlocked the shop and set to work. A few regular customers were understanding of the circumstances and took up her offer for free delivery. The rest would have to wait until morning.

She took time to ring the hospital, spoke to Ana, then Luc, and learnt her sister would be discharged the next morning.

It must have been after seven when she realised she'd hardly eaten all day, and she rummaged in the small refrigerator beneath the counter, discovered a pot of yoghurt and an apple, demolished both, then continued working.

At nine she locked up the shop and began deliveries. Fortunately they were contained within a fifteen-kilometre radius. Consequently it was almost ten-thirty when she entered her apartment, and she fed Millie before heading for the *en suite*, where she shed her clothes, then she took a leisurely shower and let the heated spray of water ease the kinks from a long, hard day.

Afterwards she donned a silk robe, then padded out to the kitchen. It was way too late to eat a meal, but something light with a cup of tea would take the edge off her hunger.

The message light on her answering machine was blinking, and she filled the electric kettle, popped bread into the toaster, then depressed the message-button in order for it to rewind.

Five, she determined as the first began to play.

A friend, suggesting they go to a foreign art film on Sunday; her doctor's receptionist with a reminder to make an appointment for her annual check-up; Luc, with an update and quietly chiding her for working late.

The fourth message sent her heart slamming against her ribs. 'Two nights in a row, darling? Unusual for you, isn't it?' A click as the message concluded. Then the fifth call ran… 'Taken him to bed yet?'

Brad.

She clenched her hands until the knuckles showed white.

Just then the phone rang, and she stood locked into immobility for a few seconds, then, mindful it could be Luc, she snatched up the receiver, muttered a strangled greeting, then sank down onto the floor as Brad's voice filtered through the receiver.

'Nice of you to pick up, darling.'

Rebekah replaced the receiver, disconnected the handset, then retrieved her cellphone and rang the telephone company's twenty-four-hour number, reported the nuisance calls, cited the restraining order, waited while her details underwent a computer check, and carefully wrote down the digits of her newly assigned private number.

Then she made a cup of tea, carried it into the lounge and switched on the television set in the hope of finding something light and humorous to view.

At midnight she crawled into bed and slept until the alarm woke her four hours later.

Habit was responsible for her mechanical movements as she dressed, drank strong, sweet coffee, dished fresh food for Millie, then she rode the lift down to the car park.

Dark streets with minimal traffic ensured a smooth drive to the flower markets, and with the day's stock stored in the van she did the return journey to Double Bay.

Rebekah worked with efficient speed, paused at seven-thirty to call Luc and give him her newly assigned number.

'Brad?' Luc queried sharply, and she cut in before he could continue.

'I've taken care of it. Don't tell Ana, OK?'

'Want me to intervene on your behalf?'

He was a force to be reckoned with, but she doubted even he could achieve any more than she already had.

'Thanks, but it's done. Give Ana my love. I'll call in to see her after I close the shop.'

'I'm taking her straight from the hospital to the beach house for a few days.'

'Good idea. Tell her I'll phone later this morning.'

'Rebekah.' His voice became clipped, serious. 'Don't be a hero. Brad calls you again, I want to know.'

'You've got it.' She replaced the receiver, dialled the hospital and was put through to her sister, whose reassurance was cheering.

'I'll be back at the shop on Monday.'

'We'll see.'

'Oh, lord, don't you start,' Ana groaned in response. 'If Luc had his way, he'd wrap me in cotton wool and confine me to the house.'

She managed a chuckle. 'That's not such a bad idea.'

'Got to go. The medics have arrived to prod, intrude and note down personal questions.'

Rebekah laughed out loud. 'Sounds like fun.'

'Oh, yeah? Wait until it's your turn, sister, dear.'

For a moment she caught a glimpse of the future, a family gathering on the lawn at Luc and Ana's home, two small children scampering in the sunshine; herself holding a baby…her own, and beside her a man whose face was obscured as he looked down at her.

The image faded, then disappeared, and she shivered.

As if! It was fanciful thinking, stimulated by Ana's pregnancy. And a desire for a child of her own? a tiny voice taunted.

Fool, she chastised as she turned back to the work table and ran a check of the day's orders.

Ana's replacement arrived at eight, a slim, dark-haired girl in her twenties named Suzie, and Rebekah breathed a sigh of relief as the girl proved to be quick and competent.

Together they coped with customers, readied orders for delivery, and Rebekah manned the phone.

When it rang for the umpteenth time she picked up and intoned her customary greeting.

'Rebekah?'

The New York accent gave him away, and the timbre of his voice sent her pulse racing to a faster beat as she managed a cool acknowledgement. 'Jace.'

'I'll be back in Sydney by late afternoon. Share dinner and a movie with me tonight.'

She tightened her grip on the receiver. 'I don't think that's a good idea.'

'Dinner, or the movie?'

'Both. Neither.' Oh, lord, she was losing it! 'No.'

She closed her eyes, then opened them again. 'I have to go,' she said with a hint of desperation, and hung up.

Ana rang mid-afternoon, her voice light, warm, *alive*. It was wonderful to hear her sound so happy, and Rebekah said as much.

'I am,' her sister assured. 'How are things at the shop? No problems? Is the temporary girl panning out OK?'

'So many questions,' Rebekah teased. 'Fine, no, very well. Does that cover it?'

'And you? Are *you* OK?'

Sisterly intuition? 'Of course.'

'Uh-huh.'

'I can take care of myself.'

'I know. With one hand tied behind your back.'

Rebekah choked back a laugh. 'Go give your husband the attention he deserves.'

'I intend to. I'll call you Sunday.'

The afternoon deliveries went out, they tidied up the shop, and Suzie left at five-thirty with a cheery wave and a promise to report early next morning.

Rebekah began moving in some of the outdoor displays, varied coloured cyclamen in decorative pots, Australian natives, ferns, and placed them inside, watered and tended to them.

It was almost time to lock up and go home, and she admitted to a feeling of relief the day was almost over.

The peal of the phone sounded above the muted

background music emitting from the CD player, and she crossed to the counter to pick up.

'I suppose you think you're smart, changing your number,' Brad intoned without preamble.

A sickened feeling invaded her stomach, and she drew a calming breath. Logic, not anger, she'd been advised. State facts clearly, then hang up.

'What you're doing is harassment, and there are legal measures in place to prevent you from bothering me. Why buck the law and invite trouble for yourself?'

She returned the receiver to its cradle, then moved towards the door, only to pause as the phone rang again.

At that moment the door swung inwards and she glanced up to see Jace framed in the aperture for an instant before he entered the shop.

No, Rebekah groaned silently, wishing him anywhere else but here, *now*.

'Aren't you going to answer that?'

The sound of his voice raised all her fine body hairs, and she suppressed the shiver of nerves threatening to visibly shake her slim frame.

Brad *and* Jace? It was too much. Without a word she retraced her steps and snatched up the phone.

'You sound agitated, darling. Am I finally getting to you?'

'You're wasting your time, and mine,' Rebekah added, and cut the connection.

'Problems?'

He couldn't begin to understand the hornets' nest

he'd disturbed, and she took a second to square her shoulders before turning slowly to face him.

Jace didn't like the tension creasing her forehead, the darkness in her eyes, or the edge of pain evident.

'What are you doing here?'

'No *hello*?' he drawled, staying exactly where he was. Crowding her right now would be the height of foolishness.

'I'm about to shut up shop and go home.'

He took a moment to scan the interior before bringing his attention back to her.

'Is there anything I can do to help?'

'Go away and leave me alone?' Rebekah posed, and saw his faint smile.

'I don't consider that as an option.'

The phone rang again, and she chose to ignore it.

'Want me to take it?' Jace queried smoothly, and saw her face pale. 'Brad?' He didn't need her confirmation, the shadows dulling her eyes were sufficient.

'It'll only make things worse if he hears your voice.'

His gaze hardened and his features assumed a grim implacability. 'How bad is it likely to get?'

You can't begin to know. Except the words never left her lips.

'Go collect your purse and we'll get out of here,' Jace commanded quietly.

'You should leave.' Please, she added silently. Can't you see I can't deal with you right now?

'I will, when you do.'

The insistent ring of the telephone proved the deciding factor, and she retrieved her purse, removed the afternoon's takings from the cash register, picked up her keys, then followed him out the door.

Locking up took a few seconds, and she turned towards him. 'Goodnight.' She stepped around him and began walking to her car, only to have him fall into step beside her.

'I thought we'd pick up a pizza somewhere.'

'You do that…solo. I've had a long day.' She unconsciously flexed her shoulders. 'Yesterday was even longer.' And tomorrow she had two weddings scheduled.

'You need to eat.'

'I plan to.' She reached her car, slid in the key and unlocked it. 'Alone.'

'In that case, perhaps you wouldn't mind dropping me off at the hotel on your way home. I caught a cab here.'

She retrieved her cellphone and punched in a series of digits, miscalculated one of them, and reached a wrong number.

Jace watched her expressive features, caught the fleeting emotions, and reached forward to open the car door.

'Who are you afraid of, Rebekah? I can promise not to harm a hair on your head.'

Why did she suddenly feel as if she couldn't breathe? 'Maybe it's not my head I'm worried about.'

A husky chuckle sounded low in his throat, and he spread his hands in silent surrender. 'Pizza, Rebekah. That's all. We both need to eat. Why not together?'

She looked at him. 'That's it? Pizza?'

'Pizza,' he drawled in acquiescence.

She made a split-second decision she had a feeling she might later regret. 'I know a place. Get in.'

King's Cross wasn't too far distant, and at this early hour it would be incredibly ordinary. It wasn't until post-midnight the Cross began to show its true colours, with the pimps, prostitutes, touts displaying their talents. In the back streets lay the dives and dens where the less salubrious deals were made. A place where a wrong move could mean a knife in the ribs, or worse.

Already the surroundings were beginning to change.

Graceful old residences were left behind, with small brick cottages appearing, terrace houses, and the element of care began to diminish.

'I get the feeling you're intent on showing me another side of this beautiful city,' Jace drawled as they neared the Cross.

'A landmark,' Rebekah corrected. 'Ana and I ate pizza here a few nights ago.'

'With Luc's knowledge?'

She began searching for a vacant space to park the car. 'I imagine she told him.'

Jace checked the flashing neon, the floodlit doorways. 'Afterwards, rather than before.'

'You're a snob.'

'No.' New York contained areas where you put your life on the line in daylight. After dark merely trebled the danger. 'I wouldn't want any woman of mine wandering around here after dark.'

'As long as you're moving,' Rebekah assured with a wicked grin. 'Standing still for more than a few minutes isn't recommended, unless you want someone to approach and ask your going rate for sex.'

She spotted an empty space and swung into it, then cut the engine.

'Pizza, you said?'

She led the way to a small shop on the opposite side of the street where the owner's oven-fired pizzas rated as the best she'd ever sampled anywhere. Bright red-and-white-checked tablecloths covered small square tables, empty Chianti bottles held lit candles in various stages of meltdown.

However, the aromas were redolent with spices and garlic, the service warm and friendly, and if you were fortunate enough to gain a window-seat it was a great vantage point to watch the people walk by.

'Rebekah! *Comè sta?*'

A tall Italian Adonis moved from behind the counter and enveloped her in an affectionate hug. '*Bella,* twice in one week?' the man teased. 'If I didn't know you visit only for the pizza, I might begin to think you fancy me.'

She laughed, a glorious, husky, free sound that caught Jace unawares. The frown that had been evident from the moment he walked into Blooms and Bouquets disappeared, and gone was the tension from her eyes.

'Angelo.' The mild admonishment held affection, and he shook his head with mock-regret.

'But I see this is not so,' he said as he moved her to arm's length. 'For you have brought someone with you.' There was a pause as he examined Jace, and something silent passed between them, then it was gone as he returned his attention to her. 'If you seek my approval, you have it.'

Jace saw the soft pink that coloured her cheeks as she smiled and shook her head in silent remonstrance.

'Jace Dimitriades, Angelo Benedetti.'

Angelo extended his hand and Jace shook it. 'Rebekah and I are friends from way back. *Friends*,' he emphasised quietly. 'The window table is yours.' His smile broadened as he held Rebekah's gaze. 'Go take a seat. I have pizza to make.' He moved ahead of them to the table, removed the *reserved* sign, pulled out a chair for Rebekah, indicated the one opposite to Jace, then he crossed behind the counter.

'I gather acquiring the window table is something of an honour?' Jace inclined.

'No one sits here without Angelo's personal invitation to do so.'

He picked up the menu and scanned the varieties listed. 'What do you recommend?'

'The works,' she said without hesitation. 'It's something else.'

It was, and when Angelo personally presented the aromatic masterpiece she watched as Jace savoured it with delighted satisfaction.

He fitted right into the atmosphere, spurning cutlery as he demolished the initial piece. 'Sheer ambrosia.'

'*La dolce vita,*' Rebekah accorded, and went on to reveal, 'Angelo refuses to get into the pizza-delivery game. If you want to sample his pizza, you have to come here to eat it. You get to drink Chianti or coffee, and watch the world go by.' She offered a warm smile. 'The total experience.'

Jace picked up another slice and bit into it. 'Worth it.'

The smile became a husky chuckle. 'I'm glad you think so.'

He stilled, and his gaze was dark, serious. 'Are you?'

The query was quietly voiced, but there was something in his underlying tone that brought all her defences to the fore.

He saw the shutters come down on her expression, and the smile faded from her lips. Such a soft mouth, so many fragile emotions. There was a brief moment when he wanted to smash a fist into her ex-husband's face for the damage he'd done. The little information he'd managed to prise from Luc had made him incredibly angry.

The silence stretched between them, and he ate steadily, aware that she pushed her plate to one side.

He could almost see the conscious effort she summoned to move the conversation on to a safe plane.

'Your trip to Melbourne proved successful?'

'Yes. I have meetings here early next week, then

it's Brisbane, Cairns, Port Douglas, Brisbane and the
Gold Coast.'

Idle conversation. The need for it beat silence and
eased the tension steadily building inside her.

'Whereupon you return to New York.'

'Yes.'

Nothing explained the sudden pain that pierced her
heart, or the sensation of impending loss. What was
the matter with her? Jace Dimitriades had no place in
her life, any more than she had a place in his. They
resided continents apart. Besides, sexual awareness
was no basis on which to build...*what*? A relationship?

Dear heaven. Even the thought of sharing sensual
intimacy with such a man fired the blood in her veins
and sent her nervous system into cataclysmic over-
load.

Imagining that strong, muscled body naked, his
arousal large, hard and pulsing with need. The touch
of his mouth on hers, his hands shaping her breasts...

Would he hurt her as Brad had? Take his own satisfaction without any thought for hers? Cruelly taunt
her to compensate for his inadequacies?

Somehow she doubted Jace was anything but an
experienced and skilled lover. He exuded the confi-
dent sensual intensity of a man at ease with himself,
and possessed of an intuitive awareness of what it
took to please a woman.

How could she explain the yearning deep inside
to discover if it was true? To give herself uncondition-

ally to his seduction, exult in the pleasure of it as they soared towards the heights of passion together, shared a mutual shattering climax, followed by the infinitely languorous warmth of drifting fingers, the gentle touch of lips to skin…the exquisite liquid feeling that accompanied lovemaking. Very good lovemaking.

'The pizza is good?'

The sound of Angelo's voice was a stark intrusion and brought her tumbling back to reality. It took a second to marshal her thoughts together and summon a smile.

'Superb, as always,' she reassured, not quite meeting his steady gaze. She needed several more seconds before she could look at Jace.

'Can I bring you coffee? Tea?'

'Tea,' Rebekah ordered. She needed to sleep tonight.

'Make it two,' Jace added, reaching for his wallet.

'Mine,' she insisted, and extracted a note from her purse to cover the bill. 'Don't take his money,' she insisted to Angelo, who laughed with delight and pushed the note towards her.

'What if I refuse altogether?' He inclined his head towards Rebekah. 'Tonight is on the house, my friend. For old times' sake.' He turned to Jace and offered a hard glance. 'Take care of her.'

'Count on it.' Jace's voice was a silky drawl laced with intent, and drew Angelo's silent approval.

The tea arrived, a fine Ceylon blend Angelo kept

for special customers, and she savoured it with genuine enjoyment.

'Do you come here often?'

'Occasionally.'

She liked his hands, the shape and texture of them, their strength. A shiver feathered its way over her skin as she remembered how they felt threading through her hair, capturing her nape the instant before his mouth lowered to hers. Magic. He had the touch, the degree of *tendresse* to melt a woman's heart.

But not hers, she determined with quiet resolve.

'I'll drop you back to your hotel,' Rebekah offered as they farewelled Angelo before emerging outdoors onto the street pavement.

It was still light, but the sky had acquired the dull patina of approaching dusk. Soon the streetlights would spring on, and the regular patrons of the Cross would begin to appear.

Together they crossed the street to her van, and she ignited the engine then eased into the steady flow of traffic.

'How will you manage at the shop until Ana returns?' Jace queried, watching her competent handling of the vehicle, the traffic.

'I was able to get another florist to fill in today, and she's agreeable to work tomorrow.' She drew to a halt at a set of lights. 'I'm seriously considering asking if she'll work part-time. I'll need to discuss it with Ana.'

'And Brad?' He slipped that in, because he felt the need to know.

'I can handle it,' Rebekah assured tightly.

'And if you can't?' Jace pursued.

She spared him a hard glance as the lights changed up ahead. 'The legal authorities will do it for me.'

It didn't make him breathe any easier. There was something primitively evil beneath the layers of Brad Somerville's projected sophistication. Obviously well-hidden to have fooled the woman seated beside him.

The cars up front began to move, and she shifted gears, then followed the main arterial road leading to Double Bay.

It was with a sense of relief she pulled into the entrance immediately out front of the Ritz-Carlton, and she looked in silent askance as Jace removed his wallet, extracted a business card, and penned a series of digits before handing it to her.

'My cellphone number. It'll reach me any time, anywhere.' He cast her a look that was serious in the extreme. 'Call if you need me.'

He reached for the door-clasp, then turned back and fastened his mouth on hers, conducting a slow sweep of the sweet inner moistness with his tongue before deepening the kiss into something frankly sensual.

How long did it last? Scant minutes, but it left him wanting more, much more than the taste of her mouth.

He stifled a sound deep in his throat that was pure regret as he gentled her lips with his own, then he broke the contact and stepped out from the van to stand watching as she sent the vehicle moving out onto the street.

Then he turned and entered the hotel lobby, acknowledged the concierge with a curt nod, and took the lift up to his suite.

CHAPTER FIVE

REBEKAH locked her apartment door and re-set the security alarm before crossing to the kitchen to feed the cat.

A sense of trepidation tied her stomach in knots as she forced herself to check the answering machine, and she expelled some pent-up breath at the sight of its unblinking message light.

Thank God. She closed her eyes, then opened them again in a gesture of innate relief.

Although how long would it take Brad to bypass the telephone company's security and determine her new unlisted number? Technically, it wasn't supposed to happen…which didn't necessarily mean that it couldn't be done.

She lifted her arms high and stretched her body in an effort to dispel kinks from sore muscles, then she moved through to the *en suite* adjoining her bedroom and began filling the spa-bath. Half an hour relaxing there with a glossy magazine and a cup of tea was just what she needed to help her unwind from the day.

It worked just fine, and she crawled into bed, snapped off the bedside light…and lay staring into the darkness as Jace's image filled her mind.

She fell asleep with the vivid memory of how it felt to have his mouth invade hers, and sheer exhaustion was responsible for uninterrupted somnolence until the alarm rang early next morning.

Saturday numbered one of the busiest days of the week, and today didn't prove any different. Suzie was a jewel, and they worked together getting the orders organised, completed, and boxed the two wedding orders ready for the courier, dealt with customers who came in off the street, and even managed to snatch something to eat at reasonable intervals.

There was no lull, little time to think, just the need for smooth efficiency.

Ana checked in around midday, and Rebekah was delighted to hear the happiness emanate from her voice.

There was the opportunity to mention Suzie's suitability to assist part-time, and Ana's *'hire her'* clinched the decision.

'Mornings and all day Fridays and Saturdays,' Rebekah offered, named the rate of pay, and gave a relieved sigh at Suzie's enthusiastic acceptance.

There was a sense of satisfaction and achievement in that Ana was fine with her life back on track; Blooms and Bouquets would continue to operate efficiently.

Two down and two to go, Rebekah rationalised, hoping, praying that her ex-husband's nuisance calls would cease and he'd fade back into the woodwork.

That left Jace Dimitriades, and she had no idea how she was going to deal with *Jace*. If she had any sense and an iota of self-preservation she'd refuse to see him and put him out of her mind.

Fat chance. He was already there, firmly embedded in the recesses of her brain. He made her want something she couldn't have. His image teased her with endless possibilities of what it would be like to *be* with him.

Take that step, and she'd be irretrievably lost. Caught up in a sensual madness that could very well lead to her destruction.

But what a way to go.

'See you Monday.'

Rebekah glanced up from the computer and smiled as Suzie caught up her bag. 'Goodnight. Enjoy the rest of the weekend.'

'Shall do. You, too.'

The glass door swung shut, and Rebekah returned her attention to the computer. She'd save the data onto disk and take it home, where she'd load it into the laptop tomorrow and key in the appropriate accounting entries.

Three customers entered the shop to secure last-minute purchases, and she tended to the last one, then just as she was about to secure the lock Jace appeared at the door.

Just the sight of him sent her pulse racing, and set the butterflies fluttering madly in her stomach. Heat suffused her body, and she deliberately regulated her breathing in a bid to control her wayward emotions. 'I'm just about to close,' she managed evenly. 'Is there something you want?'

His answering smile did strange things to her equilibrium. 'You, to join me for dinner tonight.'

Forget control. His *you* sent her imagination into a tailspin, and she banked down riotous images of tangled sheets, naked bodies…his, *hers,* coupled together in the throes of passion.

What was *wrong* with her? The silent castigation was heartfelt. Had she been locked too long in denial? Was that it? And if so, why *this* man?

Don't answer that.

Her only weapon was humour. She lifted a hand to her chin and tilted her head.

'Ah, you're all alone in the city with no one to call, and I'll do?' What was she doing, for heaven's sake? One didn't tease men of Jace Dimitriades' calibre. 'What if I've made other plans?'

'Have you?'

Honesty came to the fore. 'No.'

'Good.'

'Don't count your chickens too soon,' she warned. 'I haven't said *yes.*'

He lifted a hand and pushed a stray tendril of hair back behind her ear. 'But you will.'

What did she have to lose? Stupid question. Maybe Ana was right, and it was time to loosen a few strings.

'Can we negotiate on a movie?'

'Done.'

'OK.'

Jace gave a deep, husky chuckle. 'You want to be chauffeur, or shall I?'

She pretended to consider both options. 'Oh, let's go for role reversal. Besides, I have a better knowledge of the city than you do.' She checked her watch. 'Pick you up at seven?'

'I'll be waiting.' He glanced around the shop's interior. 'Now, let's get you out of here.'

'I've done it a thousand times on my own.' More, if anyone was counting.

'Then indulge me and let's do it together.'

Five minutes later Rebekah walked to her van as Jace slid behind the wheel of his car.

Neither of them noticed the man seated in a vehicle thirty metres distant. If they had, it would have taken more than a casual glance to determine his identity. A cap worn backwards and wrap-around sunglasses provided a very good disguise.

There were no messages recorded on the answering machine, and Rebekah hit the shower, stepped into clean underwear, tended to her make-up, swept her hair into a smooth knot, then dressed in black evening trousers, a red camisole and matching evening jacket. She added stiletto heels, caught up an evening purse and her keys, then she took the lift down to the underground car park.

The MG was parked in its customary space, and she fired the engine and sent the sleek little sports car onto street level, then drove the few blocks to Jace's hotel.

He emerged from the lobby as soon as she drew into the entrance bay, and within minutes she rejoined the traffic.

'Where to?'

'Darling Harbour.'

'Yessir.'

Jace wondered if she had any idea how her features

lightened? Or how the darkness that was a lurking constant in her eyes disappeared when she smiled?

'Don't be sassy.'

She shot him a grin. 'Just acting out the *chauffeur* part.'

It was a beautiful evening, cool, but not uncomfortably so, and they ate seafood at an elegant restaurant overlooking the inner harbour, drank a little chilled white wine, then took in a top-rated movie guaranteed to earn the lead actors, the producer and director major award honours.

'That was great,' Rebekah accorded as they emerged from the cinema complex and began walking to where she'd parked the MG.

Fine food, beautiful ambience, fantastic movie… great date, *great man,* she reflected, aware this was her first date in a long while. Too long.

She'd played her private life so carefully since her divorce. Brad's erratic behaviour had diminished her self-image, damaged her trust in men, and left her with a heightened sense of the need for self-preservation.

Rebekah reached the MG, unlocked both doors, and slid in behind the wheel as Jace folded his lengthy frame into the passenger seat.

It wasn't a car for a tall, well-built male frame, and it brought him far too close for comfort. She was supremely conscious of his thigh close to the gearshift, making it difficult for the edges of her fingers not to brush against him each time she changed gears.

There was an acute awareness of his clean male scent combined with the hint of his exclusive brand of cologne. Above all was the intense sensual chemistry apparent…a latent entity that threatened her libido, not to mention her peace of mind.

'Shall we stop off somewhere for coffee?'

Rebekah brought her jangling thoughts together and focused on his words, faltered for a few telling seconds, and offered hesitantly, 'It's late. I—'

'Just…coffee,' Jace reiterated quietly, aware of her escalating nervous tension. 'There are a number of cafés close to the Ritz-Carlton. We'll choose one, and when we're done I'll walk back to the hotel.'

It sounded reasonable, no strings, just the sharing of coffee as a pleasant conclusion to a very enjoyable evening.

Double Bay was known for its trendy cafés, where the day-time clientele lunched and the social élite met and lingered over coffee during the evening. Whatever the time, it was an opportunity to be *seen*.

Finding a parking space took a while, and they strolled along the street-front, chose a café and selected a table.

Coffee at its finest, Rebekah acknowledged silently as she savoured the sweet, aromatic brew. Discussing the merits of the film they'd just seen seemed a safe topic of conversation, and they engaged in an interesting exchange of views.

'You have tomorrow off?'

She stilled, and for a second her eyes assumed a wary expression. 'Yes.'

'I've booked a harbour cruise. It takes approximately six hours and leaves at ten.'

Such cruises were very popular among the tourists, and crew served lunch on board as well as morning and afternoon tea. 'You'll enjoy it.' It was a great way to see the many coves and bays around the inner harbour, view prime real estate, and relax in pleasant surroundings.

Jace held her gaze. 'Join me.'

She was willing to swear her heart stopped for a few seconds before racing into a thudding beat. 'There'll be a running commentary informing passengers of various vantage points throughout the day. You won't need me along.'

His smile held warmth and something she was reluctant to define. 'I want you along.'

'Jace…' She paused, then stumbled over the words, 'I can't keep seeing you.'

'Can't, or won't?'

Oh, lord, this was getting out of hand. *'Why?'*

There was despair in the query, and it angered him to think her ex-husband had done such a number on her.

'The truth?' His gaze speared hers. 'I want to spend time with you.'

To what end? The obvious one wasn't an option. 'I won't have sex with you.' Stark words that matched his in honesty.

'If I just wanted sex, there are several numbers I could call.'

So he could. Numbers listed in the trade papers, the telephone yellow pages…and failing that, all he had to do was ask a discreet question of the hotel staff to have the relevant information supplied.

'So,' he drawled silkily. 'Shall we start over?'

She took a deep breath and slowly released it. 'I usually do domestic chores on a Sunday.' Go to the gym, meet a friend for coffee, take in a foreign film, read, relax. It was a token excuse, and they both knew it.

Oh, *dammit*. She spread her hands in a gesture of surrender. 'All right, OK.' She was angry, with herself, *him,* for being manoeuvred into a position where it would seem churlish to refuse. 'I'll go.'

Rebekah glimpsed the gleam of humour in that dark gaze, and she could have sworn the edge of his mouth twitched. 'Such a gracious acceptance.'

She drained the last of her coffee. 'I think it's time I went home.' She stood to her feet. 'Thanks for an enjoyable evening.'

He duplicated her movements, extracted a note and anchored it on the table. 'I'll walk you to your car.'

'I'll be fine,' she stated firmly. 'Goodnight.' She turned away from him and quickened her steps, aware that he fell in beside her.

'Has anyone told you you're impossible?' she flung tersely, and missed the fleeting amusement apparent.

'Rarely to my face.'

'Obviously it's high time someone did.'

There were people seated outdoors beneath large shaded umbrellas, and she was conscious of background chatter, music emitting from speakers, and cars cruising the street searching for a parking space.

Within minutes they reached the MG, and she unlocked the door, then slid in behind the wheel, slipping the key into the ignition without pause.

Jace leaned down towards her. 'Join me for breakfast at the hotel. Eight. Then we'll head for the pier.'

Rebekah looked at him steadily. 'I'll eat at home, and meet you in the hotel lobby after nine.'

She fired the engine as he stood upright and closed the door. With consummate skill she eased the car out from its parking space and resisted the temptation to check the rear-vision mirror as she entered the flow of traffic.

Rebekah slept well and woke feeling refreshed and ready to meet the day. Choosing to wear dress-jeans and a T-shirt, she tied a sweater over her shoulders, applied sun-screen beneath her minimum make-up, and swept her hair into a careless knot atop her head.

Shortly after nine she slid her feet into joggers, caught up her shoulder bag, her keys, then took the lift down to the underground car park.

Jace had also chosen casual attire, and her heart jolted at the sight of him in jeans and a polo shirt. He held a jacket hooked over one shoulder, and he was something else.

He walked towards her, and she admired the way the jeans moulded his thighs, hugged his hips, while the polo shirt clung to his hard-muscled torso, emphasising an enviable breadth of shoulder.

'Hi.' As a greeting, it fell short by a mile, but it was the best she could do with her breath caught in her throat as he slid into the passenger seat.

'Morning.' His appraisal was swift, encompassing. 'You slept well?'

Oh, my, how did she answer that? Admit his image had filled her imagination and her last waking thought had been of him?

'Yes, thank you.' Why was she sounding so excruciatingly polite? 'And you?'

'Fine.'

His smile broadened, and her stomach curled as the grooves slashing each cheek became more defined, and tiny lines fanned out from the corners of his eyes.

Rebekah moved the gear-shift and sent the MG out onto the street, driving with practised ease as she headed towards the city pier.

He exuded latent strength…not only of the body, but of the mind. A man who went after what he wanted with steel-willed resolve, she perceived, and wondered at his strategy with regard to *her*.

A convenient but brief affair while he tended to business? Why go for emotional entanglement when he could pay for sex, then walk away?

It didn't make sense. None of his actions made sense.

Unless… No, she dismissed instantly. He wasn't attracted to her. *Intrigued,* possibly. Was he aware of the sexual chemistry that shimmered between them? Or was it one-sided and all *hers*?

Oh, for heaven's sake, get a grip, she mentally chastised. He's Luc's cousin, he's in Sydney on business, you're the sister of his cousin's wife. He's simply being kind.

So why didn't it feel like *kind* when he touched her? *Kissed* her?

So how *did* it feel? a tiny imp taunted.

Like she'd caught a glimpse of heaven on earth. Something she dared not hope for, in a place she was afraid to occupy.

Fear of rejection? Afraid it wouldn't, *couldn't* last?

She'd experienced one particular taste of hell. She wasn't keen to sample another.

But what if you're wrong? What if you're choosing to deny something incredibly wonderful simply because one man fooled you with a Jekyll-and-Hyde personality?

Just enjoy the day, why don't you? she admonished silently as they walked out onto the pier and boarded the large cruise boat equipped to carry up to fifty passengers and crew.

The sun shone brightly with the warmth of an early summer, and the sky was a clear azure. A breeze became evident as the boat moved out into the harbour, and Rebekah pointed out prime real estate built on the rocky cliff-face that bordered the many coves and inlets.

There were numerous craft moored, some small, others large and luxurious, and she indicated various landmarks, homes of the rich and famous as the boat cruised the inner harbour.

For a while they moved out on deck, and she was conscious of Jace's presence, the light touch of his hand on her arm, the way her body reacted to his as he leaned in close to follow her line of vision as she indicated certain focal points of interest.

Way out in the distance a huge tanker was slowly making its way in, and as they returned city-side there were two tugboats steaming out to meet a luxury liner, a solid, oft-used ferry boat chugging towards the North Shore, and a sleek hydrofoil bringing passengers in from Manly.

Where better to view the wide, distinctive arch of the Harbour Bridge, the graceful architectural curves of the Opera House?

Sydney was a beautiful city with one of the finest harbours in the world. Today, looking at it from a visitor's viewpoint, there was a sense of pride in the familiar, an innate feeling of patriotism.

The sun had moved overhead and was now shifting towards the west, washing the buildings, some old, some new in towers of concrete, steel and glass.

Glorious by day, stunning at night when electric light shaped the many buildings against an indigo sky, and multicoloured flashing neon added colour and interest to an intriguing night-scape.

'Beautiful.' Jace's voice was quiet, almost husky, and Rebekah turned towards him, words of agreement escaping her lips.

Except he wasn't admiring the view, he was look-ing at her.

For one brief minute it seemed as if the world shifted slightly, and she barely refrained from reach-ing out a hand to steady herself.

Crazy. Perhaps she imagined it, and it was the boat?

But no, it was moving steadily, there was no back-wash, and the harbour waters were as smooth as glass.

This was bad. Really bad.

She leaned forward against the railing and concen-trated on a small liner as it lay moored, then she shifted her attention to the row of city buildings.

Most all of the passengers had emerged onto the deck, and she gave a surprised start as Jace moved to position himself behind her.

It was, she realised, a polite gesture to allow others room to share the view, and his arms caged her body as he fastened his hands on the railing.

His body wasn't touching hers, but she was su-premely aware just how easy it would be to lean back against him. Have him link his arms at her waist, and rest his chin against her head.

For a moment she felt as if she couldn't breathe, and panic that he might sense her discomfort forced her to regulate every breath in an effort to slow her rapidly beating pulse.

The cruise boat docked at four, and the passengers lined up ready to disembark. Jace stood behind her, and he put a hand to her waist to steady her as they stepped down the gangplank.

She felt the heat of his touch, and her stomach executed a backward flip.

Nerves, she decided, were hell and damnation. Her body seemed to be in a permanent state of flux whenever Jace Dimitriades was within touching distance.

'We're not far from the aquarium,' Jace declared. 'I checked out its location this morning. We've time for a quick tour before it closes.'

'*We?*' She shot him a startled glance. 'I don't think—'

'You have an aversion to sea creatures?'

'No.'

'You visited last week, and can't bear to do it again so soon?'

Dammit, he was teasing her. Well, two could play at that game. 'Fish?' she queried sweetly. 'You want to go see *fish*?'

His warm smile tore the breath from her throat. 'With my favourite tour guide for company.'

Rebekah gave a small mock-bow. 'Australian residents have a duty to please their overseas visitors.' She indicated a flight of steps. 'Shall we proceed?'

The staff member manning the aquarium ticket box shook her head doubtfully and reminded there was less than an hour before closing time.

'We'll walk very quickly,' Rebekah assured as Jace picked up the tickets.

Some exhibits were exotic specimens, others fearsome, especially in the large aquarium housing various predators. The enclosed areas held a damp salty smell, and Rebekah breathed in fresh air as they emerged out into the sunshine and began walking to where she'd parked the car.

'How dedicated are you to playing tour guide?' Jace queried as he slid into the passenger seat.

She turned towards him. 'You don't want to go back to the hotel?'

'I'd like to explore the Rocks,' Jace declared, and saw her eyes widen.

The area was in an old part of the city bordering on the harbour and held a variety of shops, stalls and numerous cafés and restaurants.

'You're kidding me, right?'

'We could grab something to eat there.'

This was going a bit too far. 'We've spent all day together,' she managed evenly.

'So, what's a few more hours?'

Common sense urged her to refuse. 'I have things to do at home.' It was a token protest.

'Want for me to help out?'

There was a part of her that was tempted to call his bluff just to see him undertake domestic chores.

'Somehow I can't summon an image of you handling a vacuum cleaner or wielding an iron.'

'I managed both during my years at university.'

Caution rose to the fore at the thought of him visiting at her apartment. Mutual ground, *public* ground was infinitely safer.

Rebekah ignited the engine. 'OK, the Rocks it is.' Two hours, she qualified.

They stayed twice as long, wandering at ease, pausing here and there, then Jace chose a restaurant where the food was superb, and they lingered over coffee, enjoying the ambience, the background music.

A sense of latent intimacy seemed to manifest itself, something she put down to the glass of wine she consumed during the course of the meal. She was acutely conscious of the man seated opposite, aware to a finite degree of the inherent vitality beneath his sophisticated façade. Primitive sexuality meshed with elemental sensuality…a dangerous combination, and more than most women could handle.

Yet it awakened something deep within her, an entity she was almost afraid to explore for fear of being burnt.

Safe meant not seeing him again. And, dear heaven, she had every reason to covet safety.

'Shall we leave?'

Jace's voice intruded, and she pushed her empty cup to one side. 'Yes. I have an early start tomorrow.'

He took care of the bill, and they exited the restaurant, choosing to walk the esplanade path to where she'd parked the MG.

Rebekah felt the touch of his hand at her waist, and she experienced a feeling of surprise, almost shock when it slid to capture her own.

For a moment she froze, her first instinct being to pull free, except she hesitated too long and his fingers shifted to thread themselves through hers in a loose linking that was warm, intimate.

It made her want to shift closer, feel the strength, the heat, of his body. More than anything, she longed for his arms close around her, to sink in against him, have his mouth capture her own and wreak sensual devastation.

Yet she hesitated, aware any move on her part would invite more than she was prepared to give.

At that moment his thumb slid against the sensitive veins at her wrist, then began an evocative caress as her pulse jumped and skidded to a heavy beat.

Could he tell? How could he not? she groaned inaudibly. She couldn't disguise the response of her body, and almost as if he knew he lifted her hand to his lips, lightly brushed them to her fingers, then let their joined hands fall.

Oh, my. She felt as if rockets were being launched inside her head, with the aftershocks reverberating through her entire body.

It was a fine kind of madness, fed by desire and fuelled by too vivid an imagination.

Rebekah was grateful when they reached the car, for it enabled her to break contact and slide in behind the wheel.

She wasn't capable of uttering so much as a word, and she didn't even try. Instead she focused on negotiating the traffic, and there was a sense of relief as she drew into the hotel entrance.

Short-lived, she discovered as Jace slid the gearshift into neutral, then he leaned towards her and captured her head, angling it as he fastened his mouth over hers in a kiss that tore her vulnerable emotions to shreds.

Seconds or minutes? She had no idea how long it

lasted, only that she felt cast adrift like a rudderless boat in the open sea.

Did she kiss him back? Perhaps she had. All she knew was that when he released her she felt totally lost.

She couldn't speak, and her eyes felt impossibly large as she simply looked at him, and she gave a start of surprise as he touched a finger to her lips.

His smile held incredible warmth, and she felt herself begin to melt…which was crazy.

'I'll phone you tomorrow.' He reached for the door-clasp and slid out from the car.

For a heart-stopping second she couldn't move, then she became conscious of the concierge standing at the entrance, valet parking staff, and she shifted gears then put the MG in motion.

Rebekah entered her apartment a short while later and crossed to the kitchen for a cool drink. It was then she saw the message light blinking on her answering machine.

Ana? Unlikely, given her sister preferred direct contact to her cellphone.

She crossed to the machine and depressed the 'replay' button, waiting as the tape automatically rewound.

'How was your day with lover-boy?' Brad's voice was low and ugly. 'Don't bother changing your silent number again.' There was a click as he ended the call.

Rebekah stood still for what seemed an age, then she located the number she'd been advised to call, day or night, and filed a report.

It did little to ease her mind. Nothing to stem the sense of frustrated anger that rose to the fore as she re-set the answering machine.

She took a shower, then slid into bed to lie staring at the darkened ceiling for what seemed *hours* before she succumbed to sleep, where nightmarish dreams invaded her subconscious, and when she woke to the sound of the alarm it was as if she hadn't slept at all.

CHAPTER SIX

'BITCH. You'll pay for this.'

Rebekah clutched the receiver as the male voice vented in a sibilant tone that held more threat than if Brad had screamed the words in her ear.

The shop held two customers, Suzie was dealing with one, and the other was examining a glorious stand of gladioli.

Rationalising with him was a waste of time, but she tried. 'You're in violation—' a click indicated he'd ended the call '—of the restraining order,' she finished to an empty line.

The electronic door buzzer sounded, and she replaced the receiver, summoned a smile and turned to see Jace standing inside the door.

Her senses stirred at the sight of him. The dark three-piece suit, deep blue shirt and silk tie indicated he'd come straight from a business meeting, and he removed the lightly tinted sunglasses, silently indicated she serve the waiting customer, then browsed the various bouquets on display.

It took a while for the customer to make a choice, and Rebekah completed the purchase, then crossed to Jace's side.

She looked pale, and her eyes bore the lacklustre appearance of someone battling tiredness and, unless he was mistaken, a headache. He doubted she'd slept any better than he had.

He lifted a hand and tucked back a stray lock of hair that had escaped the knot atop her head. And watched her eyes dilate at his touch.

'Feel up to sharing one of Angelo's pizzas?'

All she wanted to do was go home, soak in a hot tub, then grab a salad, veg out in front of the television for an hour, and make up on lost sleep.

'I'd planned on an early night.'

'You've got it. I've at least an hour's work on the laptop, and I'm due to take the early-morning flight to Cairns.' He didn't add that he'd originally intended flying out tonight, but had shifted the booking to tomorrow. 'I'll be here when you close.'

His smile made her toes curl. She should refuse, but she didn't. 'OK.'

'Wow,' Suzie said with genuine awe when Jace had left the shop. 'Who *is* that man?'

Rebekah explained the connection, and Suzie rolled her eyes.

'Is your sister's husband equally attractive?'

'Equally,' she assured solemnly.

'I don't suppose there are any more male cousins here or abroad?'

'A few.'

Suzie gave an impish grin. 'I *know* I'm going to enjoy working here.'

Jace reappeared just as Rebekah was about to lock up, and gone was the formal business suit. In its place were jeans and a casual chambray shirt left unbut-

toned at the neck. He'd rolled the cuffs back and discarded shoes for joggers.

'All done?'

Luck saw them park close to Angelo's pizzeria, and
they ordered, choosing take-out rather than electing
to eat in, and strolled along the main street while they
waited on the pizza.

'Tough day?'

Jace caught hold of her hand, and she didn't object.
'Not really. Ana insisted on putting in a few hours,
against Luc's and my wishes. Fortunately Suzie is
good at taking up the slack.' She spared him a direct
glance. 'Yours?'

'Bearable.' He didn't add he'd spent most of it
wanting the day done so he could spend time with
her.

A tout called out to them from an open doorway,
only to halt his outrageous spiel as Jace directed him
a chilling look.

Angelo had the pizza boxed and ready to go when
they returned to the shop.

'Where do you suggest we eat this?' Rebekah
asked as she eased the van into the flow of traffic.

'Your apartment?'

It was her own private domain, and only family
visited her there. When it came to joining friends, she
chose a restaurant, café, cinema or shopping complex
as a meeting place.

'I don't think that's a good idea.'

'My hotel?'

A park bench? Drive out to one of the beaches? By then the pizza would be cold.

'We'll go to my place.' She shot him a direct look. 'Just be warned I intend chucking you out at nine.'

'So noted.' His drawl held an element of husky humour.

Minutes later she used her key to unlock the sliding steel grille guarding entrance to the underground car park, eased in beside the MG, then they rode the lift to the seventh floor.

As soon as she opened the apartment door Millie was there, rubbing her head against Rebekah's leg, only to back up and regard Jace with feline curiosity.

'The kitchen's through the lounge to the right.' She led the way. 'I'll show you where the plates are kept, and you can apportion the pizza while I feed Millie.'

The message light on the answering machine was blinking, and her stomach tightened.

'You want to get that?' Jace asked, indicating the machine, and she shook her head.

'It won't be anything that can't wait.' If it was Brad, she'd prefer to run it when she was alone.

They ate pizza seated at the dining-room table, and she unearthed a bottle of red Lambrusco, extracted two wine glasses, filled both, and handed him one.

There was an easy familiarity in the gesture, although nothing discounted the electric tension fizzing along her nerve threads.

'How long will you be away?' It was the only thing she could think to offer, and he finished the mouthful he was eating before responding,

'Four days. I fly direct to Cairns tomorrow, visit Port Douglas Tuesday morning, take the late-afternoon flight Wednesday to Brisbane, visit the Gold Coast Friday morning, and return to Sydney late afternoon.'

'Real estate?'

'Shopping complexes, warehouses,' Jace added as he reached for another slice of pizza.

'You assess, buy at a low price, move in a team to upgrade, promote, then sell when they're showing a handsome profit.' It was just a guess, but she imagined it to be a fairly accurate one.

Rebekah demolished two slices, then slowly sipped her wine.

'Something like that,' he declared indolently. He didn't add that he headed a family consortium with global business interests, and he kept a personal check on all of them. The Sydney arm had initiated some major staff changes at its top level, and he'd chosen to cast a personal eye over the new MD's purchase proposals. And check out if his attraction for Ana's sister was as tantalising now as it had been a year ago.

The answer was easy. The solution, however, was anything but.

The women in his life had been eager, willing, and practised in the art of seduction. Relationships clearcut, boundaries established and recognised, and while affection formed a base, *love,* the everlasting kind, had never rated a mention.

Until the event of Luc and Ana's marriage he'd

been content with the status quo. There were any number of women he'd be satisfied to have as his wife. But none he'd covet as the mother of his children. Which had to tell him something.

For the past year he'd immersed himself in work, dated few women more than a token once or twice, indulged in selective sex, and become very aware that while it might satisfy his libido, any emotional pleasure was sadly lacking.

'Would you like some coffee?'

'Thanks. Black, one sugar.'

Rebekah stood to her feet, gathered up the plates and cutlery and carried them through to the kitchen.

The headache she'd fought against most of the afternoon intensified, and she opened a cupboard, retrieved painkillers, popped two from the pack and swallowed them down with water.

'Headache?'

She hadn't heard him leave the dining room, and her hand shook a little. 'It's nothing a good night's sleep won't fix.'

His mouth curved into a faint smile. 'Is that a hint I've outstayed my welcome?'

'No,' she managed quietly. 'No, of course not.'

The smile reached his eyes. 'Good.' He moved round the servery, took the glass from her hand and put it down, then he captured her face in his hands and began gently massaging her temples.

She opened her mouth to protest, only to have him press his thumb against her lips.

'Shh. Just relax.'

It felt like heaven as his fingers moved to massage her scalp, and she instinctively lowered her lashes so her gaze fastened on the hollow at the base of his throat where a pulse beat so strongly there.

His touch held a mesmeric quality, almost as if a part of him was invading her senses, and she swayed slightly, caught in the sensual magic he was able to evoke.

A slight sound brought her lashes sweeping wide, and she almost died at the magnetising warmth evident in his slumberous gaze.

Her lips parted involuntarily, and she glimpsed the warmth turn to heat, then his mouth slanted over hers, gently at first as his tongue took an exploratory sweep before tangling with her own in an evocative dance that demanded more, much more.

One hand fisted her hair while the other slid down past her waist to hold her fast against him, and she lifted her arms and linked her hands together at his nape as she leaned into him, exulting in the feel, the taste, the sensual heat of him.

It was like nothing else she'd experienced before as he wrapped her close, so close, his hands shaping her waist, her hips, buttocks.

His mouth left hers and nuzzled the sensitive curve at the edge of her neck, then trailed a path to nibble her earlobe before seeking her mouth as he took her deep in a sensual imitation of the sex act itself.

Almost as if he sensed he was going too far too fast he eased up a little, locking her hips close to his own so she couldn't help but be aware of his arousal.

Its potent force took her breath away, and she wondered what it would feel like to have him inside her, moving in an ever-increasing rhythm until he reached his peak.

There was a part of her that wanted to be swept away by the tide of passion. To have no thought, no scruples, no reservations. Just follow wherever he chose to lead.

Would the reality exceed the limits of her experience, and prove to be as mesmeric as she imagined it could be?

Somehow the answer had to be *yes*. This man possessed the touch, the sexual expertise to indulge a woman in a feast of the senses. From acutely sensitive to the raw and primitive.

A shiver feathered its way over the surface of her skin, raising all her fine body hairs in anticipation as treacherous desire pulsed from deep within.

She wanted the tactile touch of skin on skin, and the need for it drove her to seek the opening of his shirt. There was a primal urge to fist the material and tug it free from his jeans then drag it off so she could rain his torso with the heated pressure of her mouth. To gently nip the hard muscle tissue close to a male nipple, then caress each one with her tongue, teasing mercilessly until he groaned at her touch.

More than anything, she wanted him to bestow her the same favour, to drive her sensually wild until there could be only one end.

Her audio-visual senses were so caught up in the mindless fantasy she was only dimly aware of a ring-

ing in her ears, and she gave a despairing groan as
Jace gently broke contact.

'Should you get that?'

The phone. Dear heaven, it was the *phone*.

The answering machine picked up, and she froze.
Please, *please* don't let it be Brad.

Jace held her loosely, his gaze intent as he witnessed her disquiet.

'Inviting him into your apartment isn't a good
move, darling.' Brad's voice was unmistakable. 'Has
he discovered you're a frigid little bitch?' There was
a click as he cut the connection, the faint whirr of the
answering machine as it rewound the tape.

Rebekah wanted to curl up and die. She closed her
eyes in an involuntary gesture of self-defence, then
opened them again to focus on the third button of
Jace's shirt.

A hand cupped her chin, tilting it so she had to
look at him, and she fought to hold back the moisture
shimmering in her eyes.

'Don't.' Jace framed her face between his hands,
and smoothed a thumb over lips made slightly swollen from his kiss.

She wasn't capable of uttering a word, and her eyes
ached with unshed tears.

He saw her lashes lower to form a protective veil,
and pain stabbed his gut as a single tear escaped and
rolled slowly down one cheek.

'Please,' she said huskily. 'Just go.'

She felt his thumb erase the trail of moisture, and

his hands were incredibly gentle as he cradled her face.

'No.'

'Please,' she reiterated as he tilted her face.

'Look at me.'

The command was softly voiced, and she felt his fingers trail the slope of her neck, linger at its edge, then return.

The peal of the phone was an intrusive, strident sound in the stillness of the room, and he felt the tremor that ran through her body.

With one economical movement Jace reached forward, lifted the receiver, listened, then ventured in a deadly soft voice, 'Don't ring again if you value your skin.' He cut the connection and didn't return the receiver to the handset.

'I suggest you change your number.'

'I've already done that twice in the past two days.' He may as well hear the rest of it. 'The police have been notified, and my lawyer.'

He understood too clearly. 'Who each advise keeping your answering machine on to record each of his calls.'

'Yes.'

'Which have only accelerated since he saw us together at the restaurant last week.'

Rebekah didn't concur, she had no need to. Brad's reaction was self-explanatory.

'Is there a possibility he might attempt to physically hurt you?'

She paused a second too long. 'I don't think so.'

'He doesn't have a key to your apartment?'

She shook her head. 'I bought it following the divorce.' And lived with Ana between leaving Brad and obtaining her legal freedom. It had been a fraught time, laced with various incidents involving her ex-husband's harassment. She'd neither sighted nor heard from him in ages. Until Wednesday of last week. Now the torment seemed set to begin all over again.

'Would you like me to stay over tonight?'

Shocked surprise widened her eyes. 'No, of course not.'

A gleam of humour lit his gaze. 'I imagine you have a spare bedroom.'

She did, but she didn't intend for him to occupy it tonight or any other night. 'I'll be fine.'

Would she? Somehow he doubted she'd sleep easily.

'Only a fool blames another for his own inadequacies.' The words slipped quietly from his lips, and when she didn't answer, he smoothed his palm along the edge of her cheek. 'And it would take an incompetent fool to allude to a woman's frigidity.' He waited a beat. 'Especially when the woman is *you*.'

He wanted to show her how it could be between a man and a woman, watch as she came alive beneath his touch. To kiss and caress every inch of her, awaken each nerve-end, and be aware only of him. Malleable, mindless, *his*.

Except he wanted her *with* him, mind, body and

soul. Not on edge with nervous tension, or emotionally shaken.

'I think you should leave.' She just wanted to be alone, secure within these four walls, where she could sink into the hot tub, then pull on a robe, view television for an hour before slipping into bed.

'Not yet,' Jace said quietly. Not until she'd regained some colour and her eyes didn't resemble huge pools mirroring a mixture of hurt and shame.

'We were going to have coffee.' A return to the prosaic was the wisest course, and he moved round her, collected the carafe from the coffee-maker and filled it with water.

Rebekah collected her shattered thoughts together and crossed to extract coffee mugs from a cupboard, coffee beans, a fresh filter, and set it all in place.

The automatic movements helped, and within minutes they faced each other across the table as they sipped aromatic coffee.

'Tell me what it was like for you as a child.'

She recognised his diversionary tactic, and cast him a level glance. 'The usual things that shape most children's lives. Love and laughter, a few tears, happy family, school. My mother died a few years ago. Dad has very recently taken a new job in New York.'

'You and Ana are very close.' It was a statement based on his own observation, and her gaze softened.

'We're best friends as well as business partners.'

It was difficult to look at him and not be startlingly aware of the way it had felt to be in his arms, his touch, the intensity of his kiss, and the way he'd been able to transport her to a place where sheer sensation ruled.

There was a part of her that wanted to be taken there again. By him, only him. Just thinking of Jace as a lover brought a flood of heat to her body, and yet instinct warned if she allowed him into her life she'd never be the same again.

Was it worth the risk? Not if she wanted to survive emotionally. This man would invade her senses, her heart, and forever leave his mark.

'You haven't mentioned your marriage.'

The sound of his accented drawl brought her back to the present with a sudden jolt, and she tightened her grip on the coffee mug.

'What do you want to hear? That I was courted by a man for several months, engaged to him for a year, and in all that time I had no inkling a few hours after the wedding he'd turn into an abusive monster?'

He was silent for several long seconds as he held her gaze. 'It must have been hell to deal with.'

And then some. 'And you, Jace? No skeletons in your cupboard?'

'A few regrets.' Everyone had some. 'None of any consequence.'

He wanted to ease the pain he glimpsed in her eyes, but knew she'd deny him if he did. Instead, he drained his coffee, then stood to his feet.

'Time for me to call it a night.' He took his mug into the kitchen and put it in the sink, then he preceded her to the door.

Rebekah caught up her keys and followed him. 'I'll drive you back to the hotel.'

'I'll call a cab from the downstairs lobby.'

'Don't be ridiculous.'

He turned towards her and pressed a finger to her lips, then he lowered his head and brushed his mouth to her temple. 'I'll phone tomorrow.'

She opened her mouth to protest, but he was already walking towards the bank of lifts, and she waited there until the lift doors opened. Then she retreated into the apartment, locked up, set the alarm, and headed for the hot tub.

CHAPTER SEVEN

'HAS Brad been bothering you again?'

Rebekah caught the fierce sisterly concern in Ana's voice, and tried to diffuse a potentially sensitive subject. 'Why do you ask?'

'This is *me,* remember? And I don't fool easily. So spill it.'

Suzie was on a lunch break, and they were alone in the shop.

Rebekah refrained from prevaricating, but she kept it simple. 'You know the score. Every now and again Brad decides to ride the nuisance wagon. So I changed my silent number to minimise the hassle.'

'Uh-huh. This wouldn't have anything to do with the fact you've been seeing Jace?'

It was a rhetorical question, and they both knew it.

'I'm not *seeing* Jace,' she refuted, paying far more attention than necessary to the bouquet she was assembling.

'OK, we won't go there just now.' Ana's gaze held a degree of anxiety. 'Watch your back, Rebekah,' she warned gently. 'Brad is a loose cannon just waiting to explode.'

She controlled the shaky sensation that threatened to visibly exert itself, and met her sister's gaze.

'I'm doing everything I've been legally advised to

do,' she assured quietly. 'It's been two years since the divorce. I'm entitled to a life of my own.'

Ana's expression softened. '*Brava.* You, more than most.' There were assurances she wanted to reiterate, but she wisely held her counsel. 'Promise you'll phone me at the slightest hint of a problem. OK?'

Rebekah offered a wry smile. 'Want me to write it in blood?'

The phone rang, and Ana picked up, intoned the customary greeting, conversed for a few minutes, then held out the cordless receiver. 'For you. Jace.'

'Hi. How are you?'

'Do you really want to know?' His voice was low and husky, almost intimate, and she barely controlled the spiralling sensation deep within.

'How was the flight? Cairns?'

'Fine. Better if you were with me.'

The breath stopped in her throat. 'I have to go, we're really busy.'

She thought she heard his faint chuckle. 'Take care, Rebekah. I'll call you on your cellphone tonight.'

Rebekah handed the cordless receiver to Ana with a lift of her eyebrows. 'Nothing to say?'

'And risk having you jump down my throat?' There was humour in her voice, and her eyes danced with silent mischief. 'No way.'

The afternoon was busy, so much so it was almost seven when Rebekah locked up shop and slid into the van. She planned a shower, then she'd fix a steak salad and eat it with a fresh, crunchy bread roll she'd picked up from the bakery, maybe watch a video she'd rented out.

Summer was definitely on its way, for the days were becoming warmer, she perceived as she swung the van into the driveway leading down to the apartment underground car park.

It took only seconds to insert her key and have the security grille lift to allow her entry, and she eased into her allotted parking bay, cut the engine and gathered her shoulder bag, the leather briefcase with the day's computer print-outs, then she slid from the van and began walking towards the lift.

'Think you're pretty smart, dating another man, don't you?'

Rebekah froze, caught in the grip of fear as Brad stepped out from behind a concrete pillar. Calm, she had to remain calm. Try logic, a silent voice screamed.

'How did you get in here?'

'Use your imagination.'

He was taller, bigger than her, and she recognised the hard glitter in those pale grey eyes, the cruel tilt of his mouth.

Instinct had her gauging the distance to the lift well.

'Forget it,' Brad advised harshly. 'You'll never make it.'

The van…if only she could lock herself in there, she'd be safe. Except she'd locked the door, and by the time she reached it, inserted the key, he'd have caught her.

OK, if she couldn't escape, she had two options. Talk first; if that failed, *fight*.

'I can't think of anything we have to discuss.'

'Wrong, baby.'

She hated his smile, it hid pure venom. 'If I don't ring my sister within five minutes, she'll call the police.'

He recognised her bluff. 'So—call her.'

Rebekah slid open the zip fastening her bag, felt for and found the small canister, then she palmed it as she withdrew her hand, aimed and pressed the spray button.

The mace hit him in the face, and his howl of pain was animal-like in its rage.

Rebekah didn't hesitate, she ran to the lift, hit and held down the button…and prayed. If only she could get inside, she'd be safe.

Oh, come *on*, she begged, agonising if she'd have been wiser to have sought the van and locked herself in. At least she could have used her cellphone to call for help.

There was a faint electronic whine heralding the lift's descent, and she felt her heart thud in her chest as she counted off the seconds to its arrival.

She could hear Brad swearing, his voice rising to a raging crescendo, and then she didn't care any more as the lift doors swung open and she raced inside the cubicle, pushed the seventh-floor button, only to see Brad put his arm between the closing doors.

A scream left her throat, and she stabbed the *close doors* button. To little avail. His strength was accelerated by rage, and she batted his hands with the briefcase, drawing blood.

Fear drove her, and for a few seconds she thought she'd won. Except one herculean burst of strength on Brad's part pushed the doors open sufficiently for him to squeeze through.

She still had the can of mace in her hand, and she used it mercilessly before he had a chance to bring the lift to a stop mid-floor.

The cubicle wasn't large, and even blinded by the stinging mace Brad roared with rage as he lurched, arms spread wide, circling as she strove to evade him in the confined space.

Her only hope was to escape as soon as the lift stopped at the seventh floor, and she quickly identified her apartment key on its keyring, and held it poised in readiness.

There was nowhere to hide, and the timing proved lousy as Brad's hand groped her shoulder, then closed over it with steel-like strength.

A random punch slammed into her ribs, quickly followed by another to her upper arm.

At that moment the lift drew to a halt, and he dragged her out into the foyer.

'Where's your damned key?'

She'd die before she willingly gave it to him, and she wrestled with him, taking a cracking slap to the side of her face.

'Give it to me, bitch!'

Rebekah swung the briefcase at him and he

wrenched it from her grasp, then tackled and knocked her to the floor.

In one desperate move she tossed the keys as hard as she could, uncaring where they landed as long as he couldn't find them.

She heard them hit something with a resounding clunk, felt the bruising grip of Brad's fingers on her flesh, then a loud voice demanding,

'What the hell is going on here?' Followed by, '*Rebekah?* George, get out here!'

There was noise, voices, the sound of scuffling, then mercifully she was free, and hands were soothing her, Maisie, her neighbour, was issuing instructions like a nursing sister-in-charge, her chosen vocation. And her partner, George, an ex-wrestler with a body that was all muscle, held Brad in a bone-crunching grip.

Maisie called the police, helped Rebekah into her apartment, called a doctor, then she collected her camera and took photos for evidence.

Rebekah didn't argue, although she was sufficiently familiar with police procedure to know they'd do the same.

When they came, she gave a statement, which had to be typed up and signed at the police station within the next twenty-four hours. The doctor arrived and examined her, dressed a few abrasions, suggested ice-packs for the bruising, and gave her a sedative to take to help her sleep.

Maisie fussed over her, plying her with water and painkillers.

'Is there someone I should call? Your sister, brother-in-law?'

'I'll do it later.'

Maisie looked doubtful. 'You really should have someone stay with you tonight. Or you should go to your sister's place.'

'I'll be fine.'

'Sure you will. You're as pale as a ghost, and as cold as charity.' She gave a derisive snort. 'If I had anything to do with it, you'd be in hospital overnight.'

Rebekah tried for a smile and didn't quite make it. 'I promise I'll ring Ana the moment you leave.'

'Hmm. Why don't you go take a shower, and I'll rustle up something light for you to eat?' She held up her hand. 'I'll be offended if you refuse.'

It was easier to capitulate. 'Thanks.'

She stayed beneath the hot spray for a while, then, towelled dry, she donned jeans, added a cotton top, and emerged into the kitchen to discover her neighbour removing a plate of delicious-smelling goulash with rice.

'Your sister rang while you were in the shower.'

Rebekah knew the answer even before she posed the question. 'You told her?'

'She had to know. She's on her way over.' Maisie indicated the plate which she set down on the dining-room table. 'Sit and eat.'

'Yes, Mother.'

'I could be, if I'd been a child bride.' She tried to look fierce. 'You need someone to look after you.'

'I have you and George just across the hall.' She

took a mouthful of food and closed her eyes at the taste. 'I know why George married you.'

'Don't change the subject. You need a man in your life.'

'I had one, and look at the way that turned out.'

'A real man, one who'll take care of you.'

'Perhaps I'm content taking care of myself?'

Maisie gave another snort, and filled the kettle to make tea.

In no time at all the intercom buzzed, and Rebekah threw her neighbour a wry glance. 'The cavalry have arrived.'

Ana *and* Luc? There were hugs, expressions of concern, reassurances given, and decisions made.

'You're coming back with us,' Ana said firmly. 'And if you argue, I'll hit you.'

'I rather think she's had more than her fair share of that, *agape mou*,' Luc chided gently, and watched his wife's face crease with remorse.

'I didn't mean— Oh, God, Rebekah,' Ana groaned out loud.

'I know, you just love me to death, is all.'

Rebekah's cellphone pealed, and Luc moved to retrieve it from the coffee-table, where Maisie had placed everything that had spilled from her bag.

'I'll take it, shall I?' He picked up, and moved to one side of the room. His conversation was muted and spanned several minutes, then he retraced his steps and handed her the unit. 'Jace.'

She closed her eyes, then she opened them again and voiced a restrained greeting into the mouthpiece.

'Rebekah—'

Even from a distance she could sense the quiet anger beneath the surface of his control. 'I'm fine.'

'And daisies grow upside-down in the ground.' His voice held an edge she couldn't define. 'Give me your word you'll stay with Luc and Ana for a few days.'

She almost said she'd suffered worse than this. 'Tonight,' she conceded, and heard him mutter something unintelligible. Suddenly she'd had enough, and there wasn't another thing she wanted to hear…much less from a man who'd caused her more emotional highs and lows in one short week than anyone she'd ever known. 'Goodnight.'

Maisie took care of her plate, Ana fed Millie and put down fresh water, while Rebekah gathered up a change of clothes, a few essentials and pushed them into an overnight bag.

Luc crossed to her side as she re-entered the kitchen. 'Ready?'

She inclined her head, thanked Maisie, gave Millie a gentle pat, then she followed everyone out into the lobby while Luc locked up.

Ana sat in the back seat of the Mercedes and caught hold of Rebekah's hand as Luc drove to their palatial home in suburban Vaucluse.

'Do you want to talk about it?'

'Not particularly.' There was little point in rehashing it.

Ana's fingers tightened, and her voice held an uncustomary hardness. 'This isn't going to happen again.'

It was nice, Rebekah had to admit, to be taken care of. Luc and Ana's home was an architectural masterpiece set in beautiful grounds high on a hill with splendid views out over the harbour.

Petros, their politically correct manservant, fussed over her as if she were a precious piece of china. Within minutes of arrival he prepared tea and exquisite bite-size sandwiches.

Luc joined them for a while, then at a telling glance from his wife he excused himself on the pretext of dealing with business email. He brushed a light kiss to Ana's cheek, then crossed to gift Rebekah a similar salutation and departed the room.

Rebekah allowed Petros to refill her cup, and declined anything further to eat.

Ana waited only long enough for the manservant to wheel the tea-trolley from the room before leaning forward in her chair.

'Tell me exactly what happened,' she insisted sternly. 'And don't leave anything out.'

Reliving the episode was emotionally draining, although it helped her deal with it.

'The *bastard*,' Ana derided huskily when Rebekah finished. 'Luc and Jace will ensure he never comes near you again.'

Hang on a minute… '*Jace?* What does Jace have to do with it?' She drew in a deep breath in the hope of assembling a sense of calm. 'While I appreciate Luc's help, I'm quite able to take care of everything myself.'

'It's done,' Ana said simply. 'And you can stop with the fierce expression.'

'Ana—'

'It's time to bring out the big guns,' her sister remonstrated gently. 'Luc and Jace have them…in spades.'

This was getting out of hand. 'Look—'

'No,' Ana declared emphatically. '*You* look. I don't want to wake up one morning and hear Brad has somehow got to you and you're just another statistic in the assault and battery records.' She leaned forward and caught hold of Rebekah's hands. 'I was *there*, remember? When you walked out on him, and afterwards.' Tears filled her eyes. 'Jace is the first man you've dated in a long time. Only to have Brad emerge out of the woodwork and stalk you.' A tear escaped and rolled down her cheek. 'No one, *no one* is ever going to hurt you again. Ever.'

Rebekah felt her stomach curl into a tight ball at her sister's distress. 'Ana, don't. I'm OK. The police have arrested him.'

'Sure, you're OK. Bruised ribs, multiple contusions. Not to mention shock and trauma.' Her voice rose. 'I hate to think what would have happened if he'd dragged you inside the apartment. Or if Maisie and George hadn't been home.'

She caught the fierce determination apparent, and stayed any further protest…for now. *She* might be the victim, but Ana was hurting too. 'You haven't shown me the latest print-out of the babe's ultrasound. Or the radiographer's video clip.'

Ana offered a shaky smile. 'Changing the subject won't change my mind.' She stood to her feet and extended her hand. 'Come on. Let's go see pictures of your foetal niece or nephew.'

It helped to take both their minds off the earlier part of the evening, and it was there Luc found them rewinding the video tape for the third or fourth time.

'Time to call it a night for both of you, hmm?'

Rebekah caught the way his features softened as he took Ana's hands in his and gently pulled her to her feet. He would, she knew, ease his wife's apprehension and be there for her when she stirred through the night.

An ache began deep inside at the thought of being able to sink into the comfort of a man's arms, have his lips brush her forehead, trail over her cheek and settle on her mouth.

'You're to rest tomorrow,' Ana insisted as they ascended the stairs. 'Suzie is competent, and we'll manage. Coming into the shop is a no-no. OK?'

'I'll see how I feel in the morning.' It was a compromise at best, and Ana shot her a dark glance as if divining her thoughts.

'I mean it.'

Rebekah caught her sister's hand and gently squeezed it. 'I know you do.'

'Petros has made up the front guest suite for you, and you're to sleep in. Just come downstairs whenever you feel like breakfast.' Ana's features sharpened a little. 'Are you sure you're OK?'

'Yes,' she reassured. In truth every bone in her

body ached. 'I'm going to have that sedative, hop into bed, and sleep like a baby.'

She did take the sedative, and she did sleep for a few hours, only to wake in the early dawn hours feeling as if her body had been pummelled like a punching bag.

Which it pretty much had, she conceded as she slipped gingerly out of bed and made for the *en suite*.

She snapped on the light and examined her face in the mirror. A bit of concealer would cover the emerging bruise. As to the rest of her…she lifted the nightshirt and grimaced at the swelling on her ribs, the blueish-purplish colour, and knew she was fortunate none of the ribs was broken. Shallow breathing was the order of the day for a while.

There were scratches on her arm, a large, reddish welt on one forearm.

Not nice, not nice at all. But the swelling would subside, the bruises yellow and disappear. Give it a few weeks and all that would remain was the memory.

Rebekah checked her watch and saw it was much too early to dress and go downstairs. Returning to bed and trying to sleep wasn't an option, so she switched on the bedside lamp and leafed through a few glossy magazines Petros had thoughtfully provided.

Rebekah waited until Luc left the house at eight, saw Ana follow him minutes later, then she quickly gathered up her bag and moved quickly downstairs.

Petros was in the midst of clearing the dining-room table, and he turned as she entered the room.

'Good morning,' he greeted warmly. 'I trust you slept well? Ana insisted I shouldn't disturb you.' His gaze took in the bag. 'What can I get you for breakfast?'

It would be useless to say she wasn't hungry. 'Orange juice, toast and coffee will be great.'

One eyebrow arched. 'Might I suggest some fruit and cereal? Eggs with a little ham or bacon? A croissant, perhaps?'

'You're bent on spoiling me.' She took a seat and poured herself a glass of juice. There was fruit on the table, and she selected a banana, peeled and ate it.

'But toast and coffee is fine.'

There was a folded newspaper near by, and she flicked through the pages, read the headlines, her horoscope for the day, and scanned the comic strips. By which time she'd eaten two pieces of toast and had almost finished her second cup of coffee.

Rebekah retrieved her cellphone and punched in the relevant digits to summon a taxi, and she was relaying the address when Petros re-entered the room.

'You intend going somewhere this morning?' the manservant asked as he began clearing dishes.

'I need to go back to my apartment and feed my cat.'

'Luc would be most upset if I allowed you to take a taxi. I'll drive you, whenever you're ready to leave.'

'Nonsense.'

'Please, in this instance I must insist. If you'll tell me which company you called, I'll ring and cancel.'

It seemed easier to capitulate, and twenty minutes

later she slid out of the four-wheel-drive Petros used for transport.

'I'll wait until you're ready to return.'

He wasn't going to like the next part at all. 'I intend remaining at the apartment, Petros.'

His lips pursed in visible disapproval. 'Luc and Ana will be most displeased.'

'I promise I'll ring and explain.' Ana she could handle, and Ana would handle Luc. *Fait accompli.* Besides, in less than half an hour she'd be at the shop.

'Ms Rebekah, I don't think this is a good idea.'

She offered him a sweet smile. 'Thanks for the lift.' Then she turned and used her key to enter the main lobby.

Home, she breathed as she entered her apartment. There was no place quite like your own, and Millie bounded towards her, curling back and forth around her ankles, purring in delighted welcome.

The apartment looked achingly familiar, and she moved through it, straightening a vase on the chiffonier as she made her way to the kitchen.

Fifteen minutes later she'd fed Millie, changed into work clothes, and was on her way to the shop.

'You aren't supposed to be here,' Ana remonstrated the instant Rebekah walked through the door.

'I know everything you're going to say,' she responded firmly as she crossed to the work table and stowed her bag. 'But I'd rather be doing something constructive than swanning on the chaise lounge, idly flipping through the pages of a magazine.'

Take control. Hadn't that been the essence of any

professional advice she'd ever received? 'OK, where are we at?' she queried briskly.

'You've got the morning,' Ana conceded, trying for a fierce look that didn't quite come off. 'Then you're going home.'

'I've got the day,' Rebekah corrected gently. 'And I'll go home when I'm ready.'

'You're impossibly stubborn.'

'And I love you, too.'

Suzie looked from one to the other. 'Are you two going to fight, then make up? Or is this serious stuff and I should take five to let you sort it out alone?'

'Stay,' Rebekah and Ana ordered in unison.

'If you insist. Shall I mediate, or referee?'

'Neither.'

The phone rang, and Ana declared *sotto voce*, 'Saved by the bell.'

The morning was busier than usual with a number of customers coming in from the street. It was late morning when Rebekah took a quick check of their stock and reached for the phone to place an order, then arrange for the courier for delivery.

The electronic buzzer heralded the arrival of another customer, and she glanced towards the door, then stilled as Jace entered the shop.

Shock, surprise were just two of the emotions she experienced. Not the least was speculation as to why he was here when he was supposed to be in Cairns. Had his meetings concluded earlier than he'd anticipated? Yet if so, why wasn't he in Brisbane?

For a moment her gaze locked with his as he stood exuding a silent power that was vaguely frightening.

She watched as he moved towards Ana and offered an affectionate greeting, then he turned and moved towards the table where Rebekah was in the midst of gathering sprays of orchids into a large bouquet.

The nerves inside her stomach gave every impression of performing a series of complicated somersaults, and her fingers faltered as he paused within touching distance.

What could she say? Anything would be superfluous, so she didn't even try as she bore his raking appraisal.

A muscle bunched at the edge of his jaw, and she saw his eyes harden briefly, then he lifted a hand and trailed light fingers over her cheek.

'Get your bag,' he commanded gently. 'I'm taking you home.' He pressed his thumb over her lips as they parted to voice a refusal. 'No argument.' He increased the pressure slightly. 'I'll carry you out of here if I have to.'

Rebekah removed his hand, only, she suspected, because he let her. 'You don't have the right to give me orders.'

'It's a self-appointed role.' His voice was a silky drawl that feathered sensation down the length of her spine.

Everything faded from her peripheral vision. There were just the two of them, fused by an electric awareness that had everything to do with heightened sensuality. Right now she didn't need or want it.

'Go away.'

'Not a chance.'

'Jace—'

'Do you really want to do this the hard way?'

He was capable of implementing his threat despite any resistance on her part, and, given the choice, she'd opt for dignity over embarrassment.

'How did you—?'

'Find out where you were?' he completed. 'It was a process of elimination. First Luc, then Petros, and Ana.'

Rebekah moved slightly, shot her sister a dark glance and was met with a blithe smile. It was nothing less than a conspiracy, and one where the odds were stacked against her.

'There's a lot of work to get through.'

'Nothing Suzie and I can't handle,' Ana assured.

'There you go,' Jace drawled with hateful ease. 'Now collect your bag and we'll get on our way.'

'I have the van. And there is no *we*.'

'Arguing this back and forth isn't going to change a thing.'

'So concede defeat and follow you like a little lamb?' She refrained from adding *to the slaughter*… To no one, least of all this Greek-born American, would she admit she ached all over, her head thumped with pain, and she was fast approaching the need for serious time out.

'I have the car double-parked outside,' Jace informed as she reached for her bag.

'I hope the traffic officer has issued you with a

ticket.' She offered Suzie a wry smile, brushed her lips to Ana's cheek, then preceded Jace from the shop.

'None of this is *your* business,' Rebekah declared as he eased the car out from the busy thoroughfare. She was unsure whether to be relieved or disappointed there hadn't been a parking-violation ticket attached to his windscreen.

'Wrong. My involvement with you started all this.'

'What *involvement*?'

'Don't split hairs, *pedhaki mou*.'

The affectionate 'little one' got to her as she turned towards him. 'You mean you postponed business meetings and flew back to Sydney because you felt *responsible*? That's ridiculous.'

He met her gaze and held it for a few seemingly long seconds. 'Is it?' He returned his attention to negotiating traffic. 'I don't think so.'

'I fail to see the reasons for everyone's concern. I'm OK.' She was tempted to tell him there had been more damaging attacks in the past, only to refrain from the admission.

'Sure you are,' Jace discounted in a dry, mocking tone. 'You were barely standing up in there, pale as a ghost, your eyes dark with pain.' There was underlying anger apparent. 'What were you trying to prove?'

Should she tell him the truth? 'I didn't want to sit and brood.' And I didn't want to be alone, she added silently.

Jace swept the car into the entrance adjacent her apartment.

'Here's fine.' She already had her hand on the door-clasp.

'The hell it is.' He eased the car down the incline leading to the underground car park, and indicated the security lock. 'Give me your key.'

'There's no need for you to personally see me to my apartment door.'

She was a prickly young woman, and one he wanted to kiss senseless one minute and shake sense into the next. 'Just…do it, Rebekah.'

'I don't—'

'Your ex-husband has been released on bail.'

Rebekah stilled at his words, then drew in a slight breath…anything other than *slight* hurt like hell. 'Why am I not surprised?'

Brad's mother was a rich society matron who engaged high-ranking lawyers to protect her only son. On the past two occasions Wilma Somerville had rushed to his defence, blamed Rebekah for instigating the attacks, and threatened dire consequences if an official complaint was filed.

The next time Ana took matters into her own hands and persuaded Rebekah to press charges, only to have Wilma's lawyer release him hours later on bail and later persuade judge and jury Brad was a well-educated, caring man who simply needed a course in anger management. A hefty fine, and he was free.

'You're determined to personally check out my

apartment to see Brad hasn't slipped past security undetected and may be lurking in wait for me?'

'Something like that.'

Rebekah handed him her key in silence, then when the security grille lifted he drove into the parking bay alongside her MG.

'I very much doubt he'd be so foolish,' she offered as they walked towards the lift.

Jace spared her a direct look. 'I'm not prepared to let you take the risk,' he assured with chilling softness.

She'd decorated her apartment in soft green, cream with a touch of apricot in muted tones. Complemented by modern furniture and same-tone drapes. Her own individual touch, rather than the ascetic perfection of an interior decorator. The ambience was calming and peaceful...her personal sanctuary.

Her small, pale grey-tipped cat sat up on the sofa, surveying him with unblinking solemnity.

'Millie,' Rebekah indicated. 'She's very spoilt, and not used to you yet.' Whereupon Millie proved her mistress wrong by jumping down onto the carpet, padding over to Jace and began winding herself around his legs.

He bent down and fondled Millie's ears. An action which sent the cat into feline ecstasy.

'Must be your natural masculine charm,' Rebekah accorded with wry humour.

Jace straightened and one eyebrow slanted in mocking cynicism. 'Why don't you sit down and relax?'

Relax, with you here? she demanded silently. Fat chance. 'Thanks for bringing me home.'

'But please leave?'

'Yes.'

'Think again.'

Her eyes flew wide. 'Excuse me?'

'Independence is a fine thing,' he opined quietly. 'In this instance, there's no way you're staying anywhere alone.'

Anger flared, and it showed in her eyes, the tightening of her mouth. 'Now, look—'

'We've done that,' Jace said in a deceptively mild voice. 'We're not going to do it again.'

'Just who gave you permission to take charge of my life?'

'The decision is mine.'

'Well, you can absolve yourself from any misguided responsibility and go leave me alone.'

'No.'

She was angry before, now she was steaming. 'Brad is unlikely to do anything while he's out on bail. Even his mother's lawyer would have a hard job extricating him from jail if he did.'

His gaze focused on her features, noting the tilt of her chin and the proud determination in those deep sapphire-blue eyes. 'I'm not prepared to risk a repeat of last night.'

She wanted to lash out at him, *hurt* as she'd been hurt. Yet this was the wrong man, and her mind was spiralling in a way that made no sense at all. 'Next you'll tell me you intend staying here all day.'

He was silent for a few long seconds, then he ventured silkily, 'That's the plan.'

It was then she noticed the laptop in his hand. 'You've brought work with you?' Her voice seemed to have acquired a higher pitch, and she met his steady gaze with something akin to disbelief.

'I can work anywhere. Why not here?'

The anger bubbled over. 'You've appointed your-self *babysitter*? I don't believe this…any of it!'

His eyes hardened fractionally. 'Believe it's not open to negotiation.'

CHAPTER EIGHT

REBEKAH reacted without thought and the palm of her hand connected with his cheekbone in a stinging slap.

An entire gamut of emotions chased fleetingly across her expressive features, and Jace divined each and every one of them.

Dear lord in heaven, she'd actually *hit* him! In her eyes it made her no better than Brad. 'I'm sorry.'

The words were huskily voiced so as to be barely audible.

The air seemed filled with electric tension, and she was hardly conscious of breathing.

'Feel better?' he drawled with deceptive mildness.

Innate honesty came to the fore. 'No.'

She missed the faint gleam of humour lurking in the depths of his eyes.

'I picked up some filled bagels on my way to the shop. Why don't we have lunch?' he suggested quietly. 'Afterwards you can rest while I put in a few hours on the laptop.'

'I'm not an invalid,' she protested at once, wanting the afternoon done with so she could be alone. His presence in the apartment unsettled her. *He* unsettled her.

He shot her a level look, then he moved through

to the kitchen, set the bagels on plates and placed them on the dining-room table.

They ate in relative silence, and washed the food down with hot, sweet tea, then Rebekah curled up on the sofa with a magazine while Jace settled himself at the escritoire on the far side of the room.

She must have slipped into a fitful doze, for she woke feeling refreshed, albeit stiff and sore. A quick glance at her watch revealed it was almost five, and she experienced shock to think she'd slept for so long.

Jace glanced up from the computer screen at her first sign of movement, his appraisal swift and encompassing as she straightened and stood to her feet.

He caught the careful way she moved, and contained a renewed surge of anger against the man who'd caused her such pain.

'Feeling rested?'

She looked better, her pale features had acquired a healthy colour, although her eyes were still too dark.

'Yes.'

'Good.' He turned back to the screen and re-immersed himself in scrolling through data.

Rebekah felt the need to freshen up, and she took her time, declining the use of lipstick as she changed into jeans and a cotton-knit top.

As soon as Jace left she'd fill the hot tub, then after a long, leisurely soak she'd grab a bite to eat and crawl into bed with a book.

Millie followed her out into the lounge, then padded towards the kitchen and waited to be fed. Jace barely glanced up from the screen as she passed through.

A slight frown creased her brow as she crossed into the laundry and extracted clothes from the drier, folded and put them away.

'I've ordered in,' Jace informed minutes later. 'I hope you like Chinese.'

She turned towards him slowly. 'I thought you'd return to the hotel.'

'You thought wrong.'

A sudden suspicion occurred. 'I'm fine, if you'd prefer to leave.'

He made two more keystrokes, then closed down the program. 'No.'

'Excuse me?'

'I have no intention of leaving you here alone.'

She felt her stomach execute a few painful somersaults. 'We already had this argument.'

'Then we'll have it again.'

'I don't need to go out from the apartment before tomorrow.' She gestured in the direction of the apartment entrance. 'There's no way anyone can get in unless I open that door.'

'It doesn't change a thing.'

'You can't stay here!'

'Why not? You have a spare bedroom.'

And she could sleep easily in her bed knowing he occupied the room directly across the hall?

'Unless, of course, you invite me to share your bed?'

The element of mockery evident brought her to flashpoint. 'As if that's going to happen!'

The apartment intercom buzzer was an insistent, intrusive sound, and after a moment's hesitation she crossed to pick up the receiver, only to have Jace lift it from her hand.

Minutes later he collected their Chinese take-out, paid the delivery boy, then he unpacked the bag onto the table.

Not long after they'd eaten she gathered clean sheets from the linen cupboard and handed them to him.

'The spare room is down the hallway on the left. Feel free to watch television. I'm going to bed. Goodnight.'

She turned and walked towards her room, closed the door, then she took a shower, slid into bed and snapped off the light.

She was running, but she didn't seem to be gaining distance in her attempt to reach a safe place. And it was dark, very dark, with only brief prisms of light.

Where was she? Nothing was familiar. Only an awareness of being outdoors, damp grass, tall trees, then there was dense undergrowth that caught on her clothes, gnarled tree roots, and the dank smell associated with the cyclic rebirth, growth and decay of plant life.

Thunder rolled across the sky, followed by forked lightning, and behind her she could hear the echo of her own frantic passage towards safety.

Except it was foe, not friend, and a mental image of Brad in the role of her attacker flooded her brain.

She tripped over an exposed tree root, and she cried out as she went down. There was an imperviousness to pain as she scrambled to her feet and staggered into a running gait, fleeing as he gained on her.

Then, miraculously, the undergrowth cleared, the trees disappeared, and there was smooth lawn, a house with all its lights blazing. A beacon offering her sanctuary.

She picked up speed and ran towards it, but no matter how hard she tried she couldn't close the distance and the house remained out of her reach.

Just as she began to despair she drew close, and she was at the front door, her hand on the knob, praying it would open and not be locked.

Her relief was palpable as it swung open to her touch, and as she turned to close it Brad was there, wrenching the door from her grasp.

She screamed, pushing all her weight against it in an attempt to prevent his entry. Except it was hopeless, her strength no match for his as he forced it open.

Then she turned and ran, blindly seeking the stairs in the hope of reaching a bedroom where she could close and lock herself in.

Only to have him catch her just as she reached the landing, and she cried out as his hands closed over her arms. Screamed as they moved to her shoulders.

She heard him swear, then his voice calling her name…

The scene began to change and fade, and she was no longer on the floor, she was in her bed in the apartment, the voice repeating her name bore an American accent, and the man grasping her shoulders wasn't Brad.

This man's features portrayed concern, his facial muscles reassembling over broad-sculptured bone as concern was replaced with relief. Chillingly bleak eyes riveted hers, trapping her in his gaze for seemingly long seconds before the bleakness faded.

'Jace?' What was he doing here? It was late, she was in bed, the bedside lamp was switched on...and then she remembered.

He caught each fleeting emotion and gauged every one. 'You were having a nightmare.'

Rebekah shivered, still partly caught up in it. All she'd need to do was close her eyes and she'd become immersed in the darkness again.

'Would you like a drink?'

She became aware of the man sitting on the edge of her bed, his jeans, the unbuttoned shirt, the slightly tousled hair.

This close she was suddenly conscious of her own attire, the thin cotton nightshirt, the rumpled bedcovers.

There was a sense of intimacy apparent, something exigent beneath the surface that would ignite and flare at the slightest touch, the faintest move.

Rebekah unconsciously held her breath, unable to tear her eyes away from his. She swallowed the lump that had risen in her throat. 'Please.' Anything to have him shift away.

Yet when he did she felt a strange sense of loss, which was crazy. There was a compulsive need to straighten the bedcovers, and she finger-combed her hair, then winced as bruised muscles made themselves felt.

Jace returned with a glass part-filled with chilled water, and she took it from him, had several sips before placing the glass onto the bedside pedestal.

'Thanks.' *Please, just go,* she begged silently. She felt acutely vulnerable, and way too disturbed by his presence.

'Want to talk about it?' His dark eyes seared hers, lingered, then trailed to her mouth.

'Not particularly.'

He lifted a hand and brushed the tips of his fingers to a large bruise on her arm, and she quivered beneath his touch.

'How often did he do this to you?'

She wanted to protest it was none of his business, except the words never left her lips. An admission would raise the query as to why she'd stayed after the first attack. Brad's tears, his apparent horror and remorse at his actions, together with his fervent promise it would never happen again had influenced her to forgive him. Until the next time.

'Does it matter?'

'Yes.' There was steel beneath the silkiness, an expression she couldn't define in those dark eyes.

His hand moved to cup her jaw, and his thumb

caressed the tender flesh Brad had slapped with a hard palm, then he threaded his fingers through her hair.

Rebekah felt as if they were enmeshed in some elusive sensual spell. 'I think you'd better leave,' she voiced shakily.

Yet the words were at variance with her emotions.

There was a part of her that ached to invite this man's touch, to reach out and seek the comfort he could provide.

Oh, dear lord, just to be held close and feel the press of his lips against her temple, the beat of his heart against her own. To feel safe and protected.

Except it was more than that, much more.

She wanted, *needed* the touch of his hands, his lips on her body. She wanted *him*.

She didn't want to analyse the *why* of it. To agonise whether she should or shouldn't, or what might come after.

There was no room for wisdom, just innate need.

Her eyes ached with it, and tears rose to the surface to shimmer in the lamp-light.

He leant forward and brushed his lips to hers in a kiss that was gently evocative, and her mouth trembled slightly as she sought control over her wayward emotions.

Her lashes fluttered down in a desperate bid to close out the sight of him. It didn't work, nothing worked, for she still did battle with her sensory perception of him...his clean male scent, the warmth and the passion. Especially the passion, *there* but held in tight control.

She felt his mouth shift to the bruise on her shoulder, then slip to caress another, and something deep inside slowly unfurled and began to melt.

Were some of the carefully erected barriers coming down? Her skin was silk, and scented with a delicate perfume he failed to recognise. He wanted to obliterate the taint of Brad's touch, replace it with his own and show her how the loving could be. The intense pleasure, the acute ecstasy experienced by two people in complete accord.

The words could come later. For now there was only the tactile sensation of touch, the silent communication of want and need in the slight tremor of her body, the fast-beating pulse at the edge of her throat, and heat…hers, his, as he trailed his lips up to fasten on her own in a kiss that dispensed with any inhibitions and encouraged her response.

It was everything she craved for, evocative, erotic, with an edge of hunger that tugged at her soul. A sigh rose and died in her throat as she angled her mouth to his and deepened the kiss.

The only part of him touching her was his mouth, and he used it to devastating effect, sweeping her to a place where there was only the moment and the electrifying sensual chemistry they shared.

Rebekah cupped his face and kept his mouth on hers until he gently removed her hands as he trailed kisses down her throat and edged to the soft swell of her breast.

He eased the edges of her nightshirt aside and savoured the rounded contours before laving a tender peak.

Sensation arrowed through her body and she arched against him, only to groan out loud as he shamelessly suckled there.

With care he freed the remaining buttons on her nightshirt and the breath hissed between his teeth as he caught sight of the bruised swelling on her ribcage.

Rebekah closed her eyes against the dark anger evident, only to have them open in stunned surprise as he pressed his lips to each and every bruise in turn.

Jace trailed a hand to the curve of her waist, then rested over her hip before slipping low to tangle in the soft hair at the apex of her thighs.

It was almost too much as his lips traced a similar path, and she cried out loud as he bestowed the most intimate kiss of all.

He sensed her shocked disbelief, the sudden stillness, and felt something twist in his gut at the instinctive knowledge her ex-husband had never gifted her this form of oral pleasure. A man who was selfishly insensitive to consider his own satisfaction without thought for his partner?

Her climax when it came took her unawares, for she hadn't imagined there could be more, much more than she'd already experienced, and she gasped as he took her high again and again until she reached for him.

His skin was smooth as thick-textured satin, and she exulted in the feel of hard sinew and muscle as she freed him of his shirt.

Dear heaven, he was built with well-developed musculature, a taut waist, and washboard midriff.

It was easy to unsnap his jeans and slide the zip down, then pull them off with his help. His briefs followed, and she had a bad moment wondering if she could accommodate him.

There was an elemental quality apparent, a base, primitive need she was unable to ignore as she became caught up in the sexual thrall of him.

His hands skimmed the surface of her skin, shaping her body as he explored all the pleasure spots with the sureness of a man who knew where and how to touch to drive a woman wild.

He took her to the brink of sexual anticipation, and held her there until she begged for release, then he entered her with exquisite care, moving slowly as she stretched to fit him.

It was like nothing she'd experienced before as she absorbed his length, and she cried out as he began to withdraw, only to ease forward in a slow rhythm as old as time, lengthening each stroke and increasing its pace until she accepted and matched it.

Together they moved in unison towards a climactic explosion that shattered all of her preconceived beliefs.

Her whole body was like a finely tuned instrument beneath a master's touch, responding as it never had before. As she'd never imagined it could, she decided hazily as every nerve sang with elated pleasure.

This...*this* was how it was supposed to be. Two

people together, sharing a sensual feast that culminated in the ultimate pleasure.

Not the quick slaking of lust that Brad had subjected her to in the name of love before he rolled off her and fell asleep.

Jace was still joined with her, his lips intent on trailing a lingering path to her breasts, where they caressed and teased, then suckled there.

Tiny darts of sensation arrowed through her body, and she traced the length of his spine with her fingertips, exploring each indentation until she reached his buttocks.

She felt them clench beneath her touch, and her lips parted in a secret smile, only to gasp out loud as he began to move, slowly stroking deep within until she caught the rhythm and joined him in the ride.

Afterwards he kissed her, taking her mouth in a gentle imitation of the sexual act itself, then he gathered her in close against him and held her until she slipped into an exhausted sleep.

It was in the early dawn hours that she stirred, and, half-asleep, began to move a little, unconsciously changing position…hazily aware something was preventing her. *Someone,* she determined seconds later.

Instant recall followed, and with it came the inevitable *ohmygod* moment. *What had she done?*

Like a giant jigsaw puzzle the pieces fell into place. The nightmare, crying out, Jace, and sex. Hell, she had a vivid recollection of the sex!

'Don't,' a husky male voice adjured close to her ear.

Rebekah stilled at the sound of that deep, slightly accented drawl, and her breath seemed to lock in her throat as one hand slid to her hip while the other took possession of her breast.

'Please. Let me go.'

His lips brushed her temple and trailed to settle at the sensitive curve at her neck. 'Stay, *agape mou*.'

'My lover'. This was all wrong. It was he who should go, not her.

'Last night was—'

'A mistake?'

Oh, God. She closed her eyes, then opened them again. It had been the most beautiful experience of her life. And she could hardly blame him for the seduction. She'd wanted him as much as he appeared to want her.

'No.'

She felt his lips move to form a smile. 'Your honesty is charming.'

'It—can't happen again,' she managed, feeling wretched. She'd never been promiscuous in her life. Brad had been her first and only lover.

'Why not, *pedhaki mou*?'

He sounded vaguely amused, and she shifted, then froze as she became aware of his arousal. 'Because it can't.' It didn't help that his mouth was intent on completing a treacherous path along the slope of her shoulder.

'Uh-huh. *Because,* hmm?'

Warmth was stealing through her veins. 'Stop that.' It was a weak admonition, and they both knew it.

'You don't want me to do this?' He shifted, drawing her to lay on her back as he leaned over her and let his lips drift over her breast. 'Or this?' He caught one tender peak between his teeth and took her to the edge between pleasure and pain.

One hand splayed over her stomach, then moved low to tangle in the soft curls, and pleasure arrowed through her body as he effortlessly located the sensitive clitoris.

It took only seconds for her to scale the heights, and he held her there, enjoying her delectation, then he took possession of her mouth as she began to fall.

It wasn't enough, Rebekah decided hazily. It would never be enough. And she reached for him, welcoming the sure, hard length of him as he slid inside her.

Afterwards Rebekah lay entwined in post-coital languor, enjoying the gentle drift of fingers in a lazy, exploratory path over his warm skin.

It felt so *right*, being here like this.

They were both adults, they weren't in a relationship with someone else... At least, she wasn't. But what about Jace?

She wasn't prepared for the way apprehension feathered along the edge of her spine. What if he was just amusing himself—?

'No.' Jace slid a hand beneath her chin and tilted it so she had to look at him. 'No,' he reiterated quietly, and her eyes widened.

'No—what?'

'I number several women among my friends, but none to whom I owe my fidelity.'

'You read minds?'

'Yours isn't difficult to interpret.' With a slow smile Jace slid to his feet and strolled naked into the *en suite*.

Rebekah took pleasure in the look of him, the breadth of shoulder, the splendid musculature of his back, the tapered waist and lean, tight butt.

Just thinking about the intimacy they'd shared brought a renewed surge of heat, and a repeated longing to experience once again the incandescent sensation he was able to arouse.

Soon she'd go take a shower, dress, make breakfast, then head into the shop. And Jace? Would he take a flight back to Cairns or Brisbane and complete his reorganised business meetings?

Then what would happen? She'd return to her day-to-day life while he tied up his Australian connection, after which he'd return to New York.

Rebekah was unprepared for the devastation that hit at the thought of him leaving. Even more unconscionable was the possibility of not seeing him again.

Maybe she could have survived with her emotions intact if it hadn't been for last night. Now she didn't have a hope in hell.

Fool, she castigated in silence. She should never have allowed him to stay, and should have banished him from her bedroom the moment he entered it.

Except she hadn't. Now she had to live with it.

Jace re-entered the room and his gaze narrowed as he interpreted her expressive features. Doubts and reflective thought he could deal with. Regret was something else.

He watched her eyes widen as he closed the distance between them, and he resisted the temptation to join her in bed. Instead he tugged the sheet free and scooped her into his arms and returned to the *en suite*.

'What are you doing?'

Another woman would have offered a feline purr, wound her arms round his neck and pressed her mouth to his.

Rebekah sounded apprehensive, and totally devoid of any musing coquetry.

A muscle clenched at the edge of his jaw in recognition of what she'd become beneath her ex-husband's hand.

'Sharing the hot tub with you.' His drawl held an element of humour, and he successfully prevented any protest by the simple expediency of closing her mouth with his own.

It was sheer magic. The pulsing water, the touch of his hands as he gently massaged scented bath oil into her skin. She wanted to close her eyes and have him administer to her forever.

How long did she have? Three, four days...a week at the most.

Rebekah knew she should stop it now. Climb out of the hot tub, catch up a towel, advise him to do the same, then say...*what? Thanks, that was great. Maybe we can do it again some time?*

There could be no doubt this was just a brief interlude. To think it could be anything else was ridiculous.

Besides, her life was all mapped out. Blooms and Bouquets was her focal priority. She had a flourishing business, a nice apartment, a late-model car. What else could she want?

A man she could trust. Someone to be there for her, as she would be for him. To share the love and the laughter, the few tears and sorrow fate might provide in their lifetime. Children. The whole package.

Was it too much to hope for?

Not just any man. *This* man.

The revelation poleaxed her. For a shock-filled second she thought she might actually have blacked out.

'Rebekah?'

Oh, God. Get a grip on reality. 'It must be getting late. I need to get to the flower market, organise the day's orders.' She was babbling, her hands already reaching for the marbled surround as she rose to her feet.

A startled yelp emerged from her throat as Jace's hands closed over her waist, and she struggled as he pulled her down in front of him, then caged her within his arms.

'I have to go.'

'No,' he refuted. 'You don't.'

'Jace...' She broke off with a groan of despair as his mouth savoured the sensitive curve of her neck.

'An hour, hmm? Just an hour.'

It was closer to two before she slid behind the

wheel, fired the engine and sent the MG up onto street level.

Jace occupied the passenger seat, and minutes later she eased the car to a smooth halt outside his hotel entrance.

'Have a good day.' It was an automatic phrase, and when he leaned forward she offered her cheek, only to have him take her face in his hands and bestow an evocatively deep open-mouthed kiss.

When he released her there was delicate pink colouring her cheeks, a soft, tremulous smile parted her lips, and her eyes held slumberous warmth.

It was a look he'd deliberately sought, and one he could easily become accustomed to without any trouble at all.

CHAPTER NINE

THE rising sun coloured the landscape, promising warmth as the day progressed, and Rebekah covered the relatively short distance to the shop in record time.

The Blooms and Bouquets van was already parked out back, which meant Ana had completed an early run to the flower markets. Something she'd intended to take care of, except something...*someone*, she corrected, had caused a delay.

The scent of flowers filled her nostrils as soon as she opened the shop door, and she breathed it in, loving the delicate fragrances.

'You shouldn't be here,' Ana protested. 'At least not this early.' Her gaze sharpened, then narrowed fractionally. 'There's something different about you.'

Rebekah crossed to the work table and stowed her bag. 'I'm fine.'

'Very much *fine*. You're almost glowing.'

Her sister was a kindred soul and far too perceptive for Rebekah's peace of mind. 'A good night's sleep works wonders.'

'Or not much sleep and a long night's loving,' Ana teased. 'Ah, you're blushing.' Her smile held a witching mischievousness. 'It has to be Jace.' The man was incredibly resourceful if he'd managed to infiltrate the emotional barriers Rebekah had erected. If he toyed with her and broke her heart, she'd kill him.

'Are you going to tell me?'

Rebekah shot her sister a steady look. 'Yes, it's Jace. And no, I'm not going to tell you.'

'Spoilsport.' Her expression sobered. 'How are the bruises?'

'It'll take a few days.'

'More like a week or two,' Ana corrected. 'Luc has employed private security to keep a watchful eye on the premises.'

It was understandable Luc wouldn't risk anything happening to his wife or unborn child.

'Shall we get to work?' Rebekah suggested.

The day proved to be busier than usual, and the phone calls many. Mostly business-oriented, but Rebekah took a call from the police relating to a required clarification in her statement, and her lawyer.

Jace rang mid-morning, and again mid-afternoon.

Just the sound of his voice was enough to send her pulse racing to a faster beat.

All day she'd been caught up with the memory of what they'd shared through the night and early this morning. After almost three years of celibacy she was conscious of highly sensitised tissues and nerve-endings as a result of his possession. Each shattering climax had been more intense than the last, and even now just the thought brought heat pooling deep inside.

There was no contact from Brad, but then she hadn't expected there to be. His mother, his lawyer, the police...each would have warned him of the consequences involved if he dared risk another personal confrontation.

Looking back, she damned herself for not realising Brad had an obsessive-possessive personality. He'd been a consummate actor, fooling everyone. Except his mother and the medical and legal advisors hired to protect him.

Jace walked into the shop just as she was about to close up for the evening, and she felt the familiar jolt of her heart at his presence as he stood waiting while she shut down the computer, checked the locks, then set the alarm prior to vacating the premises.

He brushed his lips to her temple. 'Busy day?'

'Yes.' Her stomach turned a somersault or two, then settled down. 'We filled more than the usual orders.'

Jace pressed a finger to the generous curve of her mouth. 'How are you?'

So intensely aware of you, I feel as if every nerve-end is fizzing with active life. 'Fine.'

His slow smile held a degree of sensual warmth. 'Feel like driving to Watson's Bay and eating seafood while the sun goes down over the ocean?'

'You don't need to do this,' Rebekah said quietly as they walked to her car.

'Take you out to dinner?' he queried as he slid into the passenger seat beside her.

'Act the part of bodyguard,' she qualified, and sensed a sudden stillness apparent.

'You want to run that by me again?'

There was silk in that accented drawl, and it raised all her fine body hairs in self-protective defence.

'I don't want you to feel obligated in any way just because—'

'We had sex?'

It hadn't been just *sex*. She'd had sex with Brad for the few brief months she'd lived with him as his wife. Last night she'd been made love to for the first time in her life. There was, she had to admit, a world of difference between sex and lovemaking.

'Want to start over?' Jace offered with dangerous softness.

She waited a beat as she released her breath. 'I think so.'

Jace caught the slight quiver at the edge of her mouth, and wasn't sure at that precise moment whether he wanted to shake her or kiss her senseless.

'Good.' He indicated the key she held poised in her hand ready to insert into the ignition. 'Suppose you drive, and we'll discuss this further over dinner.'

The restaurant Jace suggested was a converted bath-house erected in the days long gone by to service the day trippers who visited the bay to swim and picnic.

Now it was a fashionably trendy place to eat, with an excellent menu and superb food.

It was a pretty beach, and the ocean waters were dappled with reflected sunlight. Soon the natural light would fade, and the moon would rise to provide a silver pathway from the horizon.

Jace managed to secure a table by the window, and

he ordered wine while Rebekah checked out the menu.

A prawn risotto and side salad appealed, and Jace selected something more substantial containing a variety of seafood.

'Let's dispense with the obligation issue,' he began as soon as the waiter retreated in the direction of the kitchen. He leaned back in his chair and subjected her to a thoughtful appraisal. 'My interest in you is entirely personal. Not a misguided sense of responsibility or duty due to an extended family loyalty. Or merely a means of protecting you from your ex-husband,' he revealed with dispassionate imperturbability, then added with deadly softness,

'What we shared last night. What was that? Just great sex, no emotional involvement?'

There was knowledge apparent in his dark gaze she couldn't deny. 'No.'

The waiter brought their starters and presented them with practised flair, while the drinks steward topped their glasses.

'I want to be with you. My hotel suite,' Jace elaborated. 'Your apartment. It hardly matters which, as long as we're together.'

She swallowed the lump that had suddenly risen in her throat. 'You're taking a lot for granted.'

His gaze seared hers. 'You think I'm playing a game? Using you for sex? *Amusing* myself with you?'

Oh, my, he didn't hesitate to spell it out. In a boardroom he'd be a ruthless aggressor, a feared adversary.

'Which one, Rebekah?' he pursued relentlessly. 'Or do you imagine it's all three?'

Dear heaven. 'I don't know.' She could be equally fearless. 'Only that whatever it is, it has a very limited time-span.'

'Does it?'

She was breaking up inside. 'Your life is in New York. Mine is here.'

His gaze narrowed, and when he spoke his voice was a silk drawl. 'With no possibility of a compromise?'

She met his gaze and held it. 'Your definition of *compromise* is what? You fly into Sydney when you can spare the time between cementing corporate deals? I take a week's break here and there throughout the year and visit New York?' She was on a roll, and couldn't stop. 'We meet halfway? Enjoy full-on sex for as long as it takes, then bid each other a fond farewell at the airport, smile and say *that was great, we'll consult our schedules and work out another date*, then take separate flights to different destinations on opposite sides of the world?'

He was silent for so long she became increasingly nervous. 'Are you done?' he queried with deceptive mildness.

'Yes.'

Rebekah picked up her cutlery and began eating, although her tastebuds appeared to have gone on strike, and she had to consciously control her hands to prevent them from shaking.

She had only to look at Jace to vividly recall his

kiss, the touch of his hands, his mouth on her body. It was almost indecent to feel the heat sing through her veins, tripping her pulse and causing her heart to thud in her chest.

The degree of intimacy they'd shared brought a tinge of soft pink to her cheeks.

After last night her life would never be the same. And that was an admission she had no intention of verbalising.

Rebekah finished her starter, picked at her main, declined dessert, and ordered coffee.

'I didn't thank you,' she ventured quietly as she spooned sugar into the dark brew.

'For what, specifically?'

Coming to my rescue? Dropping everything and flying to Sydney? Putting me first above important business meetings? 'Ensuring my safety.' It didn't seem adequate. 'It was kind of you.'

He considered the word, reflected on it a little. 'I think we've gone way past *kind*.'

'I hope it hasn't interrupted your business meetings.'

'So polite,' Jace gently mocked. 'I have an early-morning flight to Brisbane, followed by an afternoon meeting on the Gold Coast. I'll be back early evening.'

She needed to ask. 'When do you return to New York?'

'Sunday.'

That left only a few days. She felt as if her whole world had suddenly shifted on its axis. Soon he'd be gone, and the thought of him not being a constant in her life affected her more than she was prepared to admit.

How could she be so contrary? Fighting against allowing him into her life for days, and now she didn't want him to leave. It hardly made any sense.

A hollow feeling settled in her stomach, and she pushed her coffee to one side, unable to swallow another mouthful.

Jace watched the fleeting emotions chase each other across her expressive features. She was a piece of work, so incredibly beautiful with a sweetness that went right to the depths of her soul. Was she aware how easily he could read her? It was the one thing that had kept him sane during the past ten days.

'Finished?' He didn't wait for her answer as he signalled the *maître d'* for the bill, paid it on presentation, then he caught hold of her hand and led her out to the car.

'I'll drop you at the hotel,' Rebekah indicated as they entered the outskirts of Double Bay.

'A token resistance?'

Her stomach executed a backwards flip at his drawled query. 'I have to be at the flower markets before five in the morning, and I need some sleep.'

'So, we sleep,' Jace said imperturbably.

'I really think—'

'We've done this already.'

'*You* might have. The jury's still out with me.'

She was aware he shifted slightly in his seat. 'All

you have to say is you don't want to share the same bed with me.'

Rebekah opened her mouth to say the words, then bit them off before the first one could escape her lips. She couldn't do it, for to deny him was to deny herself.

Millie greeted them as soon as they entered the apartment, miaowing in protest because she hadn't been fed. Something Rebekah attended to at once, and was rewarded with a brief purr and a swishing tail as the cat tucked into her food.

The message-light on the answering machine was blinking, and showed three recorded messages. The first was her father in New York, then Ana with a reminder for the morning. Brad followed with sibilant invective damning Luc and Jace Dimitriades, and promising Rebekah would pay, big-time.

'Don't erase it,' Jace commanded quietly. 'Let it run in case he rings again.'

'He will.' She was certain of it.

'Each call will become another strike against him in court.'

Not too much of a strike, she accorded silently. His mother and her lawyers were a formidable team.

'I'm going to hit the shower.' Rebekah turned and moved down the hall to her bedroom.

Minutes later she stood beneath the warm spray of water, soap in hand as she lathered her skin. The subtle rose-scent misted with the steam, and she gave a startled yelp as the door slid open and Jace stepped behind her.

She didn't have a chance to say a word as he turned her round to face him, then his mouth captured hers in a gentle, evocative kiss that tugged at her heart-strings.

'You shouldn't be here,' Rebekah managed the instant he lifted his head a little, and she glimpsed his musing smile as he shaped her face with his hands.

'Uh-huh.'

He angled his mouth over hers, and this time he went deep, sweeping her emotions to unbelievable heights where there was no sense of time or place, just the heat of intense eroticism.

How long had they remained like this? she wondered with bemused bewilderment when he slowly broke the kiss. Long seconds, or several minutes?

He had the most beautiful face, she decided, taking her fill of him. Dark eyes merging from the deepest grey to black, a facial bone structure to die for, and a mouth that was heaven on earth.

She possessed the strongest inclination to lean in against him, press her head to the curve of his shoulder, and just rest there. To have him close his arms around her, and know nothing, no one, could touch her.

Jace put his hands on her shoulders and turned her away from him, then he began massaging her nape, the tense muscles at the edge of her neck, her shoulders.

There were kinks, and he eased them out, working at each one until she sighed in gratitude.

It felt so darned good, she simply closed her eyes

and went with it, exulting in his touch, the magic he seemed able to generate without any effort at all.

'Better?'

Rebekah lifted her head and breathed an almost inaudible, 'Yes,' as he gently turned her round to face him. 'Thanks.'

He caught up the soap and placed it in her hand.

'Return the favour, *pedhaki mou*.'

Her eyes widened as she registered a delightful mix of surprise and reservation.

'Too big an ask?'

To soap that masculine frame…all over? Maybe she could skip certain parts of his anatomy… Although it seemed ludicrous to feel reticent after last night.

She didn't trust herself to speak, and began lathering his chest, completing the upper part of his body, his arms, shoulders, then she stepped behind him and rubbed the soap over the muscular curve of his back, his buttocks, the backs of his thighs. Then she moved in front of him and handed him the soap.

'You can do the rest.'

His arousal was a potent force, and a soft pink coloured her cheeks.

'Too shy?'

The pink deepened, and she reached for the shower door, only to have him halt her escape.

'Stay, *agape mou*.' The husky plea undid her, and she looked at him blindly as he drew her round to face him. 'I want to pleasure you a little, then I'll take you to bed…to sleep, I promise.'

She stood mesmerised as his hands shaped her breasts, and brushed the tender peaks with the pad of his thumbs.

Liquid fire coursed through her veins, and a husky groan sighed from her throat as his lips sought the vulnerable hollow at the base of her neck, savoured there, then gently bit the soft flesh, soothed it, then trailed to the slope of her breast, where he suckled until she dragged his head away and pulled his mouth down to hers.

Her mouth was firm, her tongue an exploratory tease, and he let her run free with it, enjoying her touch as his hand trailed low over her hip, then slipped low to caress the sensitive moist folds, felt the clitoris swell and harden...and absorbed her cries as she went up and over. Again, and again.

She *ached* to feel him deep inside her, and in one fluid movement she linked her hands together at his nape, then lifted herself to straddle his hips, where she created a sensual friction that had him groaning out loud.

'Witch,' he accorded in a husky voice an instant before she sank down onto him, absorbing his length to the hilt in one slow slide. His hands cupped her buttocks as they began to rock, long, leisurely movements that increased in pace as they scaled the heights, poised at the brink, then tumbled together into a glorious free fall.

Afterwards they stepped from the shower stall, and Jace caught up a towel, fastened it at his hips, then he caught up another and dried the moisture from her body.

The bruises had become more colourful, and looked vivid against the paleness of her skin.

Jace swore low in his throat and would have said more in castigation, except Rebekah pressed a finger to his lips.

'Don't. It's done.'

He swept an arm beneath her knees and carried her into the bedroom, then he pulled back the covers, settled her down onto the mattress and slid in to curl her close in against him.

Exhaustion brought an easy sleep, and contentment kept her there until the alarm buzzed loud in the early pre-dawn hours.

'Stay there,' Rebekah bade as Jace slid from the bed and pulled on his trousers.

'I'll make coffee while you dress.' He snapped the waist fastening closed, and she gathered up fresh underwear and headed towards the *en suite*.

There was coffee perking in the coffee-maker when she entered the kitchen, and she tried not to be caught up by the look of him as she collected a cup and filled it with the aromatic brew.

Lean-hipped, bare-chested, olive-textured skin covering splendid musculature, his hair tousled, and a night's beard shadowing his features, he was something else.

'Problem?'

He was the problem. A very big problem. And it was getting worse with every day, and *night*, that passed.

Sunday. The word seemed to reverberate inside her head. On Sunday he leaves. Two nights he'd stayed over, and already she couldn't bear the thought of him not being here.

How could she become so attached to someone so soon? It didn't make sense. None of it made any sense.

Rebekah finished her coffee, then she crossed to the sink, rinsed the cup, then caught up her shoulder bag.

'I have to go.'

'You didn't answer the question.'

How could she say she'd miss him dreadfully? Or that her heart would break a little when he left?

His gaze was steady, his eyes dark with an expression she couldn't define as she stumbled to find the words.

'I appreciate you being here.' It was as close as she could get, and his mouth curved at the edges.

'I'll come down to see you safely into your car.'

He glimpsed her slight confusion. 'Have you got a spare key I can use to get back in here?'

She did, and she fetched it, gave it to him, then walked to the door.

The basement car park was well-lit, and as silent as a concrete tomb. This morning it seemed eerie, and she suppressed a faint shiver as she slid in behind the wheel.

Jace shut the door, and watched as she reversed out, then drove towards the ramp leading up to street level.

CHAPTER TEN

FRIDAY was always a busy day at the shop, with numerous orders to fill, deliveries to be ready on time for the courier, and they had two weddings booked for Saturday.

'We'd like to have you and Jace join us for dinner tonight,'

Ana issued soon after she arrived. 'Luc spoke to Jace before I left and he's deferred the decision to you.'

It sounded a lovely idea. 'Thanks, that'll be great. What time?'

'Seven?' Ana's eyes sparkled with humour. 'Petros said to tell you he'll make moussaka.'

'And dolmades?' Rebekah said hopefully.

'I'll ring and tell him.'

With Ana manning the telephone and the computer, Rebekah and Suzie worked with efficient speed, taking minimum breaks for lunch. By day's end everything was done, preparations were in place for Saturday, the market requirements tabled.

'All done,' Suzie said with satisfaction. 'Will you be OK if I leave now?'

'Sure. See you tomorrow.'

Jace was waiting as Rebekah locked up, and she

handed him the keys to the MG while she slid into the van.

Ten minutes later they rode the lift up to her apartment, and after a quick shower she selected a simple bias-cut dress in topaz-blue, added stiletto-heeled pumps, applied minimum make-up, then she caught up an evening purse and emerged into the lounge.

Jace was intent on televised news coverage, and he turned towards her as she entered the room. His smile was warm and her pulse tripped then raced to a faster beat.

'Ready?'

It was a few minutes before seven as Jace brought the MG to a smooth halt immediately adjacent the main entrance to Luc and Ana's home.

Petros opened the front door before they had a chance to ring the bell, then Ana was there with Luc to greet and usher them indoors.

'We'll have time for a drink before Petros serves dinner,' Ana informed as she moved into the lounge.

True to Ana's promise, Petros served dolmades as a starter, followed it with moussaka and delicate slices of lamb, and presented a magnificent fruit flan for dessert.

Rebekah chose to join her sister and accepted mineral water, leaving the men to drink superb red wine with their meal.

Petros was in the midst of clearing the table prior to serving coffee when the house cellphone rang, and he moved to one side, extracted the unit, spoke briefly, then handed it to Luc.

The conversation was brief, and Luc's tone sufficiently serious to warrant concern as he ended the call.

'That was the police reporting a break-in at Blooms and Bouquets. Someone was seen hurling a brick through the front window.' Luc spared Rebekah a level look. 'The culprit's been caught and identified.'

'Brad.' It was more of a statement than a question, and Luc inclined his head in acquiescence.

'We need to organise for someone to board up the window,' Ana said at once. 'Is there any other damage?'

'I'll go down with Rebekah,' Jace indicated as Luc put through a call to an emergency repair service.

Please God, don't let it be too bad, Rebekah pleaded silently as Jace drove down to the shop. It wasn't any great distance, and he pulled the car to a halt on the opposite side of the road.

A police car was parked adjacent the shop doorway, and Rebekah presented documentation as proof of ownership, then she unlocked the front door and entered the shop.

It was a mess. Vases were overturned, flowers strewn on the floor, and there was water pooling everywhere.

She felt sick, sickened at the degree of vengeance that had caused Brad to go to this extreme. The risk of being seen and caught was high, for the area bordered on the trendy café district, and was consequently well-lit and frequented by several passers-by.

Had he wanted to hurt her so much he was prepared

to go to jail? She doubted even his mother and her high-flying lawyer would be able to save Brad this time.

Maybe it would turn out to be a good thing, and he'd finally get the help he needed. But at what price?

Police procedure took a while, an emergency contractor arrived to board up the window, then Rebekah received clearance to clean up.

There was a sense of unreality, that the whole episode was merely a bad dream from which she'd awaken.

With methodical efficiency she began noting down ruined blooms, and made a list of what she'd need to re-order. Now it was a matter of physical work, clearing broken glass and floral debris.

'Where do you want me to start?' Jace asked as he discarded his jacket and began rolling up his shirt-sleeves.

She fetched a broom and handed it to him. 'You sweep, I'll dispose of the glass.'

They worked together, and it didn't take as long to clean up as she'd first thought. When it was done, she rang Ana and gave her sister a personal report, then she checked the locks and preceded Jace to the car.

'Thanks for your help,' she said quietly as she slid into the passenger seat.

'You imagine I'd have let you come down here and tackle this alone?'

His voice held a quality she didn't want to examine right now, and she retained silence for the short ride back to her apartment.

Inside, she moved straight through to the bedroom, stepped out of her stilettos, slipped off her clothes, and donned a silk robe.

Bed had never looked so good, and there was the temptation to slip between the sheets, snap off the light and drift into a dreamless sleep.

'I've made coffee.'

Rebekah turned at the sound of Jace's deep drawl, and tried for a faint smile, only to fail miserably.

He closed the distance between them and gathered her in against him. He'd expected reaction to set in, but hadn't bargained on it leaving her dark-eyed and white-faced.

'That bad, huh?' He felt a tremor rake her slim body and rested his cheek against the top of her head.

Just hold me, she begged silently. She needed to borrow some of his strength for a while. Even a few minutes would do while she replenished her own. Then she'd sip coffee, maybe put on a video in the hope of losing herself in a light, frivolous movie.

At that moment the phone rang, and she stiffened, wondering who could be calling at this hour. Then common sense prevailed as Jace released her.

'Want me to take that?' He didn't wait for her to answer as he crossed to pick up the bedroom extension.

His end of the conversation was incredibly brief, just a word here and there in confirmation, and she stood quietly as he replaced the handset.

There was a part of her that noticed the broad set of his shoulders, his stance, the way he exuded an animalistic sense of power. Inherent vitality meshed with blatant sensuality to compile a forceful image any sane person would prefer as friend rather than foe.

'Luc,' he revealed. 'Brad has been denied bail.'

The relief was palpable. This time he'd gone too far, and he hadn't been able to slip free of the legal net.

'It's over,' Jace assured quietly. 'Your statement and the evidence is sufficient to ensure he'll go to jail.'

'His mother—'

'Even her lawyer won't be able to swing anything. That's a given.'

'You can't be sure of that.'

'Yes,' he said with grim inflexibility. 'I can.' Brad Somerville would never have the chance to hurt her again. If he so much as tried, the law would come down on him so hard life as he knew it would never be the same again.

'Now,' Jace inclined as he pulled her close. 'Where were we?'

'I think we should go to bed.'

A husky chuckle sounded low in his throat. 'My thoughts, exactly.'

She shook her head. 'To sleep.'

'OK.' He swept an arm beneath her knees and carried her through to the bedroom, switching off lights as he went.

'I can walk,' Rebekah protested.

'Indulge me.'

Yet it was he who indulged her, and for a while she forgot the ugliness of the earlier hours, then he held her as she slept.

Saturday proved to be exceptionally hectic, and a few of the regular clientele called in to commiserate over the broken shop window, the break-in. Rebekah and Ana were circumspect in their explanation, even to Suzie, and it was business as usual as the orders were met, deliveries made.

It was late when Rebekah finished for the day, and she walked out of the shop into Jace's arms, laughing a little as he drew her close, bestowed a lingering kiss, then caught hold of her hand as he led her to the car.

Did he have something planned for his last night in Sydney?

She hoped so. She felt like dressing up, going somewhere special in order to hold the memory of the night forever in her mind.

He didn't disappoint. An hour later she sat sipping champagne in one of the finest restaurants the city had to offer.

The food was exceptional, the ambience fantastic, and the man seated opposite was the embodiment of everything she could ever hope for.

Yet there was a sad poignancy to the night. This was their last meal together, the last time they'd share the same bed.

Unless… No, she wouldn't even go there. Their lives, where they resided, they were too far apart for it to be possible to sustain a successful relationship.

Sure, they'd call each other. Email, fax, phone. For a while. Then the contact would dwindle down to practically nothing, and eventually cease.

But it had been great while it lasted. Better than great, she admitted. So much so, she wasn't sure she'd be able to exist without him.

They lingered, and returned late to her apartment.

The loving was the sweetest, the most sensual experience of her life. He made it so good, it was all she could do not to weep from the joy of it.

They slept for a while, then woke to pleasure each other again before hitting the shower.

'I'll make breakfast,' Rebekah declared, and he pressed a finger to her lips.

'We'll do it together.'

Bacon, eggs, hash browns, juice and strong black coffee. Except she could hardly eat a thing as she conducted a mental countdown to the time they'd need to leave for the airport.

They talked, although afterwards she couldn't recall a word she'd said, and she cleared the table, stacked the dishes, blindly forcing herself to focus on the mundane as he collected his wet-pack from the *en suite*.

She heard him re-enter the kitchen, followed by the soft sound of his overnight bag hitting the floor, then his hands curved over her shoulders as he turned her round to face him.

His hands slid up to cup her nape, then he covered her mouth with his own in a kiss that seared her soul.

When he lifted his head she could only look at him

in silence, too afraid to say the words bubbling up in her throat.

'Marry me.'

Rebekah's jaw dropped, and she struggled to find her voice. An impossibility with a host of random thoughts chasing each other inside her head.

'What did you say?' she managed at last.

'Marry me,' Jace reiterated quietly, and witnessed the gamut of her emotions. Shock, confusion, fear. He could accept the first two, but he wanted to wipe out the third.

'You can't be serious.'

'I am. Very serious.'

She was lost for words. There was one part of her that wanted to shout an unconditional 'yes'. Except sanity demanded a different answer.

He didn't give her the chance to utter it. 'You stole my heart when I partnered you at Luc and Ana's wedding. If I could have, I'd have swept you off to live with me in New York then. But it wasn't the right time…for you.'

'And you imagine it is now?' she queried sadly.

'I want to make it the right time. The question is…do you?'

'Jace—'

'I love you,' he vowed gently. 'The everlasting, "till death do us part" kind.' He made no attempt to touch her. He could, he knew, use unfair persuasion. But he wanted nothing she'd regret on reflection. 'I want to be in your life, and have you in mine.'

Was she brave enough to reach out with both hands

and accept what he offered? She wanted to, desperately.

The thought of never seeing him again was earth-shattering. Yet...*marriage*?

Rebekah met and held his gaze, aware of the strength, the perceptive quality apparent and the integrity. This man wasn't of Brad's ilk, and never would be.

Dared she take that step forward? She didn't think she could...at least, not right now. Maybe in a few months' time, when she'd become used to the idea.

'No conditions, Rebekah.'

He was adept at reading her mind, and to offer him anything less than total honesty wasn't an option.

'I can't do that.' She was breaking up inside. 'I love you.' She felt her mouth tremble, glimpsed sight of the sudden darkness in his eyes, and recognised the effort it cost him to retain control. 'The past week with you...' She faltered, unable to find the words. 'I couldn't bear to lose what we share.' She was dying, slowly, as surely as if the lifeblood was flowing from her body.

'*But?*'

Rebekah wasn't capable of saying a word.

A muscle tightened at the edge of his jaw. 'You must know I find ''no'' unacceptable.'

'Jace...' His name emerged from her lips as a husky entreaty.

He caught up his bag and slid the strap over one

shoulder. 'I have to collect my stuff from the hotel, check out, then get to the airport.'

'I'll take you.'

'No.' He leaned forward and kissed her, hard, briefly, then he straightened and walked to the door. He turned and cast her a long, steady look. 'If you want to make it "yes"…call me.' He opened the door, and closed it quietly behind him without so much as a backward glance.

Rebekah stood there in stunned silence, battling with herself to go running after him. Except she hesitated too long.

It seemed an age before she gathered sufficient energy to re-enter the lounge, and she curled up in a chair, buried her head in her arms and cried…for everything she'd just lost.

At least half a dozen times during the next hour she picked up the phone to call him, only to cut the connection before she'd keyed in the requisite digits.

Then it was too late, he'd already have boarded, and his cellphone would be switched off.

Millie jumped up into her lap, padded until she found a comfortable position, then settled and began to purr.

Rebekah abstractedly fondled the cat's ears, and didn't even try to stem the silent tears.

She had little idea of the passage of time. Eventually she stirred and began taking care of household chores, then, not content, she embarked on a thorough spring-clean of the apartment.

Food was something she couldn't face, and at seven she curled up in a chair and switched television channels until she found something that held her interest.

She must have slept, for she woke to the distant sound of the alarm ringing in the bedroom and she scrambled to her feet to go switch it off.

CHAPTER ELEVEN

ANOTHER day. Her first without Jace. Where was he now? On a stop-over at Los Angeles?

Oh, dear God, *what had she done*?

It was a first to display uninterest at the flower markets; at the shop she assembled blooms and bouquets automatically, devoid of her usual enthusiasm. At night she ate little, showered, then climbed into bed in the spare room after lying awake in her own for hours agonising that Jace wasn't there to share it with her.

Two, three days, four. Each one becoming more unbearable. She couldn't sleep, she didn't eat.

On the fifth day Ana took her by the shoulders, shook her a little, then demanded,

'OK, what gives?' She took a deep breath. 'And don't feed me any garbage about missing Jace. It's more than that.'

Sisterhood was a wonderful thing. Rebekah didn't know whether to laugh or cry. She did neither, and went straight to the truth.

'Jace asked me to marry him, and I said *no*,' she said starkly.

'You *what*?' Ana demanded in disbelief.

'I said no,' Rebekah reiterated, adding, 'For now.'

'Jace asked you to marry him, and you *refused*? Are you mad?'

'Wary. Scared,' she qualified wretchedly.

'Of loving him, and being loved in return?'

'All of that.' And more. 'His base is New York. It's a long way from home.'

'If you love him,' Ana began, then clicked her tongue in silent remonstrance. 'You *do* love him?'

Did she breathe? 'Yes.'

'Then what in hell are you doing here? Book the next flight out and go tell him.'

In her mind she was already winging her way there. 'The shop—'

'Suzie and I can manage.'

'Luc—'

'Leave Luc to me. Maybe we need to consider our options,' Ana suggested. 'Whether we want to sell, or have someone manage the place on our behalf.'

'But Blooms and Bouquets is—'

'Ours? It can still be ours, if that's what we both want. Just not run exclusively by us.'

'We've put so much into this place.'

'Maybe it's time to move on. I have a husband and soon there'll be a child. Both of whom are my life.' Ana drew in a deep breath, keyed in a few strokes, and brought up an internet site.

'What are you doing?'

'Booking you on a flight to New York.'

'I can't—'

'Yes, you can.' Her fingers flew over the keyboard, poised, then she added keystrokes, muttered to herself, added a keystroke or two more, then waited for confirmation. 'Done,' she said with satisfaction a short while later. 'You fly out tomorrow morning.' She named the airline, the flight number and departure time. 'Your electronic ticket will be despatched by courier within the hour.'

It was all going too fast, and she opened her mouth to say so, except Ana got in first.

'Don't,' she cautioned. 'For once in your life take hold of the day and go with it. What do you have to lose?'

What, indeed? she queried as she checked her bag, showed her passport, and moved through Customs into the departure lounge early next morning.

Her initial protest that Jace might be in another city…hell, another country, were dispensed with at once by Ana, who'd assured she'd already checked such details with Luc.

'Surprise him,' Ana had insisted. 'You have his office address, and that of his apartment. If by chance he's not at either place, you have his cellphone number. You can call him.'

So here she was, in a state of high anxiety, about to board a flight to the other side of the world.

Was she doing the right thing? Worse, would he still want her? They were questions she'd asked herself constantly during the past fifteen hours. Twice, she'd almost cancelled out.

The agony and the ecstasy, she accorded wryly as the plane soared into the air. Knowing that it was mostly of her own making didn't help at all.

If she'd listened to her heart instead of her head, she'd have shouted a joyous *yes* when Jace asked her to be his wife. Instead, she'd applied numerous reasons why she shouldn't be with him, rather than all the reasons she should.

Dammit, she was a fool.

Words that sprang to mind repeatedly during the long flight, the disembarkation process, and the cab ride to her hotel.

If you want to make it 'yes', call me. Except she hadn't called, nor had he called her.

What if he'd decided she was too much work, and had taken up with another woman?

If he could do that in so short a time, he wasn't worth having, she decided as she slid from the cab and followed the concierge's direction to Reception.

Her suite was on a high floor overlooking Central Park, but she barely glanced at the view before she unpacked a few essentials, then took a shower.

Ring him, a silent voice urged when she emerged dressed and feeling marginally refreshed.

It was crazy to be so nervous, she decided as she checked his cellphone number, then keyed in the digits.

Her hand shook a little as she waited for him to pick up.

'Dimitriades.'

Hell, he sounded different. Hard, inflexible.

Rebekah swallowed, then found her voice. 'Jace?'

There was a second's silence. 'Where are you?'

Oh lord. 'In a hotel.'

'*Where,* Rebekah?'

For a moment she couldn't think. 'It's opposite Central Park.' Memory kicked in, and she named it, then added her room number.

'Don't move. I'm on my way.'

He ended the call, and she replaced the handset, aware she had no idea where his office was situated in relation to the hotel. Or even if he was in his office.

It could take him up to an hour or longer to get here.

Time she could use to call her father, and catch up. On the other hand she could leave it until tomorrow to ring him. A call to Ana held more importance, and she checked the time difference, calculated it was the middle of the night in Sydney, then opted to send a text message instead.

As the minutes ticked by she was conscious of the onset of nervous tension. Her stomach felt as if it was tying itself in knots, and she couldn't keep her hands still for longer than a few seconds.

Rebekah examined the contents of the bar-fridge, checked out the cupboards and drawers, leafed through the complimentary magazines, and scanned the hotel directory folder, the breakfast menu.

Perhaps if she made herself a cup of coffee—

The doorbell rang, and she almost dropped the cup.

Then she was at the door, unfastening the lock with fingers that shook a little.

Jace seemed to fill the doorway, and her gaze became trapped in his. Held there by some mesmeric force.

For a moment neither of them moved, and everything faded from her peripheral vision. There was only the man, nothing else.

'Are you going to ask me in?'

His slightly accented drawl broke the spell, and she stood aside.

'Of course.'

He closed the door carefully behind him, then turned to face her, seeing her uncertainty, the nervousness, knew he could dispense with it, and would any time soon.

'Would you like coffee?' Rebekah asked in a strained voice.

Whisky would be more appropriate. Had she any idea what he'd gone through in the past week? The hour it had taken for him to get here?

'Coffee isn't a priority right now.'

Oh, to hell with it. She hadn't come all this way to play verbal games. If he was waiting for her to make the first move then, dammit, she would!

Without thought she reached out a hand, fisted it in his shirt and pulled him close. Then she drew his head down and sought his mouth. Her heart and soul went into the kiss, slaking a need that had been denied too long.

It took only seconds for his hands to settle over her shoulders, then ease down her back to cup her buttocks as he held her against him, and it was he who took control in a devastating oral supplication that tore the breath from her body.

Her lips were soft and slightly swollen when he

lifted his head, and he traced the lower curve with a gentle finger.

'What took you so long?'

'Stupidity,' Rebekah said with innate honesty, and Jace smiled as he pressed a light kiss to the tip of her nose.

She locked her arms around his waist and pressed her hips in against his, felt the power of his arousal, and exulted in his need.

'Are you going to say the words,' he drawled gently, 'or do I have to drag them out of you?'

'Yes. The answer's *yes*.'

His mouth found hers, and this time there was such an element of *tendresse*, her heart softened and began to melt.

'Good.' His hands shaped her body, lingered, then moved up to capture her face. 'When?'

'When…*what*?' she queried, definitely distracted by the way his lips were caressing her closed eyelids, a temple, before trailing down to the edge of her mouth.

'Will you make an honest man of me?'

His fingers were toying with the buttons on her blouse in seemingly slow motion. There was all the time in the world, and he was in no hurry.

'Early next year?' she posed, not really focusing on planning a wedding date right now.

'Uh-huh.' He tugged the blouse free from the waistband of her skirt, then gently pulled it free.

'The end of the week.' He began working the zip on her skirt. 'A traditional ceremony in Sydney.' The skirt slid down to the carpet. 'I initiated the requisite paperwork while I was there.'

'You're crazy,' Rebekah said huskily as he undid her bra fastening.

His mouth closed over hers fleetingly. 'Crazy in love with you.'

She was willing to swear her heart stopped for a few seconds before kicking into a faster beat. 'Thank you.'

Jace lifted his head. 'For what?'

'For having enough faith in what we share to walk away and let me realise for myself that what I feel for you is *love*.'

He brushed his lips to her cheek. 'I don't think you have any conception just how hard it was for me to do that.'

She thought of the long, lonely nights when she woke and realised he wasn't there. How she jumped at every ring of the phone. The meals she wasn't able to eat because of an aching heart. And the knowledge that life without Jace in it would be no life at all.

'Yes, I do.' She eased his jacket off, then began unbuttoning his shirt. 'You're wearing too many clothes.'

'Want some help?' he asked quizzically, and she shook her head.

'Believe me, the pleasure is all mine.'

· And it was. She took it slow, savouring the removal of each item until he stood naked before her. Then she pushed him down onto the bed and straddled him, watching in delight as his eyes dilated and became heavy with passion.

Instinct ruled as she tasted him, and she savoured each moment the breath hissed between his teeth, the faint groan, the slight tremor as she embarked on a sensual feast where boundaries and inhibitions didn't exist.

Then it was Jace's turn, and he showed no mercy in his pursuit of gifting her the ultimate in primitive pleasure. It was she who cried out, she who reached for him and begged his possession.

When they came together it was with raw, primeval desire. Brazen, tumultuous. *Magic*.

The long aftermath held a dreamy quality, a gentle, tactile exploration with drifting finger-pads, soft kisses, and such an acute sensitivity it made her want to cry.

'Hungry?' Jace murmured as he nuzzled the soft hollow at the edge of her neck.

'For you, or food?'

She felt his mouth curve against her throat.

'When did you last eat, *agape mou*?'

'On the plane.' How many hours ago? Eight, ten?

'I'll order Room Service.' He bestowed a brief hard kiss. 'Then we'll shower, and you get to grab some sleep.'

He chose a light meal, and he extracted a half-magnum of champagne from the bar-fridge, opened it and poured the contents into two flutes.

'To us.'

He touched the rim of his flute to hers, and her

bones melted at the wealth of passion evident in his dark gaze.

'I love you.' She wanted, needed to say the words, and Jace took hold of her hand and brought it to his lips.

'You're everything to me,' he vowed quietly. 'More than I ever dreamed it was possible to have.' He turned her hand over and buried his lips in her palm. 'My life.'

She wanted to cry, and the tears welled up and shimmered there, threatening to spill.

He lifted his head, saw them, and pressed his lips to each eyelid in turn. 'Don't.'

The long flight, the nervous excitement, the love-making had taken its toll, and she was helpless to stem the flow as they spilled over and trickled down each cheek in twin rivulets.

He smoothed them with his thumb, then fastened his mouth on hers in a gentle, evocative kiss.

Their meal was delivered a short while later, and they fed each other morsels of the light, fluffy mushroom omelette, the salad, and Rebekah alternated the champagne with bottled water.

She was almost asleep on the chair, and it was all she could do to remain awake as they showered together, then, dry, she let Jace carry her to bed, where she curled up against him and was asleep within seconds of her head touching the pillow.

It was a while before Jace gently freed himself from her embrace and slid from the bed. He extracted his cellphone and made a series of calls. Then he rejoined her in bed and gathered her close.

There was, Rebekah accepted, nothing quite like the power and prestige of serious money.

Jace used it mercilessly to ensure everything went according to plan, and she experienced a sense of stunned disbelief as he organised return flights to Sydney the next day for them both, accepted Luc and Ana's offer to have the wedding at their home, gave them carte blanche to have Petros arrange caterers and liaised with the guest list.

The phone calls were lengthy and many, with Ana relaying she'd seen a wedding gown to die for, and everything down to the finest detail would be successfully organised in time for *the* day.

The fact that it was seemed nothing short of a miracle.

Even the weather was perfect, with brilliant blue skies, sunshine, and the merest hint of a breeze to temper the day's warmth.

'Ready?'

The gown, as Ana had promised, was something else.

Ivory silk with an ivory lace overlay that had a scalloped hemline resting just below the knee. Elbow-length sleeves in ivory lace, and a high neckline. The headpiece was a pearl band with a short fingertip veil bunched at the back of her head, and she carried a single long-stemmed white rose. Her only jewellery was a diamond pendant and matching earrings.

'Yes.' Rebekah turned to her sister and gathered her close in an affectionate hug. 'Thanks for everything.'

'You're welcome,' Ana responded gently. 'OK, let's get this show on the road.'

Luc was waiting downstairs to lead her out into the grounds, where the guests were assembled on chairs either side of a red carpet facing a delicate wrought-iron gazebo.

'Beautiful,' Luc complimented quietly as he took her arm. His gaze slid to his wife, and the warmth of his smile brought a lump to Rebekah's throat.

Together they walked out onto the terrace, traversed the short flight of steps, and made their way towards the gazebo. The guests stood and those lining the red carpet threw rose petals in Rebekah's path.

She saw Jace standing at the assembled altar, and she caught his gaze and held it as she made her way towards him.

A light, husky laugh escaped her lips as he drew her close and kissed her, thoroughly.

The celebrant cleared his throat, and they broke apart.

It was a simple ceremony, the words deeply moving, and Rebekah fought back the faint shimmer of tears as Jace slid a wide diamond-encrusted ring onto her finger.

There was the flash of cameras, voiced congratulations, and a shower of rose petals as they trod the red carpet as man and wife.

Champagne and food were served in a marquee

erected close by, guests greeted and thanked, then all too soon it was time to change and leave for the airport.

Ana helped her remove the headpiece and veil, then assisted with the zip fastening of the gown.

Rebekah freshened up, then slipped into an elegant trouser suit, added comfortable heeled shoes, then turned towards her sister.

'I'm going to miss you dreadfully.'

'We'll email each other every day, and talk on the phone. Jace has promised me you'll both visit at least twice a year.'

Rebekah's expression sobered a little. 'A month ago—'

'Don't look back,' Ana cautioned gently. 'You have today, and all the tomorrows.' She brushed her lips to Rebekah's cheek. 'Embrace them and be happy.'

'How did you get to be so wise?' Rebekah asked shakily.

'If you cry, I'll hit you.'

'Sisterly love,' Luc drawled from the doorway, whilst Jace offered,

'Shall we divide and conquer?'

'I think so,' Luc said with musing indolence as he crossed to his wife's side and drew her close.

Jace extended his hand, and Rebekah's toes curled at the way he looked at her. 'Ready, *agape mou*?'

'Yes.' And she was. Ready to go anywhere he chose to lead.

Together they made their way downstairs, and as they reached the car Rebekah turned to her sister.

'OK, this is it. The last goodbye.' She gave Ana a quick hug. 'I'll ring you from Paris.' Then it was Luc's turn. 'Look after her,' she said fiercely.

'Every minute of every day,' he promised solemnly.

'Go,' Ana pleaded, on the verge of tears.

Two sisters, two destinies, Rebekah mused as Jace took the main road leading towards the airport.

'We'll visit soon. And you have my word we'll return for the birth of Ana's child.'

Rebekah felt something begin to soar deep within, and she turned to look at him. 'Have I told you how much I love you?'

She had, several times through the night. They were words he'd never tire of hearing. Words he'd say to her, over and again for the rest of his life.

'If you do, I'll pull the car to the side of the road and kiss you.'

Her eyes assumed a wicked sparkle. 'An act that would probably cause a public spectacle.'

'Count on it.'

'Then I guess we need to wait for a more appropriate moment?' She began counting off each finger. 'Let's see, there's the long flight, with a brief stopover in Los Angeles. Thirty-six hours in total before we reach Paris.'

'Forty-eight,' Jace corrected with a musing smile. 'We have a not-so-brief stop-over in Los Angeles.'

Rebekah gave a laugh that was part delight, all mischief. 'Can't keep your hands off me, huh?'

He shot her a gleaming glance. 'Want me to try?'

Her expression sobered. 'No,' she assured quietly. 'Not in this lifetime.'

He waited until he passed the hire car in at the airport before he gathered her close and kissed her, thoroughly. So thoroughly she temporarily lost any sense of time or place.

Then he unloaded their bags from the boot, hefted the strap of one bag over his shoulder and gathered up the other, and caught her hand in his.

Together, as they would always be, for the rest of their lives.

EPILOGUE

SYDNEY in the spring reminded Rebekah of new beginnings as seasonal plants came into bud with the promise of life and colour. The trees began to blossom as nature prepared for yet another rebirth.

The gardens in the grounds of Luc and Ana's beautiful home were carefully tended, the lawns fresh and green and clipped with manicured precision.

It was a glorious day, the sun shone and there was only the merest drift of cloud in a stunning blue sky.

A baby's wail pierced the air, loud and protesting, as the celebrant performed the naming ceremony of Luc and Ana's young son. Marcus Lucien Dimitriades possessed a strong pair of lungs, and at three months of age he was his parents' pride and joy.

'Beautiful,' Jace accorded softly as he curved an arm along the back of her waist, and she turned to him with a smile, about to concur, when she saw he was looking at her, not the babe Ana held in her arms.

It was almost a year since their marriage, and there were times when she felt the need to pinch herself to see if she was living in a dream or the real world.

'Definitely *real*,' Jace assured quietly as he brushed his lips to her temple, and she lifted her face to slant her mouth into his, briefly savoured their warmth and reluctantly broke the contact.

'I love you.'

She felt his arm muscles tighten at the back of her waist. 'You certainly pick your moments, *agape mou.*'

'Bothers you, huh?' she teased, and almost drowned in the passion evident in his dark gaze. 'You can exact your revenge later.'

'Count on it.'

Later that night she lay in his arms, replete in the aftermath of lovemaking.

'Have you told Ana our news?'

Rebekah pressed her lips to his shoulder, nibbled a little, then soothed the love-nip with a soft kiss.

'Today was special, and very much her day. I'll tell her over lunch tomorrow.'

Jace's hand shifted to her waist and settled there, and she covered it with her own.

A child, theirs. A unique gift they would nurture and watch grow. Share the joys, the fun, the laughter, and hopefully few tears. And love unconditionally for the rest of their lives.

'No regrets?'

'None,' she vowed gently. 'You're the love of my life. My present, my future. Everything.'

Brad, her brief marriage, and its repercussions no longer existed.

'As you are mine,' Jace reciprocated gently.

Modern Romance™
...seduction and
passion guaranteed

Tender Romance™
...love affairs that
last a lifetime

Sensual Romance™
...sassy, sexy and
seductive

Blaze™
...sultry days and
steamy nights

Medical Romance™
...medical drama on
the pulse

Historical Romance™
...rich, vivid and
passionate

27 new titles every month.

*With all kinds of Romance for
every kind of mood...*

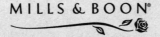

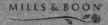

Don't miss *Book Five* of this BRAND-NEW 12 book collection 'Bachelor Auction'.

Who says money can't buy love?

On sale 3rd January

MILLS & BOON

CHRISTMAS SECRETS

Three festive Romances

CAROLE MORTIMER   CATHERINE SPENCER
DIANA HAMILTON

Available from 15th November 2002

*Available at most branches of WH Smith,
Tesco, Martins, Borders, Eason, Sainsbury's
and all good paperback bookshops.*

FREE
2 BOOKS
AND A SURPRISE GIFT!

We would like to take this opportunity to thank you for reading this Mills & Boon® book by offering you the chance to take TWO more specially selected titles from the Modern Romance™ series absolutely FREE! We're also making this offer to introduce you to the benefits of the Reader Service™—

★ FREE home delivery
★ FREE gifts and competitions
★ FREE monthly Newsletter
★ Exclusive Reader Service discount
★ Books available before they're in the shops

Accepting these FREE books and gift places you under no obligation to buy; you may cancel at any time, even after receiving your free shipment. Simply complete your details below and return the entire page to the address below. *You don't even need a stamp!*

YES! Please send me 2 free Modern Romance™ books and a surprise gift. I understand that unless you hear from me, I will receive 4 superb new titles every month for just £2.55 each, postage and packing free. I am under no obligation to purchase any books and may cancel my subscription at any time. The free books and gift will be mine to keep in any case.

P2ZEC

Ms/Mrs/Miss/Mr ....Initials ....
BLOCK CAPITALS PLEASE

Surname ....

Address ....

....

....Postcode ....

Send this whole page to:
UK: FREEPOST CN81, Croydon, CR9 3WZ
EIRE: PO Box 4546, Kilcock, County Kildare (stamp required)

Offer valid in UK and Eire only and not available to current Reader Service subscribers to this series. We reserve the right to refuse an application and applicants must be aged 18 years or over. Only one application per household. Terms and prices subject to change without notice. Offer expires 31st March 2003. As a result of this application, you may receive offers from Harlequin Mills & Boon and other carefully selected companies. If you would prefer not to share in this opportunity please write to The Data Manager at the address above.

Mills & Boon® is a registered trademark owned by Harlequin Mills & Boon Limited.
Modern Romance™ is being used as a trademark.